Capitalism and Socialism

John Vaizey

Professor of Political Economy, Brunel University

Capitalism and Socialism

a history of industrial growth

Weidenfeld and Nicolson
London

First published in Great Britain by
George Weidenfeld and Nicolson Ltd
91 Clapham High St, London SW4

ISBN 0 297 77848 X cased

Set, printed and bound in Great Britain by
Fakenham Press Limited, Fakenham, Norfolk

Contents

Foreword

This book is a history of what came to be called capitalism, that is an economic system based upon the pursuit of profit in free markets, from which industrialism emerged. Industrialism transformed the world and provided the first truly world-wide culture, where similar artefacts and habits of business were to be found from London to Tokyo, from New York to New Delhi. In this industrial system, modern constitutional democracy emerged.

That development did not lead, however, to world-wide constitutional democracy. The dark forces of authoritarian nationalism proved very strong and produced Hitler in Germany, and many lesser Hitlers in almost every continent. Above all, however, a fundamental challenge to the idea of capitalism came from the heart of capitalism. This is socialism. The major doctrine of socialism was developed by Marx. There is, however, a liberal variety of socialism which has little to do with Marx. It is the attempt by social democracy to combine state control of the economy with political freedom. It is a major issue whether the two are compatible with each other.

This book uses material taken from two earlier books, *Capitalism* and *Social Democracy*, now out of print, but which have been much used in schools, colleges and universities. The themes have grown together, as the opposition of liberal capitalism and social democracy (on one side) and communism and authoritarianism (on the other) has developed in the 1970s. The political forms of liberty which are compatible with a technologically advanced economy seem to be on the defensive at the time of writing, but this will not necessarily always be the case.

Introduction

Peace and prosperity are what most people want much of the time. Since modern machinery came into widespread use two centuries ago, prosperity has depended upon the technology of the machine. We live in the first world-wide civilization. Artefacts like the transistor, the car, the aeroplane, metals like steel, plastics, are to be found in all but the most remote corners of the world. Prosperity depends upon this technology. And of course the technology has brought dreadful problems with it. Used destructively it could end the world by nuclear war, and pollution means that the sea casts up plastic bottles even in uninhabited regions. No serious alternative to the technology exists, however. At most suggestions for its modification are proposed.

This modern technology has been compatible with long periods of peace and with terrible wars. It has been compatible with tyrannies as foul as history has ever known, and with unparalleled liberal freedom.

In my judgement liberal freedom based on prosperity represents the best form of society yet known. It may not be ideal. But Utopian visions, like those of Marx, have led to hellish societies.

I have traced the history of modern industrialism, and of the various political forms that it has made possible. Constitutional democracy and social democracy are both based on prosperity. But tyranny has also emerged in prosperous countries.

In this book I have examined the links between the emergence of modern technology and the system of economic organization broadly known as capitalism. It is common ground to liberals and social democrats that the survival of some sort of decentralized economic system is necessary for continued technological progress and for the survival and development of constitutional and democratic government. The rough ride that the development of technology, and of capitalism, has given many people in many places at many times has led to the development of a series of theories about an alternative way of life. This alternative has been broadly labelled 'socialism', though it is composed of literally hundreds of disparate theories. Much of the practice that these theories have led to has been nevertheless incorporated in 'capitalism'.

The book begins in very early times, the classical civilizations of Rome and China, because economic behaviour with advanced technology has early roots, and there is no reason to believe that our ancestors were less clever or adaptable than we are. Why did they not invent industrialism? The book examines this question and sees capitalism emerging from the disruptions of medieval society to take a breath-taking leap into modern technology and world-wide industrialism.

It is this industrialism and its consequences which *are* our modern world. In it there are two main versions of liberal freedom – that usually known as liberal capitalism and that known as social democracy.

It becomes increasingly apparent that the compromise between the public and private sectors that has been achieved in North America and Western Europe since 1945 is a possible solution to the realities of life and people's aspirations, if constitutional democracy is to survive and develop. It has, however, yet to prove that it can survive the stresses and strains of the apparently limitless capacity of mankind for embracing tyranny, the forces of nationalism, and the environmental consequences of technological advance.

1 Early capitalism

What is capitalism?

Capitalism is a word that has had many meanings, and is still in dispute. It arouses opprobrium and adulation; violent opposition and enormous support. It can be interpreted socially, economically, or politically; it can be described in engineering terms or in human terms.

Capitalism is mainly a feature of the North Atlantic. It probably started in Italy, spread into Holland, then England, and across the Atlantic to the North American littoral. After that it spread until its tentacles embraced parts of every continent. Capitalism, therefore, though based on the North Atlantic, was the first world-wide civilization.

Its main feature has been steadily accelerating technical progress. As the early sections of this book will show, it would be a mistake – a grave mistake – to think that before capitalism the economies of the world were stationary, flat, and stagnant. Imperial Rome and Mandarin China reached peaks of technical achievement in some fields that were not reached again till the seventeenth and eighteenth centuries; the same is probably true of national income per head. Yet it is only since that time that continuously accelerating technical change has been a central feature of civilization.

The causes of this continuous technical change are manifold. The application of science and technology to human problems is probably the key factor; it was the invention of modern science (based on the rediscovery of Greek learning) that supplied the dry kindle, for which technological innovation provided the flame. The beginnings of modern technology centre on changes in energy production and changes in transport; and the linking of these at first small but crucial changes to generally acceptable scientific principles invented a mode of changing human society that has proved irreversible.

The continuous technical change – which is the central feature of capitalism – had to be embodied in physical capital and in the skilled labour force. The first condition, then, for the application of science and technology to human affairs was the accumulation of a surplus – capital that could be embodied in new machines and buildings. The accumulation of this surplus and its application to useful arts was therefore the economic condition that had to be established, before the scientific and technological changes could be firmly grounded. How to accumulate this surplus and apply it to the useful arts is the next question. The answer to that is the evolution of a number of separate groups or classes in society which could play important roles. The rich and powerful had always accumulated wealth; but so long as they used it on war, on ostentation, on religion, on themselves, it was not capable of application to useful arts. So somebody had to accumulate profits, or surpluses, by way of trade; somebody had to see openings, opportunities, occasions for profits to be made; somebody had to be prepared to employ large bodies of men and women; somebody had to be prepared to invest in factories, transport and production. These were not always the same people, because the functions were diverse. But in a world of landowners, farmers, soldiers, aristocrats, priests and other feudal beings there appeared a new phenomenon: merchants, traders, bankers, manufacturers, employers and retailers, as a self-conscious group, were now borrowing money, investing it, getting profits and spending their profits on further investment. It was their concern with profit, and its reinvestment to yield still more profit, that differentiated them from other social groups. It is their ascension to a dominant social and cultural position which is the hallmark of capitalism.

The corollary of this is the rise of money, and the market system, to a dominant mode of relationships. Mankind moved from status to contract. It was money values, the anonymous arbiter of the price system, that tied all the different parts of the capitalist economic system together. It was not, as in Rome, allegiance to an emperor; or allegiance to a pope; or allegiance to a creed; or submission to a military tyrant: it was an acceptance of a link, via prices, to the profit and loss system of the market economy which indicated that a country, a region, a port or a city had gone over to capitalism.

A further feature of the capitalist system was the evolution of a group in the community – eventually to be numerically dominant – who were propertyless, not tied to the soil or to any specific place, who depended for their existence upon wages. The wages were paid to them by capitalists for work done; and when there was no work, there was no pay. In earlier societies, whether slave societies, Asian societies, or feudal societies, the subsistence of the worker and his family was implicitly guaranteed by his status and was (to a greater or lesser degree) divorced from his work. Not so with capitalism. Work for wages and no other obligations was the order of the day. This propertyless, wage-earning, often unemployed group of people was christened by Marx 'the proletariat'. It was the proletariat which was to overthrow the bourgeois, or capitalist, state. It was the proletariat, it seemed, that in the North Atlantic world refused to overthrow the bourgeois state, and became itself a bit bourgeois.

What was the bourgeois state? The early capitalists saw it as a referee, and no more. Its functions were to dwindle. Its swaddling clothes were to be thrown off so that the capitalists could be free to pursue profit. But eventually the state was rebuilt in a new form: first, to wage war and to occupy colonial territories, and second, to cope with the immense social and technical problems of running the proper environment for a prosperous industrial society. Far from withering away, the state has become the most dramatic and important feature of capitalism. And it is the state, allied to nationalism, that has moved the world out of capitalism into the era of scientific-militarism.

When did it begin?
Capitalism has many faces and many aspects. Its start, therefore, can be assigned to many periods. It was in full bloom over most of the world between 1880 and 1914. Thereafter its geographical area began to contract. Its early blooming could be seen over most of Europe and the east of North America (as well as in a few offshoots like South Africa and the Australasian

colonies) in 1820. It was coming into wide acceptance in Europe, and especially in Britain, by 1770. Most of this book, therefore, is concerned with the period post-1820. But much of the major manifestation of high capitalism – capitalism in full bloom – could be seen in embryonic form from very early times.

Take, first, the advance of science. The rediscovery of Greek knowledge and the adaptation of Arab learning spread through western Europe after the fourteenth and fifteenth centuries. Galileo, Copernicus, Newton began a tradition of scientific enquiry that, with a few hesitations, became ever stronger, until its victory was assured at the time of Darwin and Huxley and the great nineteenth-century chemists and physicists. The triumph of the scientific spirit, which spread into history, biblical studies, the study of the classics, can be dated to the mid-nineteenth century; and its main foci were Britain and Germany.

The unleashing of continuous technological innovation is a little harder to date. The complexity of French clockwork, the ingeniousness of many Chinese devices (and they invented gunpowder), was matched to a degree by some of the achievements, especially in civil engineering, of the Greeks and Romans. By comparison, much of the engineering associated with the industrial revolution, such as the invention of the steam engine and its use to draw trains along the rails, was crude and unimaginative. But the industrial revolution, and especially its embodiment in energy and transport, was linked closely to scientific principles, and through the development of both mechanical and civil engineering it became a continuously accelerating process applied to more and more walks of life. It would be wrong to think that change had not occurred before the invention of the steam engine. The sailing ship, for example, had evolved from a small, bulky and inefficient vessel, mainly propelled by oars, as used in Roman times, to fast schooners whose rate of travel was many times that of their predecessors. Each generation of ships embodied some improvements over what had gone before. But steam and steel meant a qualitative difference in the adaptation of techniques, and the process of change was rapid. As soon as an apparent plateau had been reached in technological design, as with the railway at the end of the nineteenth century, a new form of equipment came along – in this case the internal combustion engine. It would be right, it seems, to assign the period of the engineer's rise to dominance as the period in which the supremacy of the technologist, and his rooting in scientific principles, first became apparent. This can be dated fairly nearly to the spread of the steam railway in Britain, in the early 1830s, which is the period when most of Samuel Smiles' heroes in *Lives of the Great Engineers* were prominent.

The rise of capitalists was much earlier than the rise of capitalist technology. In all recorded time there have always been merchants and traders, and they were prominent in organizing the trade routes (which reached India and China) of the Ancient World. The Arab traders were famous. The rise of Venice in the wake of the Crusades is well documented. By the thirteenth and fourteenth centuries the Italian city states and some northern cities were active centres of trade, with rich traders. By the seventeenth century whole countries – Holland and England – were ruled partly by merchants, whose family interests were linked to all the recognized sources of authority and power.

The application of farming surpluses to trade, and of manufacturing profits to agriculture, is a well attested phenomenon of eighteenth-century England. The brewers, who were among the first big industrialists, put some of their profits into farming, and big farmers put some of their profits into brewing. It is this sort of process – the utilization of surpluses, through country banks, and the lending of the surpluses to industrialists – which is a central feature of capitalism. A well developed banking system existed in western Europe by the mid-eighteenth century. A tradition of engineering-minded entrepreneurs evolved, at first mainly in England but then elsewhere, who began to transform the economy. Wedgwood in pottery is an example of a name that became world-famous for the application of new techniques to a traditional occupation; and he became rich in the process, while his products were transported all over the capitalist world. It had been the same with Chinese pottery, but this had not been produced by Wedgwood's methods of bulk production, nor had it been financed and transported in the same way.

Marx and Engels have written vividly of the rise of the

working class – the spread of the landless labourers. As methods of agriculture changed and as the birth rate rose, so the surplus of population congregated in the cities and worked for capitalists, for wages. By the mid-nineteenth century this was the most common way of earning a living in England, in northern France, and in parts of the United States. By the end of the nineteenth century it was the landed peasant who was untypical in western Europe and North America.

The emergence of the bourgeois state is associated with the overthrow of the feudal regulation of trade – Free Trade in England in 1846, the Cobden treaty with France in 1860, the abolition of slavery in America in 1863, the abolition of serfdom in Russia in 1861 – and the rise of a small bureaucracy wholly or partly responsible to a Parliament elected mainly by the business classes.

Engineering, the rise of capitalists, the emergence of the working class, and the transformation of the state all point to the early nineteenth century as the very period when capitalism, as it became known, finally emerged.

The Ancient World

It may be assumed that whatever mankind's particular genius may be, it was not less present in the time of the Ancient Greeks and Romans than it was in nineteenth-century western Europe. Yet the Ancient World, which had many of the preconditions for capitalism – that is for continuous technical progress, revealing itself in the steady accumulation of the means of production – did not achieve capitalism. Consider what Greece and Rome had. Science reached a peak that was certainly not recovered till the seventeenth century, and possibly even later. Roman roads were technically in advance of any means of transport till the canals of eighteenth-century England. Roman agriculture produced crops which in yield and quality were possibly not equalled till the eighteenth century. The aqueducts and roads, temples and houses were triumphs of civil engineering. The Roman Empire, especially, produced huge surpluses, which were available for investment. There was a large class of merchants and traders, which traded as far as China and India (the caravan route for silks was used by the Greeks in the fourth century BC). At the height of the Empire civil peace prevailed over an area which reached thousands of miles – from Gibraltar to Asia Minor, from Scotland to Africa. The process of governing such a vast Empire was developed to the highest degree of sophistication.

But it never developed into capitalism. Historians of classical times have long pondered the reasons. One is that the technology, though advanced, was not systematically linked to a body of scientific principles, so that a brilliant innovation was not necessarily part of a cumulative, reasoned process.

Another reason is that the ancients never operated a full money economy. Money, to them, it seems, was used in the way that small change is used. It was valued because it was made of gold, silver, or copper, not because it was a medium of exchange on which credit could be built. It was not the basis of credit; it was not accumulated in banks; surpluses were not systematically lent by one sector of the economy to another sector, so that, while there were merchants and traders, they did not occupy the same social role that a modern capitalist fulfils. There was no class of men organizing production on borrowed money and selling the produce at a profit, though apparently there were individuals, or small groups, who did so.

More important, the Ancient World was a slave economy. The spread of conquest brought in continuing supplies of slaves, and their labour was the basis of much production. When the supply of slaves dwindled, production languished. The significance of this is that the 'free' wage bargain, between a propertyless worker and an employer producing for profit (and using borrowed capital or credit to finance the process), was not capable of becoming a significant feature of Greek or Roman society so long as the slave owner could legally possess all the fruits of the slave's work. The productive possibility of the free wage bargain was not foreseen; nor could it be, until the crude exploitation represented by slavery was ended.

Above all, perhaps, the secularization of the world that accompanied capitalism was never achieved by the Greeks and Romans. It was an era of militaristic triumphs and defeats, of gods and goddesses, of a society utterly unlike anything that has been consonant with capitalism. There is little point in arguing what is cause and what is effect; the fact of the matter is that in Greek and Roman life the community was dominant over the individual. The community's aims were not high production or individual profit, but the pursuit of military glory, social achievement, and religious satisfaction. These clever, achievement-motivated, remarkable societies (in many respects the most remarkable the world has ever seen) were not capitalist societies.

Might Rome have become one? Its embryonic monetary institutions were destroyed by a disastrous inflation, under Valerian in 256, which spread and could not be stopped. There were more large estates, and gradually the agricultural basis of the society diminished. The government extended its operations to cover many aspects of life; it was an autarchic and arbitrary society. Then the barbarian invasions began to erode the Empire, until large parts of it collapsed. The slaves and the serfs merged into a class which bore the brunt of the economic and political crisis. A combination of attack from without and problems within brought economic activity to a lower level, from which capitalism ultimately emerged.

China

In the eighteenth century China may have had double the population of Europe, and it probably had a higher standard of living even than Holland, the richest country in the West. This fortunate economic position had lasted for many centuries; even at the time of the Roman Empire it seems probable that China was more populous and that its people were richer. The Chinese had relatively settled government, with a complex administrative system. Their scientific and technical achievements were ahead of those of the West. Their agriculture was more intensive. They had a skilled workforce.

China was a world in itself, of many kingdoms, as early as the Egyptian and Babylonian civilizations. The country was a unity, but a unity as a civilization (like medieval Christian Europe) rather than as a political entity like the Roman Empire. By the second century AD China had contacts with Persia, Rome and southern Asia, both by sea and by land.

The conquest of China by alien Buddhist nomads unified it politically, but the culture (which was Confucian, with ancestor worship at its centre) absorbed the conquerors, as the Indian culture absorbed conqueror after conqueror. Unlike Europe,

China did not pass through a period of the 'Dark Ages'. The culture continued to grow richer, not thinner; the population continued to increase; and the bond of a common language grew tighter.

During the T'ang Empire (618–907) China extended its links with Byzantium, Japan, India and Persia. By this time it was clear that China had the most advanced civilization in the world, and it was during this period that the Chinese came to regard all other civilizations as barbarous, akin to the barbarian nomads of the steppes, the foreigners with whom they were most familiar. The Chinese had a civil service recruited by competitive examination. They had widespread literacy and cultivation of the arts. They had a relative abundance of food, provided from a carefully managed agriculture which relied on complex irrigation works, and they had advanced methods of manufacture of cloth and pottery and utensils.

Even when the Mongolians overthrew the T'ang dynasty and broke with its traditions, within a century the old order was re-established. But the condition of the restoration was respect for the past, in every particular, and contempt for change and the outside world. By the fifteenth century, when America was rediscovered by the Europeans, China had a population of two hundred million (probably three times that of Europe) and was living a settled, complex life, with a rich culture and moderate prosperity. Western visitors like Marco Polo were astonished at the wealth and vitality of Chinese cities and the complexity of their science and mechanical contrivances. The Ming civilization, the civilization which came into contact with Europe (chiefly the Portuguese), was not only an imitation of the T'ang traditions. In its porcelain, pottery, architecture and metalwork its developments were magnificent. But though these developments can be seen as representing a break with the past, generally it is true that the hierarchical nature of the society and its predominant tone of respect for the past (centred on the veneration of ancestors) were not conducive to a class of entrepreneurial innovators.

Gradually the Portuguese, the Dutch and the English established themselves on the coasts of China, in enclaves. It was from these enclaves that they brought back Chinese tea, porcelain and silks, and other rarities. But, because they traded from enclaves, their trading habits did not spread like an infection, as they did elsewhere.

European technical and commercial development, then, went on independently of China; and the isolation of China from the rest of the world meant that it fell relatively behind Europe, technologically. The Manchu conquest from the north, in the seventeenth century, was absorbed, like all other conquests. But it enfeebled the political and administrative structure of the Empire, and as the threat from the north disappeared – since Manchuria and China were now one, and Manchuria, though the conqueror, adopted the ways of the conquered – China's military strength decayed. Consequently, when European imperialists arrived in strength, the Chinese were unable seriously to resist. The opium war of 1842 was based on a pretext: tired of trading with the Chinese mainly in silver, the East India Company insisted on exporting opium, and on the Imperial government's refusal to trade on this basis, gunboats were sent. There followed a series of rebellions, exacerbated by the pressure of population on land, which finally brought the Chinese Empire down.

Thus the great Chinese civilization did not produce the scientific technology that was to transform the world, nor, having seen it, did it find that technology interesting or acceptable. The reasons were a combination of legitimate satisfaction with things as they were and a social structure with no room for entrepreneurs.

The Middle Ages

The Middle Ages stretch from the end of the Ancient World, in the fifth and sixth centuries, to the beginnings of capitalism, in the sixteenth and seventeenth centuries. The changes into capitalism began in western Europe in about 1500. It would be absurd, of course, to imagine that this period of a thousand years, followed by two to three centuries of preparation for full-blown capitalism, could be considered as a homogeneous unit; but certain central points stand out which are essential for a full understanding of capitalism as it emerged in western Europe.

First, the Roman Empire never wholly died, either in the East or in the West. The Byzantine civilization continued many of the

practices of the later Roman Empire, though it lost the aggressive expansionist militarism of the Romans, turning more to
trade. Constantinople became the centre of trade for the Middle
East, for distant Asia and for Europe. Next, the Latin successor
societies to Rome in western Europe seem to have kept to a
degree some of the urban life that had been characteristic of
Rome; in France and Italy, some of the rural life probably
survived substantially. The Arab invasions which swept across
Asia, across North Africa, and into Europe, up to the Pyrenees
and beyond, cut off western Europe from much of the Byzantine trade, but the Arab traders in their turn developed a
substantial land and sea trade across Islam. In Spain, where the
Arab and Latin cultures mingled and to some extent merged,
the Arabs and Jews became the centre of diffusion of Greek and
Arabic scientific and philosophical works, so that Greek science
and culture penetrated Islam and in turn penetrated the Latin
cultures. The characteristic of later medieval society, therefore,
was that it was unusually open (in comparison with other
societies) to ideas from a variety of cultures.

Next, the development of sailing vessels, especially under the
impact of Arab achievements and navigation, and small but
significant improvements in many of the mechanical arts,
gradually increased the productive potential of medieval
society, which though less rich and powerful than Imperial
Rome was less vulnerable to outside attack and inner collapse.
During the period of the Crusades (roughly 1096 to 1204) the
Venetians and their associates entered significantly into
Mediterranean trade, both with Arabs and Christians. The
Fourth Crusade, indeed, was marked by an attack on Constantinople, the capital of the Greek Orthodox Church, which gave
Venice access to trading links that stretched across to China,
where a Venetian merchant, Marco Polo, travelled in the late
thirteenth century. Thus the Italian city states grew in wealth
from trade with the whole Euro-Asian land mass, as well as with
North Africa, and the level of intellectual, artistic, technical
and scientific achievement rose significantly as the Greek, Arab
and Latin cultures came into contact.

Northern Europe developed a similar sea-borne trade,
stretching from Ireland to Russia, with links round and across
Europe to Italy. It was based on goods like wool, fish, timber,

grain and cloth. Again merchants made fortunes, and cities like Bruges and Antwerp grew rich. A characteristic of medieval society, then, was the independence of trading cities; the fact that these cities – Genoa, Venice, Bruges, Pisa, and, a little later, London and Paris (in fact many of the great cities of modern Europe) – were rich, and powerful, and centres of intellectual life, was to become central to emerging capitalism. A network of trade existed all across Europe, with links round the world. There were vigorous intellectual centres at the key points of this trade network. At the heart of this intellectual activity were moneyed men, making profits by buying and selling, who dominated their cities.

They bought and sold partly on behalf of their fellow citizens and partly on behalf of the rural population. Late medieval life was predominantly rural (as was most of the world until the late nineteenth century), but it differed from classical times in that the central government was weak and the local lords were powerful. The feudal structure – oversimplified and formalized of course – consisted of a territory belonging to a feudal lord, a class of tenants, or yeomen, owing some feudal dues to the landlord, and a class of labourers, owing substantial dues, but in return expecting a living from the land. When a catastrophe like the Black Death took place, causing wages to rise, or when a substantial price inflation occurred, the feudal system began to break down. Some feudal lords began to use some of their surplus to enter trade, while some labourers were expelled from the land and began to form the beginnings of a class of landless labourers seeking employment in the towns. As prices rose and new knowledge began to affect production techniques, so agricultural relationships began to change. But in all this loosely organized medieval system tightly linked by trade, there was room for the towns to grow and prosper, and for the spirit of profit to dissolve feudal bonds.

It was in this fertile soil that the seeds of the new geographical and intellectual discoveries of the late fifteenth century were sown.

The rise of trade
Many medieval towns were based mainly on trade, and the trade network was to grow and become increasingly far-flung.

The rising incomes of the towns and their rural hinterlands demanded more and more silks, spices and other treasures, as well as basic commodities like wool and timber, salt and grain, wines and hides. The technology of the sailing boat and the art of navigation improved, so that expeditions were made along the shores of Africa, to India, and across the Atlantic to America. Vasco da Gama, Cabot, Christopher Columbus, Sir Francis Drake, are among the best known of scores of sea captains who pioneered new trade routes and discovered, or rediscovered, civilizations not known to the medieval world. Trade was extended to India and most of Asia on a big scale, and whole civilizations, like those of the Aztecs and Incas in South and Central America, were plundered. Wealth flowed into western Europe. Though initially some of the wealth went to maintain and develop the splendour of kings, princes, and bishops, as in Spain and Portugal, much of it enriched the merchants of the thriving cities of Italy and northern Europe.

At the same time, feudalism was breaking down. The rise of wages after the dreadful population losses of the Black Death and the Hundred Years War (about one-third of England's population died in two years, 1348 and 1349, during the Black Death) was but one of many causes of the decline of the manorial system. The growth of local trade made it profitable to produce agricultural commodities – especially grain – for local markets. Increasingly, feudal dues and services were commuted for money, and the landowner became a moneyed man as well as a lord. In some countries the feudal lords attacked each other, destroying their own power, as in England; elsewhere, as in France, they consolidated it with the monarchy. In those countries where the traders were allowed freely to operate, or where they were able to ally themselves with the political authority, the landowners began themselves to drift into trade. Allied to this shift in the importance of trade, which was promoted by an apparently noticeable rise in national incomes, was a shift of political and religious ideas.

The great trading routes rapidly spread across the Atlantic, the Indian Ocean and the whole of Europe. The early capitalists – people like the Fuggers in Augsburg and the Medicis in Florence – were merchants turned bankers. As banking developed, together with significant advances in commercial practices such as double-entry book-keeping, it became possible to finance large-scale trade, enabling the products of large-scale industry to be exchanged. The earliest industrial revolution was probably in the manufacture of cloth, with the development of the watermill to enable mechanical fulling to take place (fulling is the process of removing grease from wool); cloth-making was the earliest large-scale manufacturing trade, in Flanders, then in Florence, and finally in England, where it formed the basis of sixteenth-century expansion. Trade in agricultural products hastened the transformation of medieval farming, to enable the production of wool, of grain surpluses, and of timber to be stepped up.

By the late sixteenth century, then, northern Italy, parts of France and southern Germany, Flanders and England were linked by great trading centres (almost all ports) into a complex process of trade. This trade was rapidly increasing inside a number of countries, though in some countries it received political setbacks, in Germany's case from the Thirty Years War, and in Spain and Portugal from the development of theocratic absolutism.

Trade carried with it new attitudes to religion and politics. The nation state came into being, as did Protestantism, which by a process of pressures also called into being a reformed Catholicism. Luther, the original heretic, was as opposed to usury as the medieval papacy had been; Calvin, however, was the archetypal Protestant whom later historians were to identify as the embodiment of the Puritan spirit of early capitalism. His emphasis on hard work, frugality, thrift and self-reliance was an essential ideology sanctioning the capitalist spirit of enterprise, profit seeking, and the utilization of retained profits in other enterprises. Early bankers made some of their income by lending to princes; though they were to continue to do this, the new and acceptable way was to lend it to finance enterprise.

By the end of the medieval period, then, with the fall of the Universal Church, the opening up of trade, the rise of New Learning and the scientific spirit, and the development of respect for a merchant-venturer class in a significant number of big cities in growing nation states, output was rising and a growing surplus was falling into the hands of families anxious to use it to develop productive enterprise, in order to engage in ever more profitable trade, both local and long-distance. The self-sufficient man was already old-fashioned; the age of specialization had begun, and with specialization large-scale production of single commodities could be undertaken. Given the existence of adequate capital, growing markets, and the possibility of a rational development of technology, the capitalist revolution was now possible. The seventeenth and eighteenth centuries therefore saw a great growth of trade, great increases in output, and a continuous expansion of western Europe's frontiers, both by means of trade and conquest. Population increased, as did the care of cultivated land. On the swelling tide of this prosperity, Europe's new limits were quickly to out-distance those of Imperial Rome; and its ideas – essentially the Enlightenment, the very spirit of capitalism – were to conquer most of the world in a way that Rome had never done.

The spread of mercantile empires

The ubiquity of capitalism in 1900 was at least partly explained by the fact that the dominance of western Europe was established by 1700. The spread of European empires was related to the spread of capitalism in a complex way. Capitalism eventually reached parts of every country in the world, and almost every country in the world was controlled by people of European stock. This may have been an inevitable consequence of triumphant capitalism (as trade developed, so the flag was bound to follow); but the evidence is to the contrary. Trade and the flag went jointly and, having conquered much of the world, capitalism rushed in to fill the vacuum. When it was a decadent or bastard capitalism, as in Spain and Portugal, then those areas of the world colonized by the Spanish and Portuguese had a decadent and incompetent colonial capitalism. When, as with North America, the conquest was by high capitalism, the consequence was an even more triumphant transplanted capitalism.

How then did Europe conquer the world? In the first place by trade and plunder. The Portuguese, Spanish, French, British and Dutch established trading posts from China to Peru, from the Cape to Newfoundland. These trading posts became centres where indigenous produce was collected, and where goods for

Europe were bartered. The home ports became great entrepôt centres, where goods were exchanged from all over the earth. In some cases, however, the trading posts became centres of immigration, as happened all up the eastern littoral of North America, in parts of South America and on the Cape of Good Hope. In America, North and South, some of the native population was murdered, part was assimilated, and the rest was driven into the wilderness, the High Andes and the mountain chains of North America. In West Africa, the population was decimated by slavery. In India, China and Japan, however, no large permanent settlements were made.

Two marked features stand out. Latin America apart, the great conquests of world trade routes were made by companies of merchant venturers, like the Dutch East India Company or the Hudson Bay Company. The profits of these quasi-military, quasi-empire, quasi-merchant bodies, gained by trade conducted against a background of superior physical force, went straight to merchants, not to governments. In Spain and Portugal, of course, the surpluses went to princes and kings. The merchants used their profits to earn more profits; the kings used their surpluses for the glory of themselves and of their God.

Secondly, the impact of trade was to dissolve existing civilizations. It has already been argued that trade had dissolved the medieval Christian civilization of Europe, just as a pertinacious weed will force apart huge stones in a great castle or triumphal arch. Trade was even more effective in dissolving the high civilizations of the Muslims, the Hindus, China and Japan, to say nothing of lesser cultures like those of the Incas and the Aztecs. The pursuit of profit in South America was transmuted to the pursuit of loot, and the dissolution of the Aztec and Inca civilizations was accomplished by a hateful force, reminiscent of the violent atrocities of our own day against the Jews, the Kulaks and the Biafrans; but the energy which caused the initial contact was the pursuit of trading routes to the east. In India, by contrast, blessedly free from hidalgos and priests, the British, Dutch and French traded; then the British conquered. But they hardly ever looted, they never massacred and they never settled. Yet the native civilization deteriorated and withered. It is this aspect of the conquest of the rest of the world which is most interesting, for what the Spaniards did in Peru was not much different from what the Anglo-Saxons had done to Roman Britain, or the Goths to Italy. The holding of India by a group of merchants, with very little force, is a remarkable feature of world history. India was not converted to capitalism, except in ports like Calcutta and Bombay. It was embraced by it, and gently milked, first of its treasure – gold, and silks and spices – and then of its commodities, like rice and cotton. It was kept like a fattening cow in capitalism's farmyard; Latin America was ruthlessly despatched in the Spanish abattoir. Latin America nominally became Catholic; nobody seriously bothered to make India Protestant. A contented Hindu cow yielded a lot of milk.

China and Japan are two more variants of a pattern which became very general. Neither was conquered, yet the high Chinese civilization virtually dissolved as its principal centres fell into the trade network. Japan, after resisting involvement for several centuries, underwent a hysterical conversion and became almost more capitalist than the capitalists. In neither case did the Europeans bother to conquer, or to convert the inhabitants to their official religion. All they wanted was for the Chinese and the Japanese to trade; and, by trading, the old ways were broken and new ways were adopted.

The merchant venturers initially sought, then, precious or rare goods – furs, spices, silks, jewels, gold and silver. By the end of the nineteenth century their trading empire had progressed from producing rare raw products, or ingenious handicrafts, to the bulk production of raw materials – wood, cotton, grains, meat, timber, coal, copper – which were manufactured in Europe or North America and sold back to the empire. Some parts of the world, indeed, were so warmly embraced that they themselves built their own Manchesters: Calcutta, Buenos Aires, Sydney, Johannesburg became outposts of industrial capitalism.

The accumulation of capital

Trade, especially trade with Asia, America and Africa, was the source of much capital. It accumulated in the hands of the merchants, who used it to finance more trade, as well as to finance the production of the goods which were taken out from

Europe to be sold. The profits from the East Indies trade and from the slave trade were enormous; the merchants engaged became some of the wealthiest men in Europe. They married, especially in England, into almost the best families, and achieved great political influence. It was in this way that they helped to create the conditions in which mercantile capitalism could prosper still further. Permission to charge interest (which offended the laws against usury), internal peace and security, the protection of the fleets of merchant vessels – all these were matters of concern to the great merchants, and in northern Europe especially they had their way.

There were other sources of capital. As some of the merchants became bankers, so the practice of extending credit spread, and it became possible to borrow to finance trade and production. This practice, which was to be the basis of high capitalism, began in a small way in Italy and southern Germany (where it was handicapped by the usury laws) but it took a qualitative forward leap in England in the eighteenth century. By 1800 there was a network of country banks, based on London, which was a viable system, accustomed to extending short-term credit to businessmen. Above all, there was a network of city financial institutions which was used for financing foreign trade.

The 'price revolution' of the sixteenth and seventeenth centuries, which accompanied the flow of gold and silver from Latin America to Europe, was a potent force in enabling capitalists to accumulate surpluses. This price revolution, which may have been due to the quite unprecedented expansion of the money base through the importation of precious metals, had a series of direct and indirect economic and social consequences which were of supreme importance. It impoverished many landowners, whose real incomes fell, and encouraged them to sell their lands, thus bringing more and more of agriculture into the capitalist sector of the economy. The wage earners certainly lost part of their incomes as a result of the inflation. Thus the poor, having increased their earnings after the population scarcity in the fourteenth century, and achieved for some of their number an escape from feudalism, now found their real wage levels falling. The relative impoverishment of both landowners and workers helped to enrich the merchants and the capitalists who employed wage earners. The great rise in profits during the sixteenth and seventeenth centuries enriched a great many quite ordinary people and encouraged more and more people to attempt to become capitalists. As the ideological temper of society changed, too, more and more people came to regard it as worthy and worthwhile to become profit earners, to become merchants and manufacturers.

The sources of capital accumulation greatly expanded, coming from overseas trade, internal trade, and a rise in the profits level. So, too, did the opportunities for the profitable use of capital. It was used first in trade and in the transport associated with trade. There was a significant advance in the technology of shipping, an improvement in ports and the safeguarding of overland routes. Capital was also increasingly applied to agriculture, manufacturing and mining; in many branches of industry there were series of small changes which cumulatively became significant. Nef has documented this for English coalmining. It was notable in European agriculture, and, to take another example, the manufacture of cloth became progressively cheaper. Thus profits were rising because technology was causing costs to fall in many lines of business.

One less obvious fact, which is none the less important, is that in many parts of the world the 'wasteful' use of a surplus was far less than it had ever been before. Europe may have been divided by religion and factions, and may hardly ever have been wholly at peace; political history is full of wars. But during this period they were minor wars. Apart from the Thirty Years War, few devastated whole territories: even the French revolutionary wars, and Napoleon, who conquered huge amounts of territory, did little damage to property or people. And when institutions were destroyed, they were often (not always) replaced by institutions more favourable to capitalism than those they replaced. Napoleon, in many respects, made Europe ripe for capitalism by giving it a framework of law, and aggrandizing the capitalist class. Also, after Islam finally lost its dynamic, Europe was free from serious attack from without; Islam's capture of Constantinople in 1453 turned out to be the last serious attack on Europe by non-capitalist forces. And the conquest of the rest of the world was achieved at little cost to Europe in blood or treasure. It is this sense of a world that was mainly secure, in which accumulation could safely proceed, which contrasts most significantly with the arbitrary tyrannies elsewhere, and the constant threats from without which had often made the tyrannies necessary for defence and security.

Flamboyant expenditure was less of a drain, too. Many of the cities were beautiful. Monarchs, princes, merchants and bishops still built ever more sumptuous palaces and castles; the baroque was one of the world's great architectural styles. But in the capitalist world more and more building was for use, and not for religion, a trend which culminated perhaps in the Empire State Building, built for offices in 1931, at a cost of $40 million, 'as a monument to man's lofty ideals', as the publicists said. It would be quite untrue to say that the rise of capitalism was accompanied by a dying down of aesthetic or spiritual achievement. But it would be true to say that less of the surplus was devoted to the equivalent of the pyramids or the medieval cathedrals. Even Versailles, or Schönbrunn, were relatively cheaper than the pyramids. And western Europe, as it entered early capitalism, was richer than almost any society that had ever been known. Its poor people were probably not much richer than their predecessors of several hundred years before, but the surplus which their labour helped to achieve was not spent on the glorification of their masters, or on the destruction of mankind, but mainly on the creation of useful objects. Capitalism may have been immoral, unattractive, destructive, but it was a furnace which forged ploughshares, not swords – and ploughshares of ever improving quality in ever increasing numbers.

The rise of a capitalist class
The early capitalists were merchants. Some of them, like the Medicis, came early to political power. In Venice they controlled the state. Others, like Sir Josiah Child in England, were powerful men of influence. In general, it is safe to say that by the seventeenth century many important international trading cities were governed by groups of merchants, who were increasingly exercising powers over the nation states in which they were found. The most vivid instance of this was the power of the City of London in England, which not only dominated the country almost openly under Oliver Cromwell, but continued

to be of supreme importance under his Restoration successors. Thus the merchant, operating perhaps in a company of merchant venturers, living with his family in a city dominated by other merchants, was one representative of the rising capitalist class. In England he might marry his daughters into the gentry, and thus gradually the influence of his family and his money would spread into agriculture.

Other capitalists, hardly worthy of the name it might be thought, were local merchants, corn chandlers, leather sellers, dealing in local commodities locally. But gradually, in England, the Low Countries and North America, such small fry became a powerful and significant group, linked as they were to the yeoman farmers by bonds of marriage and credit. It is worthy of note how important the family was in capitalism. The essence of credit is trust: you have to have faith that your loan will be repaid. A tight-knit family was often the best guarantee of security. Thus capitalist families, great and small, were built up, linked with each other by marriage, and, usually, by common religious convictions.

To this growing class of big and small merchants and bankers the early capitalist industrialists and farmers must be added. The essence of a capitalist industrialist was that he was an organizer. The earliest industrialists were 'putters out'. A clothier, who has been claimed to be the origin of the industrial capitalist, was a man who owned the wool from the time it left the sheep's back till the time it went to a tailor. The specialization of labour usually entailed at least a dozen stages between shearing the sheep and selling the cloth, each performed by a different group of people. The clothier organized the whole process. To do so he needed organizing – 'entrepreneurial' – skill, capital, and good business contacts. It was, of course, by modern standards a technically extremely inefficient system. The rate of loss was very high. Efficiency eventually dictated that some of the stages at least should be performed under one roof. That roof was owned by the capitalist, and the machinery that came to be invented was installed and owned by him as well. The early industrial capitalists, therefore, evolved from merchants who acted as coordinators of an industrial (or agricultural or extractive) process into owners of fixed capital who employed workers by the hour or day or week, on their own premises. Some of the earliest capitalists in this sense were the coal owners (for the demands for energy soon grew as industrialism began), and the capitalist farmers. But the industrial revolution as commonly understood first manifested itself in the consumer goods trades, of which textiles, pottery and brewing were the most important. The capitalist owned not merely the materials used in production, but the tools and the buildings. The fixed capital (as opposed to the 'circulating capital' represented by the raw materials being processed and the wages advanced to the workers before the final goods were sold) embodied the technological progress known as the industrial revolution. The fixed equipment, which used energy derived ultimately from coal, was extremely expensive, and the industrial capitalists often therefore became big capitalists. By the mid-nineteenth century the term 'capitalist' applied at least as much to manufacturers as it did to traders, to industrialists as much as to bankers.

These industrialists had to have high technical ability. So, too, a successful banker or farmer had to be up-to-date in his knowledge and skilful at his business, to survive in an increasingly specialized and competitive world. For a feature of capitalism, compared with the societies that preceded it, was the high degree of specialization that took place. It was the market system that permitted and encouraged specialization. As soon as there was a market, and people could charge what the market could bear, and could make new products rather than selling conventional products at a 'just' price fixed by a guild of producers, then the competitive skill of a producer became of dominant importance in determining his personal fortune. If he was to keep ahead of competitors, he had to try to modify and improve his products. Thus the early capitalists came to be highly technically qualified people.

The capitalist class, then, included merchants, small and big traders, bankers, manufacturers and farmers. Through their family networks they came to include many of the members of the professions; but their central focus was 'business'. The capitalist class was differentiated on the one hand from the landowners and peasants by deriving its income from business rather than mere ownership – 'business' being defined precisely as buying and selling goods and services – and on the other hand it was differentiated from the working class by the possession of capital. Its members lived mainly in the towns, and their connections came to occupy prominent – even dominant – positions in society. And as the 'bourgeoisie', or those who controlled the towns, were the rising class, it tended to be their cultural values that became the dominant values of society as a whole. Thus the bourgeoisie came to control more of the state; it was their tastes that determined the market for art; and it was their thought that became the fashionable thought.

So the capitalist class was much wider than the group of businessmen who ran the capitalist economies. It was a group which formed the elect in many walks of life, from the Church to the arts. Yet it would be wrong to think that the bourgeoisie was unopposed, or that it was itself homogeneous. As late as the 1860s, even in England, Parliament was still numerically dominated by the landowners, though the landowners had long been intermarried with the bourgeoisie. In Germany the princes and the hereditary aristocracy were the governing class until the 1860s. Indeed, in France, in many respects a pre-industrial capitalist country, the Second Empire and the Third Republic were remarkable for their bourgeois character, compared with other European countries. The trappings and often the realities of power rested with the landowners, especially in Russia, the Iberian peninsula and other parts of Europe. The workers and the peasants too provided occasional rumblings against capitalism which broke out into violence from time to time, as in 1848 and 1871 in France. The bourgeoisie itself was deeply divided: first by nationality, and then by religion and cultural allegiance. Despite the international character of capitalism, it was associated with the rise of nationalism and ideologies, which, ultimately, brought it several times almost to the ground.

Technical innovations

Capitalism was synonymous with technical progress. For millennia, of course, technical change had taken place, but had done so fitfully and with frequent regressions, as civilizations rose and fell. Only such basic discoveries as fire and the wheel seem to have survived from civilization to civilization; more complex techniques had to be reinvented. From the fifteenth and sixteenth centuries, however, technical progress moved forward with increasing rapidity. The significant advances were in transport, energy, textiles and other consumer goods, metalwork and agriculture.

The evolution of the sailing ship has already been mentioned. It made possible rapid, frequent and reliable sea journeys, carrying bulky cargo and considerable numbers of passengers. Road transport improved quickly with the coming of the turnpikes in England. Thus when the steam engine was introduced to railways and ships, it came into a situation where a big transport system already existed, visiting all continents, and enabling substantial trade to be carried on.

The second acceleration of technology was in energy. Windmills and watermills were not new, windmills having been used in Europe since the twelfth century, and watermills probably a little earlier, though both had a Chinese ancestry. By the seventeenth century both windmills and watermills were ubiquitous. Coal had been used for centuries as a domestic fuel, before it became widely used in England as an industrial fuel in the seventeenth and eighteenth centuries. To mine coal for domestic use from deep seams, the first steam engines were developed by Savary and Newcomen to pump out water. Newcomen's engine, developed in 1712, was the first successful steam engine. Carlo Cipolla, the brilliant economic historian, points out that by the time of its invention, western Europe's per capita consumption of energy was already greater than Roman society had ever known; he attributes this higher rate of energy consumption to the absence of slavery (or muscle power). It is also attributable to the steadily rising demand for manufactures which created conditions where technical improvement steadily paid off the cost of innovation. It was against the background of rising energy consumption that James Watt's development of the steam engine occurred; and with that development the enormous forces of the industrial revolution were let loose. Watt's engines, and those designed by his successors, had become prevalent by 1800 in the textile industries and in brewing. By 1850 'the age of steam' was well under way. Thus the end of the eighteenth century saw a rising output of coal and a steady development of steam power. This revolution in energy consumption was the clue to the nature of the industrial revolution, and hence to the nature of industrial capitalism. For the consumption of energy now rose to unprecedented levels, and at a continuously accelerating pace. Capitalism can almost be defined as the range on the curve of per capita energy consumption where it rises above 15,000 calories per day (according to Cipolla): derived to the extent of eighty-five per cent from plants, animals and men. (This 15,000 calories includes food.) By 1900 energy consumption was mainly from mineral fuel (except, again, for food).

Textiles and consumption goods were rapidly changing at the same time. Compare the roughly constructed medieval house, with little glass and rough carpentry, with an eighteenth-century brick villa, full of windows, careful carpentry and metalwork. The improvement in workmen's tools – saws, chisels, adzes – is as important as the improved quality and reliability of the bricks, glass, door furniture, sash-cords and water closets that went into the house. Almost any other commodity would show a change from rude individuality to sophisticated smoothness. The rise in technical proficiency is obvious. The methods of production became increasingly mechanized, with a steady improvement in the reliability and consistency of the products. The invention of more and more machinery to process wool and cotton textiles – to spin, to weave, to dye – required a substantial development of the engineering trade. It was this mechanization, too, which raised the demand for energy. The energy was derived first from watermills and then from steam engines. The immediate demand for more energy, then, was caused by the rapid growth in the volume of manufactures and by the mechanization of the means of producing them. This is why the textile industry – especially the cotton industry of Lancashire – may be regarded as the pioneer of the industrial revolution. It was the first to become mainly mechanized, the first to use steam engines widely, and the first to congregate substantial numbers of workers in factories. The story of the Lancashire cotton industry is the story of early capitalism. But cotton was not the only consumer goods industry to be revolutionized. It was significant because it was an apex of a trade triangle: cotton came from North America and the Caribbean, it was sold overseas, and slaves were transported from Africa to America. Cotton, therefore, combined mechanization, a labour force, capitalists, merchants, and use of the new reliable trade routes, in an entirely pathbreaking way. But similar tales can be told of other products – beer, wool, iron and brass goods, for instance. All demanded machinery, energy, capital, markets, labour and entrepreneurs.

Timber was of course used in making the machinery, but above all iron was needed. Therefore, the growth of the iron trade was significant. It used wood and coal as a source of energy and was essential for many small artefacts – nails, joists, hinges – for machinery, and (when railways came in) engines and rails. It was round the iron industry that major technological innovation based on science was centred. The use of coal to convert ore into pig iron was not possible before the middle of the eighteenth century; its use was an early application of chemistry to manufacturing. Iron manufacture was one of the earliest American industries, because of the abundance of timber in North America; but it was above all in England that the process most rapidly developed. As a result of Abraham Darby's discovery of the method of converting iron ore into iron by using coke, the use of coal was possible. Then Cort invented the puddling process, which gave a purer product in larger quantities, and he next invented the rolling mill which enabled large quantities of iron to be pressed and shaped. This raised the output of iron tremendously, because costs fell and the technical conditions for producing large quantities now existed. Huntsman then invented a process which enabled steel to be made with greater reliability. The engineering industry was now able to call on cheap iron and reliable (though not cheap) steel. The consequences of the manufacture of large quantities of cheap iron were tremendous; the coal and engineering industries were based upon the abundance of iron.

Lastly, all this industrial activity took place with an emerging market and an ever growing labour force. Apart from the Irish Famine of 1845–50 and Stalin's Ukrainian famine of the early 1930s, Europe no longer knew mass hunger. For this and other reasons the population was growing rapidly. It was fed by an ever increasing agricultural production. More and more land was brought into production, in Europe and America, as forests and woodlands were cleared. New crops, especially root crops, were developed. Tropical products, like tea and sugar, became more common. Above all there was an improvement in agricultural methods. This came partly from an improvement in knowledge. The principles of selective breeding became pragmatically clearer. Animals grew bigger and were better tended. Crops improved. The land was scientifically enriched by manure and by rotation of crops, and by new techniques of ploughing, hoeing and sowing. To enable these new principles of farming to be applied, England pioneered the principle of enclosing fields with hedges or walls, to replace the medieval system of strip cultivation in large open fields; it seems that, outside England, such principles were first adopted in Holland. As the animals were improved by selective breeding, their feeding was also improved by the use of root crops and turnips, enabling them to be kept through the winter. Continuous meat production, instead of annual autumn killings, became possible. Thus all over Europe, and eventually all over the colonies, progressive landowners became capitalist farmers, applying a developing agricultural technology, by means of capital, to their land. The consequence was a growth of agricultural production on a scale that had never been seen before. It was on this abundant food that vast new populations were enabled to live; and they formed the labour force for industrial capitalism. In the process, some parts of agriculture itself became increasingly capitalist. But in some countries, notably France, where the peasants gained possession of the land after the revolution, they were resistant to change, as were many Russian landowners. In these countries the progress of agriculture into capitalism was barred by institutions which were eventually overthrown by a combination of low prices and revolutionary change. Despite its progress into capitalist forms of production, agriculture remained, in almost all countries, a reservoir of hostility to capitalism.

2 Capitalism and industry

The explanations of capitalism

Adam Smith, a Scot, was born in 1723 and died in 1790. He was a well-known though not a distinguished professor of philosophy in Glasgow, but in 1776 he published *The Wealth of Nations*, which was to become the cornerstone of the philosophical interpretation of capitalism. Adam Smith was almost the first economist (itself a capitalist occupation) and the first serious analyst of the process of economic growth. His work became the basis of the capitalist programme.

Economic growth, he reasoned, depended on the division of labour, which improved the skill of the labourer and enabled different specialist occupations to be developed. As the market economy spread, so the possibilities of the division of labour increased. The key to specialization, therefore, was the growth of the market. Technology developed as fast as the market allowed it. Wage labour in capitalist occupations yielded a surplus (which labour engaged in service occupations – such as government – did not). It was the surplus, invested by the capitalists, which was the engine of capitalist progress, since it was this surplus which enabled them to feed the labourers in the interval between buying the new materials (or sowing the seeds) and selling the finished goods or crops. For Adam Smith, labour was the source of value, and it was differences in inputs of labour which explained differences in the prices of various commodities. Therefore, labour for Smith was the factor of production which yielded the means which enabled progress to occur. The surplus fell into the hands of the capitalists, who used it as capital both to employ (and feed) more labour and to construct plant and machinery. The landowners took their toll of the surplus but their use of it was worthless, mere idle consumption, as was the share of the surplus appropriated by the Church and the government. A society, once provided with a framework of law and order, would achieve its greatest level of economic welfare if the product of labour were divided between subsistence wages for labour and the profits of capitalist enterprise.

Smith's argument yielded several important conclusions for policy. One was that anything that limited the spread of the market limited the exploitation of advancing technology (which he called the division of labour). He was a free trader, and looked forward to a world whose goods would be freely exchanged with as few restrictions as possible and where prices would find their true level. A second conclusion was that landowners were unproductive drains on the economy except where they acted as capitalist farmers. Thirdly, government should do as little as possible, except to keep the peace, because every penny not used by a capitalist in productive enterprises was a waste.

It should be said at this point that Smith was probably more right than he was wrong. Eighteenth-century governments were organizations for finding jobs for unemployed aristocrats, and a few landowners apart the huge incomes of the aristocracy were wasted on ostentatious consumption. The great mass of the growing population would have starved unless they had been given the opportunity of employment, and the only way they could be given employment was by the accumulation of a productive surplus which could be used to create fixed capital and finance the stocks of raw materials and semi-finished and finished goods that an advancing economy requires. What is happening in India now is what would have happened in nineteenth-century Europe if Adam Smith's arguments had not prevailed. His doctrine of free trade, and of the essentially productive nature of profit and unproductive nature of government activity, became the central points of the capitalist doctrine. It was with this manifesto that tariff barriers were lowered all over the world and that the free movement of capital and labour was not only allowed but encouraged. It was with this manifesto that governments were everywhere exposed to reform, with a reduction of their activities ensuing.

Smith's brilliant arguments were carried further by two English economists, T. R. Malthus and David Ricardo. Malthus (1766–1834), a Cambridge clergyman, was concerned with the rapidly rising population and extended Smith's reasoning to argue the proposition that the population tended to rise in geometric progression, while food supplies rose only in arithmetic progression. The supply of labour therefore tended constantly to exceed the means to feed it; and the pressure of the supply of labour tended constantly to push the wage level down to subsistence. Philanthropists who sought by private philanthropy or government action to redistribute income to the poor were self-defeating, because the population would automatically increase to eat up the surplus. The only hope lay in population control (by voluntary restraint) and in the accumulation of a productive surplus. There is little doubt that one of Malthus' main arguments was correct: the way to cope with the population increase was not philanthropy, but to extend production. However, he underestimated the possibility of raising production. In fact, his mathematics could almost be reversed, to suggest that food supply under capitalism would tend after a certain period constantly to exceed population. But the way that food supply was increased was through the productive investment of the surplus produced by the wage labourers and invested by the capitalists.

Ricardo (1772–1823) was a stockbroker, drawn from the world of finance, and his contribution to classical economic theory was a fundamental one both because it was the highpoint of classical economics and because it formed the basis of the most ruthless refutation of capitalism, by Karl Marx. Ricardo adopted Adam Smith's position, but assigned a heavy role to the rate of profit. According to Ricardo, there was a tendency for the rate of profit to fall and so for the rate of economic expansion to slow down, since the rate of expansion was determined by the surplus available for investment in the means of production. The only factor offsetting this fall was technological progress; and technological progress depended, in turn, upon the capitalist class's spirit of enterprise. Ricardo was in effect saying that wages could not rise, that the rent of land (the income of the landlords) was unproductive, and that the engine of capitalist progress – profits – had a tendency to run down. Therefore, it was implied, profits must be carefully preserved. He was against the Poor Law, against the Corn Laws, and against any restriction on the free forces of the market.

The steam engine and the energy revolution
Capitalism, then, according to Smith, Ricardo and Marx, is the story of the creation of industrial hardware, of which the steam engine was the essential apparatus. James Watt developed Savery and Newcomen's steam engines by separating the condensing chamber from the chamber in which steam was generated; and by the use of a piston, forced forward by the pressure of the steam, he was able effectively to transform heat into usable energy. By applying the piston to a rotary motion he could take advantage of the procedures used in the watermills, at that time the main source of industrial energy. After many technical and financial struggles Watt teamed up with Matthew Boulton, and in the years between 1785 and 1800 (when their patent expired), their enterprise built 289 steam engines for cotton mills, breweries and other factories. Steam engines rapidly became technically more efficient as boiler-making developed as a craft, as pig iron quality improved, as new high-grade steels came into use, and as the size of engines (measured in horsepower) increased.

The English coal industry was the first large-scale extractive industry organized on a capitalist basis, and it provided the biggest single new source of energy to mankind probably since the windmill became generally used, and possibly since the horse was first used as a draught animal. The main centre was in Northumberland and Durham, where for the first time deep mining was developed. The men (and until 1842 some women) were lowered by cable; then they worked with a pick and shovel, and used gunpowder occasionally at the more recalcitrant spots. There were light tramways, pulled by human labour, to take the coal along the mined seams to the shaft. The working conditions were appalling and the dangers – from rockfalls but above all from explosions – immense. In the pits, employment ranged from very small numbers to hundreds of people. The mine owners were often big capitalists and sometimes wealthy landowners from whose soil the coal was extracted – men like Lord Fitzwilliam, Lord Crawford, Lord Durham, Lord Londonderry and the Bishop of Durham. They gained a reputation for ruthlessness which was wholly deserved. Yet the colliery workers were amongst the highest paid wage earners in the country, and were to become part of the aristocracy of labour, leading the field in forming trade unions and in political activity. Their villages were closed, tight-knit communities, where there was a common consciousness of hardship (especially when demand for coal fell and there was unemployment) and of comradeship in an exceptionally hard life. All over northern England – Lancashire, Staffordshire, Yorkshire, Cumberland – and in Scotland and South Wales, the coal industry grew rapidly, from about 10 million tons of coal output in 1800 to 44 million tons in 1850, an amount which was tripled again by 1880. As coal was virtually the sole source of industrial energy (and increasingly of domestic heating), especially with the invention of coal gas for commercial use (Regency London had gas lighting), coal output is an excellent index of the spread of industrialism – though as the efficiency of engines improved it progressively understates industrial expansion as the nineteenth century went on. By 1850 there was a substantial export of British coal, showing the rise of overseas industry, and the Belgian, French and American coalfields were coming into serious production.

British coal was exceptionally cheap at this time and it formed a basis for low cost energy. The demand for coal – good quality steam coal – came from the stationary engines increasingly applied in industry. The development of engineering skills enabled the steam engine to be used in different branches of trade. Maudslay developed the technique of manufacturing cylinders and valves, of screw-cutting lathes, of planing and milling machines. Steam hammers, accurate measuring machines, all increased the power and precision of steam-equipped tools, so that identical machines could be produced in large numbers, enabling large-scale production units to be equipped. Engineering became an industry which was strongly localized in London, Lancashire, Glasgow and some midland towns like Birmingham. Machines were developed to produce rails, struts for bridges, iron beams for factories; mechanized printing became possible; and iron ships.

Thus the steam engine not only harnessed coal power but by the development of the engineering industry enabled energy to be applied to a wide variety of occupations. The revolutionary development of the application of steam power to transport enabled the railway and the steamships to reduce transport costs, increased the availability and speed of communications, and enabled bulk cargoes to be easily carried. The expansion in coal consumption after 1830 is attributable in some large part to the rapid spread of the steam train; and then the development of the steamship and steam tram increased the market for coal still more rapidly.

Despite the early industrialization of the Belgian coalfield, as well as of the adjacent part of northern France, a few small areas in Germany and a few places in America, by 1850 the British coal and engineering industries dominated the world. Over two-thirds of the world's coal was mined in Britain; some went for export; and about half the world's energy produced by steam power was produced in Britain at that time. It is no wonder that the economic and social drama being played out in Britain was the model from which capitalism's nature was deduced, both by Ricardo and by Marx, and that the political and social doctrines evolved in Britain were widely adopted as the doctrines of capitalism.

England adopted, in the age of steam, the policies of laissez-faire. The Poor Law of 1834 left the poor to a bare and intolerable relief when they were destitute – otherwise they had to fend for themselves. Free trade was enacted and agricultural protection was eliminated. The state machine was reformed. The bourgeois spirit infiltrated venerable institution after venerable institution.

Notable among the consequences of this steam revolution was a relocation of economic, social and political power in the country. The steam revolution was mainly based on the coalfields (since it was cheaper to transport finished manufactures than to transport coal), and the bulk of industry therefore was located on the coalfields. (The older trades continued to be located in the big cities of the pre-steam era – notably in London.) It was to these coalfields and the industrial areas adjacent to them that populations flocked. Living conditions in the towns were so bad that the death rate exceeded the birth rate, but the population was continually sucked in from the adjacent countryside and from Ireland, so that huge concentrations of people grew up round Manchester, Liverpool, Birmingham and the smaller industrial towns of the north. It was within these industrial areas that new political and social movements had their base. Both the ardent free-trade doctrinaires and the early socialists were products of the industrial districts – John Bright and Richard Cobden, laissez-faire's chief political spokesmen, were Manchester Liberals, and Peel, the prime minister who first achieved a substantial degree of free trade, was a Lancashire cotton mill owner's son.

The introduction of steam thus occurred first in Britain, giving Britain a world leadership which it exercised throughout the nineteenth century, until it was overtaken by Germany and the United States. Within Britain, and more especially within England, it relocated economic power, and consequently the social and political balance shifted. The composition of Britain's exports moved to manufactured goods (especially cotton and engineering goods) and coal; its imports became, increasingly, basic foodstuffs and raw materials. The unleashing of steam's energy was the prime cause of the spread of capitalism, by railway and ship, throughout the world.

Transport
If early capitalism is synonymous with the rapid increase in per capita energy consumption associated with steam power, it is also synonymous with the development of a speedy, secure and unsurpassed network of communications. It was the railway and the steamship which fully integrated the steam revolution with the spread of capitalism, but the early years of industrialism in England were pre-railway and pre-steamship. The steady improvement of sailing ships has already been mentioned: the American merchant navy reached its apotheosis in the 1830s and 1840s, with the development of the beautiful clippers and schooners which sped across the Atlantic and round Cape Horn. But the development of sailing ships was a continuum from the original Viking sailing ships that had gone to America a millennium before. The steamship in an iron hull was a radical

advance which did not become at all widespread until the 1860s, though it was used on American rivers from the 1810s. Railways became the basic means of transport in Britain in the 1850s and somewhat later in Europe and North America. Until then capitalism spread by water, helped by radical improvements in the road system.

The internal means of transporting goods in most countries before 1800 were mainly by river and canal. The canalization of rivers to make them navigable had been going on from the Middle Ages, but canals (which the Romans had constructed) were not generally dug until the seventeenth century, when Colbert built the Languedoc Canal. This, together with the improvement of the French road system by Henri IV, was primarily defensive in origin, whereas the English canal and road building of the eighteenth century was almost wholly commercial. England, surrounded by sea and with navigable rivers stretching far inland, was well placed to develop commerce in bulky goods, and did so; the next step was to connect some places to the rivers by canal, or to connect the rivers with each other. The Duke of Bridgewater had a canal constructed by a civil engineer (formerly a millwright) called James Brindley, to connect his collieries at Worsley to Manchester. This was then linked to a project of Josiah Wedgwood, and others, to join the potteries in Staffordshire by canal to the Mersey, the Trent and the Humber. This Grand Trunk Canal was the first major canal system; it enabled coal, salt (from Cheshire) and pottery to be transported easily and cheaply to Liverpool and Manchester and down through Hull to London. A further canal linked the system to the Severn, and so to Bristol. A link through Coventry and Oxford to the Thames, completed in 1790, meant that most of the major manufacturing towns of England were linked by the internal canal and navigable river system.

The canal mania, when canals were started all over Britain, came in 1790–4, but canals continued to be built until the 1830s. Ireland was crossed by two canals, from Dublin to the Shannon, and Scotland was bisected by the Caledonian Canal. Thus by 1830 the British enjoyed an internal transport system linking their excellent ports and rivers with each other and enabling goods like wool, timber, clay (for bricks), iron, manufactured goods and stone to be transported quickly and easily. The effects of this transport revolution (for it was no less) in speeding up the movement of goods, people and ideas were notable. 'Sea coal' became a common domestic fuel; bricks became cheap, enabling a wide development of housebuilding, and markets became ever wider. Not less important, the canals were owned by companies, which accelerated the process of the creation of financial institutions. The institution of transferable 'shares', which earned profits, was not entirely new (it had played its part in the founding of the great mercantile companies) but it was first widely developed by the canal companies and was a notion that was developed to embrace the concept of a permanent company, owning considerable installations and operating them on a continuing basis as generations came and went. This was the form with which the railways were launched; the company was soon to replace the one-man family business and the partnership as the typical form of capitalist enterprise.

Europe also built canals, based on the great river system, which increased the level of commerce significantly, especially after the Belgian development of the 1820s, which used the Scheldt estuary as its means of transport. The American river system was used extensively as the interior was conquered. In 1807 the Hudson was the site of the first commercially satisfactory steamboat, the *Clermont*, on the Hudson River between Albany and New York, and the Mississippi and the Ohio began to be successfully used by steamboats in the 1820s. The first major canal system was the Erie Canal, which links the Hudson River and New York City to the Great Lakes at Lake Erie. This linked Ohio, the Great Lakes and New England, and so stimulated New York's development as a great port and as the centre of industrialization in New England.

The energy revolution reduced the costs of energy. The canal system reduced the costs of transporting energy potential, always the biggest costs in energy production. The fall in costs per ton mile was probably to one-tenth, and even one-twentieth, of what it had been by road; and transport was technically possible for large bulky commodities, which it had not been before.

There was a significant improvement in road transport simultaneously with the building of canals; by the beginning of the seventeenth century the European road system was in a worse condition than it had been under the Romans. The horse was strengthened by selective breeding and better feeding. Wheels were improved, carriages were lightened, and springs were introduced into them. Above all, the roads themselves were made on new principles. In the Middle Ages pack horses proceeded in convoy along stone causeways, which ran along the roads. The roads were deep muddy tracks in wet weather, dusty paths in dry. The French constructed a national system of roads for military purposes, just as the road from London to Holyhead was a military highway. The French *routes royales* were built by the *corps des ponts et chaussées*, and were well constructed. But it was the British, through the turnpike trusts, who advanced technologically in road construction. The turnpike trusts, bodies of local worthies, kept the roads in repair by charging tolls for passage. John Metcalf, a northern roadbuilder (1717–1810), dug ditches by the roadside to drain them and put foundations underneath. Thomas Telford (1757–1834), who built iron bridges, strengthened the foundations; John McAdam built up the surface from stone chips, so that it was not broken by the iron rims of the wheels of the fast carriages, which had destroyed the surfaces of earlier roads.

It was on road administration that all attempts at road reform had previously broken down: the road was either ill or well constructed, but it was almost always ill maintained. Most of the turnpike trusts saw to it that repairs were undertaken. Consequently road travel times were cut to about one-third of what they had been early in the eighteenth century. This speeded up communications, and the movement of people became faster and safer. The amount of travel was by modern standards very small; and only Britain, the Low Countries, France and the United States had a passable road system. Where there was industrialization there were improved roads. Elsewhere, communication was exceptionally difficult.

Thus by 1830 canals and improved rivers had made industrial loads technically and economically possible to transport. Steamships were beginning to be used on rivers and for coastal traffic (from Britain to Ireland, from England to the continent, in the Mediterranean). Sailing boats were far quicker and bigger than they had been. The roads in industrial areas had cut travel time by two-thirds. The effect of this transport revolution may be seen in the greater volume of trade, both overseas and inland. But it was the steam engine that really revolutionized the world.

Railways were made of iron and were first laid to solve the problem of bearing the weight of carts full of coal drawn by horses from the mines to the nearest point for loading on to a barge. Northumberland, Durham and South Wales had several hundred miles of track before 1820, and there were also a few miles of track in northern France and in America, chiefly for coal. Steam engines were first used on roads, but their weight and power destroyed the road surface. After two other pioneers had made attempts, with some success, George Stephenson began on his famous railway steam engines; in October 1829 his *Rocket* won the competition, established by the new Liverpool to Manchester line, for the best engine, stationary or loco-motive. Suddenly it was clear that the alternative to costly roads and slow canals had been found.

The railways were very expensive to build. A new technology had to be pioneered; land had to be bought; canal interests had to be bought out. By the end of the 1830s the outline of England's trunk system had been completed. Before 1860 Parliament in London had authorized the building of over a hundred lines; and over eight hundred Railway Acts were passed in the twenty-five years between 1825 and 1850. The first lines were solidly profitable: the volume of traffic, both of goods and of people, rose at geometric rates. By 1850 there were 6,625 miles of route in operation, linking nearly all the principal British towns. Railway shares had become a major form of investment, held by almost the whole middle class. There was a railway mania (discussed in the following section), which caused speculative booms and slumps, virtually the first of a recognizably 'modern' kind.

The economic effects of the railways can scarcely be exaggerated. First, their cost of construction was high. In England, the first country in which they were built, thousands of 'navvies' were employed. Great civil engineering concerns, headed by Brunel, Peto, Brassey, Locke, and others, organized large gangs of highly paid workers and a flow of materials and equipment to the line, which spread across the country on embankments and in cuttings like a series of scars. This raised employment and disturbed existing social patterns.

Next, the demand for iron and coal speeded up the development of iron works and coal mines, which also reduced their costs as the costs of transport fell. Whole new coalfields came into operation. The demand for engines and equipment, for carriages and wheels, for signals, for many iron and steel goods, provided a great new opportunity for the engineering industry. The electric telegraph was introduced in 1839 to keep stations in touch with each other, and this led to a further development of engineering. The great firms of Napier, Armstrong and Whitworth and Maudslay (to name but a few) developed heavy and light engineering techniques to a new degree of precision. The railway companies themselves set up locomotive repair and engineering departments.

The railways employed a great many people – clerks, drivers, porters, engineers – by 1851 reaching in Britain a total of sixty-five thousand. New towns, like Swindon, were created for and by the railways.

Above all, however, the railways speeded up transport and reduced its cost. The passenger time was reduced to one-third of that prevailing on the fast turnpike roads, and then to one-fifth. Transport time for goods was one-tenth of that by the canals, and the loads could now go to parts of the country not connected with the canal and river system. The consequences for industrialism were obvious. The movement of population became far easier, travelling now being within the reach of all but the very poorest of the working class. The price of industrial goods fell, and the price of bulk goods (raw materials and food) fell even more dramatically. The railway engine brought full-blown capitalism to Britain as well as to other countries.

The railway spread quickly to Belgium, France and Germany, though their route mileage was less than Britain's till the last quarter of the nineteenth century, America, however, introduced the railway only a little later than Britain, and there it spread even more quickly. By 1865 the American railway mileage was three times that of Britain. Also, the significance of the railway outside Britain was even greater (if that is possible) than in Britain. It was a unifying force: it helped to create a nation out of the United States, out of Germany and out of Russia. In America, by spanning undeveloped lands, it speeded up pioneering, hitherto virtually confined to areas near a great waterway. In Europe, where capitalism had not yet spread over virtually the whole country, as it had in Britain, the arrival of the railway helped to break down the isolation of local markets and to create national economies.

The spread of the railway in North America (for it was not widespread in Africa, Asia or Australasia till the last part of the nineteenth century) changed the balance of world trade. It enabled the population of America, fed by huge emigrations from Ireland, Germany and England, to spread over the continent and enormously to increase the production of food and new materials. These not only permitted the growth of American industry, but by reducing the costs of production and transport the railway allowed cheap food and materials to flow to Europe. This ultimately transformed European (and especially British) agriculture, but, of more immediate importance, allowed the industrial population to be fed. Adam Smith's division of labour appeared to be working in a splendid way: the fertility of America reduced food costs, while European ingenuity led to an outburst of industrial production, spreading to more and more products, driving out the handcraft producers, reducing costs, standardizing goods and killing the old society. The time was not far distant when the brassware of Benares would come from Birmingham.

To complete the transport revolution, the steamship became internationally acceptable. By the 1830s steamboats were chugging up the Mississippi and crossing the English Channel. After 1840 the iron steamship began to cross the oceans, making for far greater regularity (it had on occasion taken three weeks to cross the Irish Sea from Dublin to Holyhead), and the improvement of the screw propeller made it possible for the weight of the ship and its cargo to be much increased. There was a period when steamships still had sails (like the five-thousand-ton vessel *Napoléon*, built in 1850), and were still partly wooden-hulled. America was the great ship-building nation. But as all-iron (and later steel) all-steam ships came generally into use, British ship-building yards came to dominate the market and the British merchant marine to lead the world. It did so entirely because its costs were low and its reliability high, for the Navigation Acts, causing British trade to be carried in British bottoms, had long since been repealed.

Steam, then, made it possible for American food to come from the prairies, via railway, steamship and railway again, to Birmingham, where it fed the workers who made the brass which the Indians sold to the English soldiers holding India. The capitalist circle was complete.

The railway mania
The railway transformed capitalism physically; it also transformed it financially and psychologically. The spread of the railway raised many, though not all, of the problems of early industrialism.

The railways had to be regulated by the government because, if they were to go across property, land had to be compulsorily purchased. The British railways were privately owned and managed. The shares were issued to the public on the Stock Exchange and attracted savings from all over the country. Because of large profits in the early days, high expectations were raised. Many companies were honestly and efficiently managed and paid regular dividends, but – inevitably in such a pioneering technology – some companies made losses, were badly run, or were plain fraudulent: in the boom of 1844 savings had flooded into the railways, and many families were ruined in the subsequent slump of 1845–7. Some dividends were paid out of capital, some companies were totally reconstructed, but after this temporary setback railway shares settled down as a secure investment. The government, of course, had to take powers to regulate railway charges and to ensure railway safety. Transport had been completely changed: it had to be regulated. Such matters as a uniform gauge for railways, standardization of techniques, a railway clearing house for travellers and freight routed through several companies, had to be settled. This was done partly by amalgamations and partly by agreements between companies. Usually a railway company was a local monopoly, because its costs were, relatively, so low that competing canals and turnpike roads went out of use and the companies owning them bankrupt. Governments had to regulate the conditions under which these monopolies conducted their business, to protect travellers, shareholders and workers.

Many overseas lines were financed by British capital, especially in Germany and the United States, and many of the European lines were built by British firms and engineers, the rails and equipment imported from England. America then developed its own rail-making industry and engineering works. The American investment was initially hugely profitable, since very favourable terms were obtained from the states – land and money grants especially – but in 1859 the initial boom collapsed and a series of defaults, even by the states, occurred. The American railway system, which stretched east–west, led to the victory of the north in the Civil War, and deflected the Mississippi north–south trade to the midwest and the northeast coast. From the vast development of railways in America sprang an American technological lead in engines and in associated work like the electric telegraph. Despite the heterogeneity of America and the large number of railroad companies, there were plans for working together on the grand trunk routes which the Civil War accelerated and formalized.

Much of Europe took a different path. The great stock market boom in railway shares which helped to establish London and New York as financial capitals for commercial stocks and shares typified the Anglo-Saxon devotion to private enterprise, and a demand for the nationalization of British railways, after the railway mania, passed almost unnoticed (though it was later unearthed by socialist apologists). In Belgium, France, Prussia and Russia, the state either built the lines and operated the railways, went into partnership with private capital, or supervised the railways explicitly as public capital utilities. In Prussia the railways were self-consciously part of the military system (it was later to be held that the First World War broke out because the railway plan for mobilizing troops, once set in motion, was irreversible and lengthy). In many countries the strategic significance of the railways was regarded as most important. In France, for example, the state engineers constructed a national plan for railways radiating from Paris, avoiding the patchwork nature of the British railway system. In many countries the cost of constructing railways was far less than in England. Partly this comparison of costs was unfair; Prussia, for instance, was flat and barren, so railways were easily built, and landowners did not have to be given so much compensation. But partly it was because the lines were more efficiently if more slowly built under state auspices.

The railway, then, offered the opportunity for continental paternalist states to create public utilities, taking the 'exploitation' out of capital assets and running the railways for the public benefit. This involved deliberately constructing unprofitable lines for strategic reasons, or, as in Bavaria, to encourage economic development. The British were capable of taking this point of view, too, because in India the government not only guaranteed the interest on railway loans but covered some of the costs. Private enterprise built and operated the railways, but on very favourable terms, and the Indian people got the benefit of greater markets; the Indian government got a strategic network which the Indian Mutiny of 1857 showed to be essential for military control.

Yet in most cases state and private enterprise collaborated, since the profits gained by capitalists on the London and New York stock exchanges appealed to financiers in Paris, Vienna and Brussels. European businessmen wanted to get into the railway business, and capital creation on so vast a scale was beyond normal government financing. Russia was, as often, an example of private enterprise running into losses, being rescued by the state, and then being run extremely inefficiently. In Russia, so far behind the rest of Europe (except the Balkans), capitalism had penetrated very little, and the railway – the very symbol of capitalism – could hardly run as smoothly as in New York or in Lancashire. But in a very few years after serfdom had been abolished, the railway in Russia was exporting Russian food and transporting the early products of Russian industry.

With the railway had come state intervention in capitalism, financial capital, booms and slumps on a large scale, and an irreversible and permanent technological advance that caused a tremendous fall in costs.

Textiles and consumer goods
The historical function of capitalism was to equip the world with capital goods. To do so it had to extract the surplus from

the workers and embody it in machines. These machines would have the capacity to produce goods on an immense scale which the workers *ex hypothesi* would be unable to buy. Certainly the railways, the smoking chimneys of the factories, the figure of the engineer, characterized the change that came over north-western Europe and the north-eastern United States in the first half of the nineteenth century. But it was the great flood of consumer goods that represented as radical a change from previous centuries as the new capital equipment: and, certainly, the capitalists themselves pointed to the increase in output as the significant fact in the expansion of the whole economic system. True, in some parts of the world it was barely keeping pace with the rise in population, but that fact in itself showed what disasters would have struck if output had not risen. Ireland, stricken by famine, was a case in point.

Industrialization first affected the Lancashire cotton industry. Cheap cotton came from America and the West Indies; Lancashire had water power, cheap labour, capitalists and technologists, and it had markets in England, Europe, Africa and Asia. Cotton textiles were the first mass-produced consumer goods and were sold all over the world, changing the habits of dress and of decoration of whole nations. After cotton textiles, other goods followed. But cotton typified the whole capitalist process. First, bulk production rivalled the production carried on by hand manufacture. The standards of the handloom weavers fell catastrophically. Then, with technical improvements in the 1820s, handloom weaving went into its death throes. By the mid-nineteenth century cotton goods were manufactured exclusively in factories, in Lancashire and the United States. In the first sixty years of the nineteenth century, English production of cotton textiles increased over twenty-fold; in 1850 three-fifths of British exports were textile yarns and fabrics, including woollens. Lancashire cotton, and, after 1850, Yorkshire woollens, achieved a world dominance on which the English export trade was based for the whole of the nineteenth century.

Wool textiles, then, were a second industry that experienced enormous cost reductions as industrialization developed. Australian and American sheep provided some of the wool – in fact a torrent of wool and cotton flowed into northern England from America and Australia and other distant lands, to be exported as manufactures. Wool lagged behind cotton, partly because it was a fibre far more difficult to deal with mechanically and partly because the domestic industry was stronger and harder to displace. Also, the demand for cotton goods was extremely income-and price-elastic – as incomes rose and costs fell, the market rose inexorably. Less so with wool.

The process of industrialization was patchy, and (as both cotton and wool illustrate) new and old techniques coexisted for long periods. The hand producers usually sank into misery, and increasingly their market shrank to that for custom-built, specialist and high-priced articles; but there was a lengthy period when the factory produced articles which were regarded as cheap and shoddy and actually were so. Old habits of production and consumption died hard and local markets for consumer goods persisted. But the tide of industrialization was inexplorable. In New England, for example, the boot and shoe industry was by 1860 predominantly a factory trade, despite a long struggle by the cobblers, who never entirely disappeared, a few remaining as shoe repairs, or high-class boot-makers. The availability of cheap boots and shoes was a major element in raising living standards.

The mechanization of boot and shoe manufacture owed a great deal to the invention of the sewing machine, which also enabled the costs of clothing manufacture to fall. In fact, the clothing industry makes an interesting example of the capitalist transformation of a domestic craft. The old tailors and dressmakers were never entirely replaced by the industry producing 'off-the-peg' garments. But the price of textiles fell, and the sewing machine greatly speeded up the process of clothes manufacture. Therefore clothiers who could buy and hold large stocks of textiles, buy sewing machines, and market the cheap goods, could either assemble their workers in a factory or engage in the 'putting-out' system, which had been familiar for nearly four centuries from Jack of Newbury's time.

Pottery was another industry which was industrialized early. The Stoke-on-Trent potteries, which exploited furnaces, and enabled standard ware to be produced in bulk and sent down the canals to the ports, became the model for potteries which reduced the price of china to levels that ordinary people could afford. Wooden platters and pewter mugs became objects more of curiosity than of use. To the new cheap china could be added a range of domestic goods almost without limit. Inexpensive furniture began to be made in factories and workshops with new and improved tools. The cast-iron heating stove became cheaper and more important in western Europe and North America, as did the cooking range. On the cooking range could be found cast-iron pots and saucepans, replacing the tin kettles and vessels produced by tinkers. Ordinary cutlery, from Sheffield, was a result of the improvement of steel. So the domestic 'revolution' could be catalogued – textile manufacture altered curtains, carpets, furniture covering; cheap timber and new machinery affected furniture; heat, light (gas was widespread by the end of 1860 in most European and American cities) and sewage disposal were recognizably 'modern' by the early 1870s. The result was a dramatic change in the standard of living of ordinary middle-class and artisan life. There was a national, indeed an international, market for many of these domestic products, which ranged from pipe tobacco and matches to articles of clothing, boots and shoes, books and newspapers. The development of mechanical paper-making and mechanical printing, the invention of mechanical binding, the evolution of commercial glues – all this made the cheap book a possibility for all but the very poorest persons. After this development society was bound to change. Applied to products of all kinds, the inferences are obvious. The range of choice of the ordinary family was enormously increased.

Nowhere was this more evident than in the revolution in domestic architecture. Brick-built dwellings, spreading out into the suburbs which were made accessible by trains and trams, contained machined doors and door handles, window glass and frames. The bricks were made in bulk. Linoleum was a common floor covering. In the more prosperous homes, especially in America, bathrooms made their appearance.

The centres of these new construction trades were Britain and the north-eastern United States, though by 1870, technically and in adventurous pioneering, America was ahead of Britain and was, generally speaking, to remain so, continental Europe lagging further behind. Machine-baked bread and tinned foods are examples of goods that were common in

England and America by the 1870s; till quite late on in the twentieth century they were rare in continental Europe. Partly this fact reflects the much larger peasant population of Europe; partly it is explained by the growth of mass markets in countries where proletarianization had gone furthest. For when a mass market was created even middle-class goods were soon produced by mass techniques and hand labour went out. In the 1920s even the English aristocracy had bathrooms, instead of skivvies carrying up pails of steaming water from the kitchen to the bedroom.

Agriculture
Agriculture inevitably became a bastion of conservative attitudes and elderly techniques. The towns were the home of capitalism and of capitalist rationality, and the rural population was intensely suspicious of changes, understandably so since for them almost all change turned out to be for the worse.

Yet agriculture was where much of it had begun. The surplus from the land had provided some of the capital for early industrialization. In England, as population rose, the development of new techniques and new forms of agricultural organization enabled output to expand faster than the labour force engaged in agriculture. The surplus population moved to the towns, in conditions of hideous misery in many cases. But, at least for the most part, the townspeople saw some of the benefits from the rising agricultural output.

New ways of organizing agriculture spread at about the time of the French Revolution, and subsequently. In England, landowners organized their land into compact farms, run (for the most part) by tenant farmers and worked by agricultural labourers. In France and in some other parts of the continent, the revolutionary redistribution of land extended the areas controlled by small peasants, often with scattered strips and patches of land, to which his rights were inalienable, and subject to further subdivision under the Napoleonic Code of inheritance. In Russia, Prussia and Hungary, the landowners brought the waste lands into their pattern of extensive cultivation. In the United States independent farmers moved on to fertile free land and organized it on an extensive basis, unhindered by historical land-tenure patterns. (Of course, the pattern was not as simple as this, since each country had several types of organization within its borders, but conceptually it is convenient to consider the question thus.)

Wherever industrialism spread fast, the market for food and raw materials rose, and despite intermittent depressions the spread of the market accelerated the radical organization changes in agriculture and led to the spread of the area of cultivated land. Britain became a big food importer; Europe was, on the whole, a string of protected markets (since it never embraced wholeheartedly the laissez-faire faith); America's costs were so low that it hardly had to consider the question of food imports. The English, with the fastest growing industrial population, pioneered new agricultural techniques – draining the soil, feeding it chemically, selectively breeding stock and plants, applying machinery to ploughing, hoeing and (eventually) reaping, binding and threshing. In a part of the kingdom where the effects of the market were not directly felt, and where the landowners were especially backward – Ireland – population rose faster than output, though the area of cultivated land extended considerably. The result, when the crop failed in 1845, was a terrible famine which killed, directly and indirectly, one million people. This shows how great was the catastrophe which the new farming techniques avoided in England and elsewhere in Europe.

America took over the lead from England in the development of agricultural machinery. American farmers had abundant fertile soil. When it was exhausted they moved on, so they had no need to develop crop rotation, deep drainage and other techniques for preserving and raising the fertility of the soil. Moreover, initially, they had no big market for their supplies; they lived in a high-level subsistence economy, except for the cotton plantations where slavery was prevalent. After 1830, with the development of transport and the beginnings of large-scale industrialization in the north-east, the wealthier agricultural workers could move west and found their own farms. Machinery was rapidly developed to save labour: John Deere developed a light plough with a steel blade, which formed the basis of a substantial agricultural machinery industry; Obed Hussey and Cyrus McCormick developed, in 1833 and 1834, mechanical reapers. Labour was scarce on American farms, and at harvest time it virtually vanished. Now large-scale grain production was possible since big tracts of land could be successfully ploughed and large prairie fields could be reaped. Other machines for threshing, drilling, harrowing and many other tasks were produced. By 1860 the United States had a large agricultural machinery industry which formed the basis of an export industry, and the huge crops were marketed in the growing American cities and in Europe.

No equivalent rise in productivity occurred in France, though there was a steady slow improvement of peasant agricultural techniques. In Prussia, however, the development of the chemical industry, the draining of marshes, and the ploughing up and improvement of sandy wastes, led to appreciable increases in agricultural output. The conquest of new lands was the chief Russian contribution to agricultural production, for the break-up of big estates and the settlement of the peasantry after the emancipation of the serfs in 1861 tended to hold back the possibilities of productivity growth. In Germany, however, the emancipation of the peasantry between 1830 and 1850 appears to have led to substantial productivity gains, especially in livestock production.

Denmark is an interesting example of a highly efficient grain-producing country whose peasantry was emancipated and which after 1860 increasingly turned to livestock production and to butter, eggs and cheese. The spread of rational techniques of livestock care and the processing of meat, eggs and butter spread throughout Europe from Denmark, and in the United States from Scandinavian emigrants (just as English emigrants had taken many of the new techniques there).

By 1850 or so the agricultural population in most countries in Europe had reached its maximum. Thereafter growth of output came from steadily increasing productivity gains; but in America the agricultural population continued to grow rapidly, and the western world was increasingly fed from American sources, and from the new farms in Argentina, Australia and South Africa. Their achievement was enormous. The European population (including Russia) rose from 190 million in 1800 to 400 million in 1900; America's population more than tripled between 1830 and 1870. By the end of the century the white populations of the world – well over 500 millions – had more than doubled since the beginning of the century and were, even so, much better fed (on average) than they had been.

The development of agriculture was accompanied, then, by an 'expulsion' of the 'surplus' population from agriculture, some of which moved on to the United States, in wave after wave, as the agricultural revolution travelled through Europe. First the British, then the Irish when their subsistence agriculture collapsed, then the Germans and Scandinavians, then the Poles and Russians, and the Italians – in all these countries population moved internally to the cities. In 1800 about four-fifths of the population of Europe and America were working at agricultural jobs; by 1850 it was down to about half and by 1900 to an even smaller fraction. At least three hundred million extra mouths were now better fed, by rather fewer hands, as a result of agricultural expansion. Even so, agricultural overpopulation was still common in Europe, especially in the southern and eastern countries, where the influence of the world market was weakest. In eastern Europe land was still relatively abundant, however, and population growth could still bend to the cultivation of new lands. In southern Europe rural poverty was widespread.

Indeed, America apart, the agricultural revolution which fed the world depressed the relative situation of the rural population. In north-western Europe, the age of the farmer was past; his reactions were to be increasingly defensive.

3 The features of nineteenth-century capitalism

Technology, education and the transmission of knowledge
The capitalist spirit was a rational one. The capitalists were
heirs to Galileo and Newton: see a problem, think about it, and
adopt the most economical answer, and be damned to past
practice and traditional theory. The capitalists, in England
originally in large numbers but then in America and north-
western continental Europe, applied this pragmatic outlook to
the problems of assessing the market and solving their own
production difficulties. Their initial response stimulated technology. The steam engine was the paradigm of a technological
answer to a practical problem – how to use new sources of
energy and apply them to machinery. Textile machinery was
the first example of a rationalist approach to production problems in an industrial context. The railway was the supreme
example of the coalescence of the solution of two problems: how
to apply steam to transport, and how to make roads capable of
bearing heavy weights.

In the eighteenth century Britain had, it seems, a relatively
higher level of technical skill and ability to 'tinker' with things
than elsewhere, though the natural sciences had advanced
further in Germany. This interest in engineering was transmitted by British emigrants to the United States. The new professions of agriculturalist and engineer developed the capacity to
solve problems. Out of their solutions – pragmatic solutions –
problems were suggested to scientists. It was not the other way
about. The science of genetics, for example, grew up to explain
the processes of selective breeding already being applied by
agriculturists.

The new industries went to great lengths to train a skilled workforce, and people with advanced skills commanded high premiums. In Britain these skills tended to be work-based: on the continent they became institutionalized, in Napoleon's *grandes écoles* and the *Technische Hochschulen*. As the nineteenth century progressed the technical problems to be solved became more complex. The movement from mass-produced iron to mass-produced steel is one example; the evolution of the chemical dyestuffs industry (based on coal tar) is another. The engineer, or his equivalent in other technologies, added to his trained experience in problem-solving a series of theoretical concepts which were necessarily linked to natural science and mathematics. It was this link that made technological progress irreversible. Even were some disaster to wipe out most of mankind and all of its artefacts, if only a few people remembered that it was possible to find out how to make things, mankind could never relapse into pre-capitalist modes of thought. Early engineering led to developments in the science of mechanics: iron- and steel-making affected metallurgy, and therefore chemistry; dyeing and other processes affected chemistry. Yet it was not till the later years of the nineteenth century that advances in the natural sciences directly affected technology. Electricity is one of the early instances, and led to physics succeeding chemistry as the major pioneering natural science. Faraday as the theorist and Edison as the practitioner were responsible for the fact that by the early 1880s electricity was a practicable tool for almost all its present uses. Geologists and chemists led the way to the great mineral discoveries of the late nineteenth century and to the exploitation of mineral oils, which formed the basis of the internal combustion engine of the 1880s.

Thus, out of engineering and the other applied sciences or mechanized arts, came a fresh impetus in the sciences of chemistry, geology and physics. Biology and zoology, which developed later, owed a great deal to agricultural techniques. By the mid-nineteenth century a reciprocal relationship between the pure and applied sciences was already at work, and this led to the formalization of the training of engineers and agriculturalists, perhaps best seen in the state colleges of the United States, which rapidly spread after the Civil War, and in the German technical high schools. It was these German and American colleges which gave Germany and America their industrial leadership in the late nineteenth century.

The relationship of these advances to education is a complex one. Most engineering-type skills were acquired on-the-job; and apprenticeship was the normal mode of acquisition. Most advances in technology were extremely small: it was the cumulative effect of these apparently insignificant changes that led to the swiftness and the magnitude of the total advance in technology. It was only as the nineteenth century wore on that a body of technical knowledge could be formally taught, and it was not till fairly late in the century that this body of knowledge could be directly related to scientific principles. An example of this is medicine: pragmatically, clinical and surgical techniques developed in the nineteenth century, but the theoretical basis of antiseptic practices, vaccination and anaesthesia could not be related to sophisticated scientific principles until physiology, bacteriology and pharmacology had solved the intellectual problems which clinical solutions to clinical problems gave rise to. Once that bridge had been crossed, modern medicine and modern medical education were possible. Thus the universities were products, rather than causes, of the capitalist technology.

There is little doubt that in the eighteenth century the general level of competence and skill of the British was higher than in other countries, and this was related to generally higher standards of literacy and education, which have in turn been linked to Protestantism. Certainly, obscurantist Catholicism was a major barrier to educational progress and so to a pragmatic approach to technical and economic questions. The high calibre of British emigrants to America (for it was mainly the skilled artisans who went) led to a rapid spread of high standards of education there; and by the early 1840s a doctrine of universal common education was accepted in most northern states. Napoleon adopted the principle of universal primary education for France; Frederick the Great did so for Prussia. The French had a setback after Waterloo, but Prussia developed its school system. Thus by the 1860s widespread primary education was common in France, Prussia, Scandinavia and America, and it was coming to be so in Britain. This provided a literate body of consumers and a labour force that could work in a rationalist capitalist environment. Out of this basic education, a few clever children could spring on to a platform of middle-level technical studies which enabled them to service the industrial machine and to act as clerks. Education for middle-class children, in Germany and America, also had a technological and scientific side, which provided the basis for their advance in high-level skills. It was the relative absence of this part of the education system in England which was much deplored by progressive opinion, and was held to be the cause of her relative falling behind in industrial advance after 1870.

New knowledge then, was developed by training and education. It was transmitted by a degree of population movement without precedent. Not only did millions of people, many of them highly skilled, cross the Atlantic, but large numbers of British engineers went to the continent, Frenchmen to Russia, and Germans to the Balkans, taking their skills with them. Trade carried the new ways wherever it went. The trader had changed his status. Feuer describes the Jewish pedlar:

this defenceless proto-bourgeois, this pioneer of trade, moving about through the uncertain apertures of closed, narrow, insulated feudal worlds, bringing goods, news, intelligence, himself an itinerant rationalist, observing people's superstitions in different places, this huckster, with his pack on his back, travelling in fear of his life, in dread danger....

Now the trader was a man of power, bringing new knowledge to another tradition. He was helped by a world-wide postal service, the electric telegraph and the invention of high-speed printing. The trader now sent books, reports and news around the world. It was the immediacy of contact and the instantaneous reactions of thousands of knowledgeable and rational businessmen to it which instituted the world-wide market.

The immiseration of the proletariat
Capitalism created modern large-scale means of production. Its purpose was to increase consumption by raising output. Yet Marx held that capitalism would be unable to solve the problems of consumption, his evidence for this being the apparent deterioration of the standard of living of the working class in mid-nineteenth-century England when he was writing. His

argument was that the wealth produced by industry would accumulate in the pockets of the industrialists while the workers, whose numbers were rising as Malthus had said they would, competed among themselves for a diminishing share of output and became steadily poorer. He called this the immiseration of the proletariat, and it was this misery which would spark off the revolution. In the long run he was completely wrong: in any straightforward comparison of conditions in the industrial countries at the beginning and the end of the nineteenth century, there can be little doubt that consumption standards had risen, in food, clothing, housing, leisure, and in the general availability of goods, including transport and public services like education. Whether other sacrifices had been made, in working conditions, in political and social alienation, are questions that will be considered later; but it is doubtful whether those sacrifices (if there were any) outdistanced the gains made in consumption. Moreover, when it is realized that the population in the white world more than doubled in a century, it is obvious that without the new means of production a terrible calamity, on the Irish scale, might have enveloped the whole world, as it still threatens to do in parts of Asia.

Initially, however, the impact of capitalism is not so clear, and controversy still rages about the period of initial industrialization. The right answer appears to be that different groups were differently affected; almost any story can be told which fits some of the facts, while the whole truth is very complicated.

Let one thing be clear. The mists of time appeared to close on a bucolic and prosperous rural eighteenth-century past, which critics of industrialism glimpsed shining in the sunshine beyond the smoke pall of Manchester, Chicago and the Ruhr. Reality was very different. Before industrialization there were patches of prosperity: New England was one; England itself reached, by about 1760, unprecedented prosperity on the basis of its extensive commerce and the improvement in the manufacturing costs already apparent at the time. The general condition of the world, however, was one of grinding poverty, interspersed with famine or near-famine conditions. Even the accounts of the arrival of the Elizabethan English in Bengal, where they found an apparently limitless prosperity, speak more of the poverty of England than of the wealth of the prosperous classes of Bengal. So it would be hard to imagine that for the typical poor person conditions could deteriorate very much.

But they did for some. The skilled hand-workers who over a period of decades struggled against the falling costs of factory competition were groups who fell into misery and pauperdom. Some of the agricultural workers, similarly, lost their status in pre-capitalist agriculture and found no new place in capitalist agriculture. They lost rights which they had taken for granted, to graze their animals, to glean, to collect firewood, and there was no work. The third group who suffered were the paupers and the beggars – the dispossessed who had immemorially been in society; these were now regarded as pernicious wastrels who had to be disciplined and who, in the words of the English Poor Law Commissioners of 1834, had to be reduced to the conditions of the 'least eligible labourer'. With wages almost by definition at subsistence level, this meant that their conditions were indescribably sad. Families were separated, their humiliation was endless. But whether it was worse than beggary is an exercise in comparative misery that it would be hard to establish.

People still died of starvation in the capitalist world until well into the twentieth century (as they died, of course, under communism in the 1930s). They did so chiefly in periods of slump, and slumps and booms, the eleven-year cycle of capitalist activity, appeared to intensify as industrialism spread. In bad years, therefore, in the 1840s for instance, many thousands were unemployed and, propertyless, without savings, with nowhere to go, found themselves homeless and starving. Only the Poor Law could provide for them. Again, these collapses were as nothing compared to the conditions in the pre-capitalist world where, as in Ireland, when the crop failed there was no social mechanism for providing relief. Despite the efforts of the government, there was no immediate means of providing relief for the Irish, except by emigration, or so it seemed.

The herding together of people into the industrial towns and cities caused a series of social problems. Infectious diseases spread easily. The absence of sewage and waste disposal facilities created conditions where dysentery, typhoid and other water-borne diseases were endemic. The death rate, especially among infants soared. There is no doubt, either, that there was a serious deterioration in the quality of food: adulteration was common (not that it was unknown in the eighteenth century) and contamination was certain.

The towns, then, were less healthy than rural life had generally been. Food supplies were more regular, but poorer in quality. Illness was greater. In slumps, destitution was common, and destitution meant homelessness and starvation. For people with redundant skills, in dying trades, conditions were terrible. The afflicted were neglected, as the common assumptions of Christian charity were questioned in the name of efficiency and self-reliance. It was the treatment of those unable to look after themselves – the children, the old, the sick and the afflicted – which first seriously called into question the ethical standards of capitalism. The reactionaries, who looked back to an age where everybody knew his place, when it was a Christian duty to comfort the afflicted, joined with the revolutionaries, who looked forward to an age when poverty would be no more. Both condemned the conditions in which society wrung a surplus out of the industrial and agricultural workers to build the means of producing abundance.

The conditions of industrial work
Discipline was the clue to working under capitalism. Pre-capitalist countries had a rhythm of work and social behaviour which were dictated by the seasons and the weather, and which reflected a ritual interpretation of life, with fiestas and fasts, high days and low days. Productivity was low; the regularity of life was the regularity of the unconscious rhythm of a traditional society. Industrial society is different. The pattern and rhythm of life is set by machinery and team work. Everybody in a working group has to start together and stop together. If the machine speeds up, the worker speeds up; if it stops, he stops. The shift from one mode of working to the other is traumatic. This is the explanation of – though it is no excuse for – the conditions of the early factories. Discipline was harsh, dismissal was instantaneous, and the atmosphere was tyrannical.

The early workers had few rights. Ignorant, desperately poor, and frightened, they depended on the factory masters for the bare conditions of life. Wages were at a minimum, and if they sought more there were others to take their place. If men were expensive, women could be used. Children worked – paupers of five or six were drafted into the factories. Hours were extremely long. Accidents were frequent. Life was cheap. In some factory barracks, or cheap lodging houses, successive shifts of workers shared beds; as one shift went on duty, their beds were taken by those coming off duty. Conditions in early industrialization always seem to have been terrible: first in England (on the basis of which Marx and Engels wrote their reports), then on the continent and in America, then in Russia and Asia, the same experience of oppression and exploitation was undergone. There is a literature, from British official publications to Maxim Gorki, from Jack London and Upton Sinclair to Fidel Castro, describing the horrors of early industrialism.

It was the cruelty of the overseers and the callousness of the managers and foremen which were most horrifying. Conditions of domestic labour were physically little better: children probably worked as long and just as unhealthily in domestic trades as in factories; but were they callously bullied to the same extent?

These conditions lasted for several generations before amelioration set in. England began to develop a group of labour managers, industrialists who were interested in labour conditions, who realized that shorter hours and more sympathetic treatment might raise productivity, and so reduce costs, increase output and not lower it. In this respect they were soon overtaken by the Americans, where the supply of cheap labour (except on the slave plantations of the south) was continually replenished by immigration but frequently depleted by movement to the west. Labour prices were continually forced up and so it was essential to deal with labour as a scarce factor of production, and not as an abundant one as it was in Europe.

The labour force, as some of its members entered their second and third generations as industrial workers, became used to industrial work and the discipline of working with machines, and therefore no longer needed to be dragooned. Machines became more sophisticated, needing more skilled people to operate them, and the general conditions of the labour force improved. Its educational levels rose perceptibly; it was composed of people aware, to some extent, of what was going on at their work and capable of working on their own initiative. Again, this was especially so in America where 'exploitation' became chiefly concentrated on vulnerable immigrant groups, the Negroes, and women. Yet 'exploitation' is an odd word to use, since the productivity of this type of labour was very low. The profits on highly paid labour employed in prosperous concerns were considerably higher. Marx was certainly incorrect in identifying surplus value with the degree of poverty of the workers.

After a time, of course, the workers began to combine in small numbers into labour unions. These unions sprang out of the growing sense of solidarity with each other. Initially, the unions in France, England, and to a small extent in America, had apocalyptic notions of a reconstruction of society on cooperative lines. The successful unions, however, were those of skilled and semi-skilled workers which could afford relatively high membership dues, engage in detailed negotiation with big employers, and seek to exclude new entrants to the trade unless they conformed to the wage conditions determined by negotiation. These bodies, similar to professional bodies, were closely allied to the concept of friendly societies and co-operative societies, which provided, in the one case, insurance against unemployment, sickness and burial costs, and in the other case reliable goods. In America, again, because of the generally higher level of the average citizen in terms of income and social aspiration, the spread of clubs, societies and communal activities was greater; the greater self-respect of the American worker was often noted both as a cause and a consequence of his higher standard of living and better working conditions.

In Britain the state began in the 1840s to regulate working conditions. The movement spread to other countries. There were safety provisions, limitations of hours, especially for children and women, and enforcement of environmental provisions for the health of the workforce. Most of this legislation sprang from the enlightened middle classes; but increasingly the workers themselves demanded legal regulation of their working lives. This movement towards state provision was to become a significant feature of later capitalist society.

Profits and their spending

As industrialism spread, so did the size and importance of the profit-receiving class. The landowner and his rent (and tribute in kind) diminished in importance as the industrialist and businessman provided more of society's savings. This arose from two causes: first, an increase in activity, which had the effect of increasing the total level of profits, proportionately with rises in other factor incomes, and secondly, the depression of real wages which probably occurred in the price rise of the Napoleonic Wars. After the end of the war, when price levels fell, profit levels probably fell as well, but as significant technical advances were occurring at the same time it is difficult to generalize.

With the coming of the railway, and the great expansion of world trade which followed the development of the British, north-west European and north-east American industrial complexes, more and more economic activity yielded a profit (as opposed to a landowner's surplus). It had two important characteristics: first, much of it was more a steady profit rather than a series of risky windfalls. Before 1840 it was customary to put money into landownership for security's sake. After the coming of the railways, holdings of railway stock became respectable. Throughout the nineteenth century, in country after country, this increasingly became the case. The London Stock Exchange, the Paris and Brussels bourses, the other continental and the American exchanges thus increasingly became the centre of a flow of capital seeking a safe haven. As the century wore on, a steady five per cent was expected. The nineteenth century, after the Napoleonic Wars, was a period of steady (and sometimes falling) prices. Thus the rise of the joint stock company, and its regular payment of dividends, became the basis for a steady accumulation of savings, expecting a regular, safe return and prepared to seek it in business. Particular pools of local capital became part of a general flood of savings. Wherever returns increased, capital flowed. The international money market, helped by international banking houses like the Rothschilds, became a reality. The flow of

British capital overseas through the City of London became prodigious. Much of American, European, Australasian, African and Latin American development was initially undertaken with British capital, which flowed out of British profits or came from the reinvestment of British overseas profits. Paris and Vienna followed suit; American capital generally found the vast opportunities of its own land sufficiently attractive to keep it there.

The second characteristic of the rise in the significance of profits was that more and more economic activity was directed to a profit-making end. The single-man business, the partnership, the firm – all of them thought increasingly of their surplus as a means of developing the market, of seeking ways to reduce costs by finding new ways of doing things.

Thus profit became a pool from which profit-making businesses took what they could usefully employ to increase profits, and those profits were returned to the pool where they were once more reallocated by the capital market. The generator of this activity was therefore the firm that increased its capital and raised its profitability. Everyone was looking for such opportunities. Railways offered them; the new mineral discoveries offered them, and capital flowed into companies in those sectors.

It would be a mistake to build up a picture of a frugal group of capitalists, reinvesting their capital with obsessive zeal. During the nineteenth century, ostentatious display like that of Louis XIV died out, even in Russia, but frugality was scarcely in fashion. The life of the great aristocrats continued, more comfortable, less violent, but still very expensive. To this was added the wealth of the new capitalist class. Some of the landowners became capitalists, by investing in industry, and some of the capitalists became landowners. There was intermarriage, especially at the edges of the classes. And there was a spread of solid comfort in middle-class lives. Houses still survive that attest to this, as do the hotels where they took their holidays, the churches, the libraries, and the universities that they built – best seen, perhaps, in the Paris of Napoleon III, almost perfectly preserved in its essentials (though the shop fronts have changed). But, even after the rising consumption of the capitalist class has been taken into account, there was still, over the period of a trade cycle, a steady rise in savings to be invested. It was this disposal of the surplus that led to the further rise in profits.

Ricardo's prediction that the profit rate would fall was, generally, refuted by experience. The discovery of new lands and the development of new techniques kept profits up. The rate of realized profits may have fallen, as riskiness decreased in the main industrial centres, but the rate of loss also fell, so the average was kept up.

Money and banking

Credit oiled the wheels of capitalism. The nineteenth century saw many remarkable inventions, but none more remarkable than the growth of the banking system and the establishment and maintenance of the international gold standard.

Banking had begun in Italy and spread to the Low Countries, as goldsmiths lent out their gold on extended credit. Gradually the habit of financing trade by bills was extended and a complex system of discounting and rediscounting trade bills was built up. Local businessmen, extending credit to their customers, found themselves moving into banking. Out of this process of creating trade credit, banking on ordinary commercial lines developed and certain principles of behaviour evolved. The credit extended by banks fulfilled some of the functions of money. Consequently, the state's regulation of the money supply was imperceptibly merged into a system of controlling the credit system.

In England a network of country banks lent locally and financed local trade. Bankers learned to separate their banking operations from their original business as merchants or tradesmen, since a run on the one involved the collapse of the other. Gradually the Bank of England, which was set up to manage the National Debt, became a central bank. In the Bank Charter Act of 1844 its powers were formally determined in a way that set the pattern for financial stability in the capitalist world.

Banks had issued credit, largely by means of notes. The French *assignats* during the revolutionary period and the English inflationary note issue had shown how easy it was for a currency to be debased. Therefore the problem was to curtail bank note issue. The currency was defined as gold. The Bank of England Issue Department was to issue notes only up to its value of bullion (plus £14 million). The Banking Department was to carry on general banking activities. The right of other banks to issue notes was gradually withdrawn.

Unintentionally, by this process, not only was the gold standard established but the banks were driven away from note issue to the development of a fully-fledged credit system (based on the cheque), whose extent was determined by the volume of credit extended to the banks by the Bank of England. For, so long as the bank could turn to the Bank of England and get credit (by rediscounting a bill, say), the Bank of England credit was – literally – 'as good as gold', and the bank could go on lending to its customers. But if the Bank of England did not extend credit, or did so only at a penal rate of interest, the bank itself could not extend credit to its customers. And when the Bank of England, managing the government debt, found that by selling securities it could contract the basis of credit, it had in its hands the weapon which enabled it to determine the level of domestic economic activity, for trade was based on credit, and contraction and expansion could be determined by the Bank of England as part of the process of managing the banking system.

These procedures were pragmatically adopted during the course of the nineteenth century, to be formalized by Walter Bagehot, the editor of *The Economist* newspaper. His principles were regarded as sound and were universally accepted. As London was the greatest centre of world commerce, the Bank of England was to a significant extent the arbiter of world economic affairs.

The principles on which it decided on expansion and contraction were relatively simple, though it is fair to say that they were interpreted with far less rigidity and far greater subtlety in the nineteenth century than they were to be in the twentieth century. The basis of the national currency was its stock of gold. If gold flowed out, the bank contracted the credit base; if gold flowed in, it expanded it. Gold flowing out was a sign that exports (including capital imports) were falling short of imports (including capital exports). It was a sign that the economy was overheated and was usually accompanied by other 'feverish' signs – full employment, rising prices and wages, and a Stock

Exchange boom. The contraction was put under way in order, directly, to safeguard gold and, indirectly, to keep prices stable and at the same level (allowing for transport costs) throughout the world.

The same recipe, religiously followed, caused chronic deflation in the 1920s. It did not do so in the nineteenth century for three reasons. First, gold was repeatedly discovered – in California, Russia, Australia and South Africa – thus expanding the volume of bullion. Second, throughout the later part of the century, a flow of British capital exports occurred, which continually raised the ability of individual countries to import without worrying about their balance of payments. So long as Britain's gold reserves were maintained by the inflow of newly mined gold, the international credit system was primed by the steady outflow of British capital. Third, the Bank of England was most flexible in its control of the economy and rarely deflated for the sake of deflating. It was an expansionist age.

It was also an age of dramatic bank crashes. Things were less well regulated and so periodically there were financial crashes in which financial institutions went bankrupt. The great crash of 1866 was an example, and in America and the other 'new' continents the credit institutions were, of course, less stable than in Europe. Fortunes were made and lost; fraud, or near-fraud, was common. It was only towards the century's end that the power of the financiers was to be seen as really sinister; and that was partly because the periods of contraction had become more frequent and more severe. Looking back, the golden age of banking was the middle years of the century.

In Europe, banking developed another side – investment in long-term capital projects – under state auspices in France. This was regarded by many bankers with deep suspicion, but the German bankers made a great success of 'mixed banking', and it was held that their practices were a useful guide to what banking should be like if national development needed to be accelerated. Both played their part in the growth of capitalism.

International trade

The growth of British exports of textiles, coal, iron and other industrial goods was a remarkable fact of the nineteenth century. It was balanced by a growth of British imports of cotton, wool, and, later, food. It was therefore apparently in the British interest (that is, the interest of those who were in the expanding trades) to promote the growth of international trade. The City of London's financial institutions progressively did so, as more and more world trade came to be financed by them; and British ships came to carry an ever growing volume of goods, not only between Britain and the rest of the world but between other countries. Britain also pioneered free trade.

Free trade had been Adam Smith's doctrine, for he looked forward to the international specialization of factors and the division of labour. This was to replace a doctrine that the aim of policy was to maximize the trade surplus in order to import gold, and that a growing gold reserve was a sign of economic victory. This belief died hard; it never died in continental Europe, and was to become the basis of Gaullist economic policy after 1958.

The English liberals, following the Scottish Adam Smith, argued the opposite. They wanted world trade to flow free of political interference. The conventional wisdom, then, was for years that trade barriers must be dismantled. First to go were the Navigation Acts, designed to protect British shipping (for strategic reasons) by ensuring that British goods should be carried in British bottoms. Thus came a series of enactments allowing the export of British strategic goods, especially machinery, which could be copied or used by the foreigner to compete with British goods. The major victory, of course, was the virtual abolition of all import duties – first by Huskisson (later run over by a railway train, steam's first sacrificial victim, a political Anna Karenina), and then by Peel's repeal of the Corn Laws in 1846. This was a symbolic triumph. The duties on corn were intended to protect agriculture, so that Peel, son of a cotton manufacturer, was proposing a symbolic as well as a politico-economic act. His proximate cause was the Irish Famine: cheap corn and free trade, it was hoped, would enable the Irish to feed themselves by exporting and importing. In fact the reverse was true. The famine killed the old subsistence economy and brought a monetary, capitalist economy to the whole of Ireland, in which free trade could work.

The next era of British policy was to spread free trade through the world. In the Cobden Treaty with France, in 1860, they substantially reduced French tariffs. Other countries had a prior task: they had to abolish internal tariffs. The American constitution had been strong on this point – the United States was a great free trade area. Germany became so after the Zollverein of 1834, and the foundation of the Empire in 1870. Austria-Hungary progressively did so, and so did Italy after the struggle for unification. The British Empire was, of course, predominantly free trade. Yet America, Germany and Russia, among other countries, did not eliminate all their tariffs. This was for two reasons. Federal governments, especially, found that levies on imports were easy to collect, and often they had few other sources of revenue. The income tax was a newfangled invention; tax systems were extremely primitive. Even if the federal government in America had wished to reduce taxes it would not have been able to do so without bankruptcy. In addition, however, the free trade doctrine was not universally accepted. Bismarck had a group of 'historicist' economists who argued that national economies gave the state a separate economic well-being from that of the bourgeoisie, and that this well-being was closely allied to military power, together with a paternalist concern for the poor by the state. This Hegelian doctrine, expressed in England by T. H. Green, was to give a basis to non-Marxist socialism; but its immediate practical result was the protection of European agriculture by tariffs and the protection of 'infant industries'. The Prussians and the Americans were very concerned to develop native industries – iron, steel, shipbuilding, chemicals – which they felt they could best do behind tariff walls. There was, of course, an element of double-talk on this position, since powerful lobbies argued in their own self-interest; but there was also an element of truth. Tariffs undoubtedly helped the development of German and American industry, though after 1830 (since American industry was firmly rooted) American growth coincided with falling tariffs.

Thus, it was only in a relative sense that the capitalist world was a free-trade world. Three things stand out. There was an extraordinary growth of world trade during the nineteenth century, in manufactured goods and primary products. It was based to a considerable extent on British capital and on sound currencies tied to the gold standard, whose basis was frequently expanded by gold discoveries. Next, the free flow of men and ideas was most impressive. Only backward governments required passports. Marx and other revolutionaries, and businessmen, could land at Dover without meeting an immigration officer; people could come and go to America (if they could afford the fare) without visas or explanations. Thus, to an extent incredible to those who began to travel after 1918, the whole world was open to travel without official intervention. It was this freedom which was the basis of the migration of peoples to the 'new lands'.

Thirdly, capital movements were virtually uncontrolled. British firms set up businesses in foreign countries; foreigners set up firms in Britain. The French built a considerable part of Russian capital equipment; the Germans spread out through the Balkans. Capital went where there was a profit to be made, and people were unashamedly unxenophobic about it. The free flow of capital was later to be identified by Lenin as the basis of imperialist exploitation. It was certainly a basis of imperialism, but in strangely international terms.

The state and the bourgeois

The state was an extension of the household affairs of the monarch, managed with futile extravagance in some countries, at some epochs, and at others (as under the Tudors, or Henri IV) with frugal care. Wars were the king's wars; charity was the king's charity, if it was not the responsibility of the Church. The result was that it was impossible to say where the state began or ended; impossible to define its functions, or to rationalize its mechanisms. It operated by corruption (which was not necessarily viewed as corruption, but as an effective way of getting business done).

Looked at through the eyes of a capitalist, the situation was terrible. The state got in his way with a series of laws and regulations, tax gatherers and licence issuers, whose original purpose, if any, was lost in the past but whose present function was to derive an income from the exercise of useless powers. First of all, then, the capitalist had to remove archaic laws from the statute book and make government less arbitrary and tyrannical. The removal of internal and external tariffs, the reorganization of government business, the removal of levies on transport, the repeal of laws against usury – all this represented a clearing of the decks which was to be found in America after the revolutionary war, in France in the revolution and the *Code Napoléon*, and in England after Bentham.

The next step was to reform the machinery of state, to separate public business from the monarchy, and to put public business under some sort of regular supervision. This was achieved by the revolution in France, by the deposition of the Stuarts in Britain (in 1688) and the arrival of the dim-witted, unattractive House of Hanover whose affairs were managed for them, and, gradually, in other countries, either by revolution or a series of gradual changes. Even in Russia, where absolutism and meddling muddle lasted longest, by the time of the 1917 Revolution the state was in fact separated from the monarchy.

Having limited and defined the power of the state and given it tolerably responsible government, the bourgeois was (until quite late on) content to leave politics mainly to the aristocracy (except in America, where the republic, once established, flourished without the hereditary principle). But, in Britain, till the 1870s, both Houses of Parliament were dominated by the landed aristocracy, though admittedly the aristocracy received constant transfusions of capitalists' blood and money. Even in France the aristocracy continued to be powerful. By the later part of the nineteenth century, however, the *haute bourgeoisie* was seeking office as well as behind-the-scenes power.

In so doing, there was a rationalization of the machinery of government (itself a characteristically capitalist metaphor). The establishment of a *carrière ouverte aux talents* was extended to the army and the civil service. Governmental efficiency was encouraged by recruiting able people and paying them adequately so that they did not have to live by bribes. Especially important was the reform of the machinery of justice. Basic to all commerce, whether internal or international, was the enforceable contract – the shift to capitalism could be defined as the shift from status to contract. Thus, a series of clearly drawn contracts, speedily enforceable at law, required a judicial system which was incorrupt, swift and predictable. Two ways were found of providing this: the first was the evolution of the English system of common law, its gradual rationalization, and the reform of the judicial system, which was finally achieved in

England in the 1870s; the other was the Napoleonic Code – the systematic rationalization of a code of law for a modern community – which Napoleon spread throughout continental Europe.

Behind both notions – the one proceeding from precedent to precedent, the other setting things out clearly – was a deep concern for the avoidance of arbitrary decisions and uncertainty. The key to the bourgeois concept of the state was that its powers should be clearly defined and that its acts should be lawful in the full sense. The most successful nineteenth-century nation, Great Britain, had no constitution, but Bagehot, in putting forward the paradox of the unwritten British constitution, argued that the constitution was in fact perfectly clear and lay on a basic foundation of total acceptability to the middle class. The consent of the governed to their mode of government and to the acts of that government was implicit in the whole way in which the community regarded its government.

What, then, did government do? It kept the peace. It saw that justice was enforced. If need be, it went to war to keep the peace or to secure the safety of trade. It 'kept the ring', as the community slogged it out by competition to get a living for itself. There was a residual Poor Law for the wholly incompetent. Eventually, it was thought then, the state should provide basic education. It laid down standards by which honest trade was conducted. That, in essence, was the Anglo-American view of government. The Prussians regarded their state differently. They did not renounce the principle of absolutism but continued absolutism with efficiency. Nor did they define the powers of the state to exclude powers over the economy. German industrialization was fostered by the state, as was the creation of the railway system; and the state took a leading part in the creation of social institutions, ranging from education at all levels to social security. The German conception of the state, then, was far broader than the laissez-faire concept prevalent in Britain and America; and it represented a model that was to be widely copied once it was realized that the interests of the high bourgeoisie did not necessarily coincide with the interests of the whole community. For the anti-liberals had always argued that the state existed to protect the poor against the exploitation of the industrialists, and this aristocratic argument, which was (it seemed) accepted and successfully implemented in Prussia, became the basis for a working-class reaction to the limitation of the powers of the state.

The state and the worker

The concept of a working class, of a group of men and women working for wages, owning no property and having a common interest against their employers which could be organized politically, grew comparatively slowly. Political reform in the nineteenth century after the defeat of the Jacobins and Babeuf meant the tidying up and rationalization of the state and the admission to some degree of power of those with property but no hereditary claim to government. In the elimination of the obstacles to progress, the aristocracy were usually able to protect themselves because almost all their assets, and some of their privileges, could be turned into cash and could be invested. Some of the greatest aristocrats became some of the greatest rentier-capitalists. It is no accident that Salisbury, Rhodesia, is named after Lord Salisbury, the British prime minister at the height of imperialism. The labouring classes, however, were in a different situation. Nobody would compensate them. Three times the Paris mob rose to seize power – in 1789, 1848 and 1871; each time it was humiliatingly defeated. The British workers did not rise, but they organized and agitated: in 1819, at Peterloo, they were defeated; in 1832, over parliamentary reform, they were cheated; in 1848 their Chartist movement evaporated.

The great mass of the workers was an unorganized, seething group of people seeking a living and enduring such desperate privations that their thoughts could hardly be turned in a political direction. So long as the authorities could control the mob there was civil peace; when the control broke down, the mob got out of hand and the working class suffered even greater privations.

Thus the attitude of the working class as a whole was essentially apolitical. Those who sought to give it a political role were small groups with many contradictory ideas and policies. Their attitudes to the state differed radically. The defenders of the old order, who became steadily more romantic about the old order as its reality faded into the distant past, saw the state as a paternalist institution, aiding the Church to fulfil its role of Christian charity, where each class knew its place and played its preordained part. This was contrasted with the chaotic vulgarity of industrialist society. Ruskin and Pugin, the European Romantics, the great Russians, believed that industrialism was an aberration.

Another group were the anarchists – those who held that state power represented oppression in a new guise, and that by ending state power oppression would end. This was sufficiently close to laissez-faire in practice to make the idea seem more reasonable than it really was, for if the state did nothing except enrich those who corruptly had their fingers in the till, then by abolishing it social life would organize itself along peaceful co-operative lines, uninterrupted by the tyranny of repressive institutions.

Thus the state could be seen not merely as an institution that was tyrannical in itself, but which was actively used by the dominant class to aid the exploitation of the powerless: in Marxist terms, the job of the bourgeois state was to aid the exploitation of the workers by the bourgeoisie, and to protect the bourgeoisie and their goods against the workers. For this reason, the early socialists wanted to overthrow the state rather than gain control of its institutions. By contrast, of course, the bourgeoisie wanted to take over the state and to curtail its powers.

The paternalists did not want to curtail the state's powers, which they saw as an essential bulwark against the remorseless exploitation of the workers by the capitalists. The early Factory Acts were introduced by Tories (that is, aristocrats) and were opposed by the supporters of laissez-faire. In England the reforms of working-class conditions brought about by state intervention were for a long period to be supported by the Tories and opposed by the spokesmen and apologists of the industrialists. Similarly in the United States the protection of the working class was left to agrarian interests who were instinctively populist and opposed to industrialism. Prussia was the supreme example of a paternalist state which both introduced industrialism and protected the workers by developing institutions for their benefit.

The radical groups in the working class gradually came, then, to take the view that the essential task before them was to extend state action, to limit hours of work, regulate conditions of employment, raise wages, and to improve social conditions by ameliorating the Poor Law, extending education, and moving into housing and health provision. The detailed construction of a welfare state began almost by accident, as the pattern established itself of some calamity being revealed (like an epidemic), its causes being investigated, and legislation being passed to remedy the conditions. The legislation was then found inadequate, a scandal would occur because it had not been enforced, and machinery would then be created for its enforcement. Once the bureaucracy had been established it acquired a momentum of its own, and a political lever existed which the working class and the reformers who were on the working class side were able to seize.

Working-class activists came to see, then, that they had to achieve some say in state policy and take part in political affairs. The Tories in Britain and the absolutists in Prussia came to see that the top and the bottom were in a position to squeeze the middle. That, in essence, became the strategy. The working-class activists, having wanted to overthrow the state, came to see it as a weapon to be used against the bourgeoisie, and they sought to put back on the political agenda the issues that the exponents of laissez-faire had religiously removed from it. The state thus moved back into the regulation of conditions of work and into the field of social security, from which it had been excluded in the bibles of high capitalism. No conversion is more dramatic on this point than John Stuart Mill's. Having begun as a disciple of his laissez-faire father, James Mill, he ended, on the same philosophical Benthamite Utilitarian principles, as a socialist – aligned with John Ruskin.

4 Early socialism

Robert Owen

Socialist theory emerged largely from working-class reaction to industrialism. It was, in essence, a philosophical creation until that time – that is, it was unrealistic, vague, Utopian – and it was the harsh reality of the steam age that gave it birth. It is possible to trace socialist thought back to Plato, to More's *Utopia*, to the Peasants' Revolt, to the Levellers in the English Civil War, but to do so is more to make myth than to trace a realistic line of descent. Robert Owen is the first genuine socialist because he was coincident with the industrial revolution and his concern was with the proletariat. Moreover he was involved in three movements which, in direct line, led to socialism: trade unions, co-operative societies, and welfare systems.

Robert Owen was a Welshman who worked in Scotland. Born in 1771, he bought the New Lanark cotton mills near Glasgow in 1800, and, as a capitalist entrepreneur, ran them profitably, while paying good wages and establishing a miniature 'welfare state' with education for the children, medical care, housing, and welfare benefits. This side of Owen was paternalist and not specifically socialist, but it marked a radical departure from the traditions of laissez-faire capitalism. More significant was his foundation of the first serious trade union in Britain, and his followers' foundation of the Rochdale Co-operative Society.

These two events, together with his benevolence as an employer, were incidents in early industrialism. The nature of industrial capitalism was revealed first of all in Britain. It required high savings, a labour force prepared to work for money under conditions of industrial discipline, a continuous stream of technological innovations, ever wider markets, and a modern system of government.

In this context, with a population explosion continually adding to the ranks of the landless poor, the working class played a passive role. In times of unrest they provided the mob; in times of war they provided the soldiers and sailors; at all times they provided the labour force for the factories and workshops, and servants for the homes which belonged to the more prosperous classes.

Radical thinkers – Godwin, Saint-Simon, Fourier – argued for the incorporation of all men into the political society, occasionally adding to this some conceptions of social and economic equality. But much of their thought (which was, of course, extremely unsystematic) was coloured by the view that a return to an idyllic pre-industrial society was possible, on the basis of peasant smallholdings. Many socialists started or took part in rural settlements, somewhat like Israeli kibbutzim, and the redistribution of land, so that men could provide for their own needs and do without mass industry, was a continuing strand in populist and socialist thought. America provided for European radicals a continuing vision of free land that could yield abundance; and a democratic society could only be built, it was thought, in such a manner.

This vision provided a leit-motif for socialist thought throughout the nineteenth century. Owen came to share it, backing New Harmony in Indiana in 1824, and establishing a settlement (on the site of an older one) which was to teach the world how to live according to new and better principles. American space, and the sense of beginning anew, combined with romanticism to suggest that a reformed society could be willed into being by a spread of new attitudes. This view (which came to be called Utopian) owed a great deal to religious revivalism and was not specifically socialist. What was socialist was the analysis of the ills of industrialism, as being due to the private ownership of capital, and the diagnosis of social and personal conflict as springing from the economic basis of industrial society. New Harmony departed rapidly from these principles and Owen, tired of the colony, left it to his younger sons.

He returned to England and found that the trade unions, newly legalized, were organizing the workers to protest collectively against social and industrial conditions. Owen then set out to realize his vision of the collectivist society through the militant working class, abandoning the paternalism of New Lanark and the private community of New Harmony. He did so first by seeking to establish producers' co-operatives which, trading with each other, would bypass industrial capitalism. These schemes, which rapidly spread, developed into a broader concept of a General Labour Union, and in 1834, after an earlier Owenite scheme for a Grand National Moral Union of the Productive Classes, there was founded the Grand National Consolidated Trades Union. The earlier Owenite scheme was for a general strike to bring capitalism peacefully to an end and to replace it by a cooperative commonwealth; the Trades Union was planned, by the same means, to achieve the more limited end of an eight-hour day of work. Owen still hoped for a common agreement by all classes to replace capitalism while the trade unionists, by class action, sought to modify it. And this was to be a recurrent socialist dilemma; they stood for goodwill among all right-minded men which they thought would inevitably bring about socialism, since socialism was the only reasonable society, but their action in practice had to be for limited objectives by class-warfare techniques, like strikes, or even occasionally by direct political violence, since in most places working men did not have the vote.

Working people also faced a dilemma. They wanted particular improvements in their daily life, that is they wanted to ameliorate capitalism by modifying it, whilst people like Owen wanted to replace capitalism by a completely new system. This is the central dilemma, indeed, of socialism.

The Union collapsed: its aims were ambitious, its organization feeble and its support evanescent. All that survived of Owen's schemes was the cooperative movement – an organization of consumers that bought goods wholesale, retailed them to its members at prevailing prices, and distributed the profits to consumers in proportion to their purchases. Owen had challenged capitalism on four fronts. He had challenged the way it organized industry; he had tried to build a visionary community; he had tried to bring it down through a trade union

movement; and he had tried to build up a consumers' organization. All of these were challenges – but the Utopian vision was
largely dropped from socialism. It concentrated henceforth on
alternative schemes for organizing industry; on trade unions;
and on consumer co-operation.

Proudhon, Saint-Simon and Fourier

Proudhon (1809–65) was a Frenchman of working-class family,
from Besançon. More than any other man he dominated French
socialism, and because of Marx's denunciation of him he
became the central figure in non-Marxist socialist thinking.
Marx, as we shall see, was a system builder, and he thought of
himself as a cold, clinical 'scientist' who predicted the inevitable
downfall of capitalism. Proudhon was not a system builder. He
was, rather, a libertarian, almost an anarchist, devoted to 'liberty' and 'justice'. He was profoundly hostile to the state, which
he thought of as essentially a repressive agency, and an
enthusiast for law, which he regarded as an abstract entity
embodying justice. The state, however democratic it might
become, would inevitably revert to repression. The law, once
established in fairness and justice, would stand unalterable and
above society. The practical work of life would be carried on by
groups or associations based on the family. Proudhon had an
organic view of society: he deeply distrusted the cooperative
societies, or companies, or free communities, that Owen had
been concerned with, and which Blanc and Fourier, his predecessors in French socialist thought, had advocated. The
family, according to Proudhon, would be able to work out its
own salvation alongside other families working for the same
end. Conflicting interests would be reconciled partly by a
change of heart, since bad behaviour was a result of capitalism,
but also by a process of combat. Marx thought the family was a
bourgeois concept, and that it would wither away when socialism came. He also thought that people's hearts did not change.
He appealed to their intellects. Proudhon had a vivid sense of
opposites and conflict; an unnatural harmony, a supremely
smooth-running system would have seemed to him a wicked
nonsense. The incentives to work and to improve one's lot were
the supreme virtues of the family, and the recognition of the
contradictions and difficulties inherent in society as a result of

the struggles of separate families lay at the heart of Proudhon's view of the good society.

In this respect Proudhon represented a radical break with the French tradition. In the French Revolution Babeuf and his followers had argued for an egalitarian commonwealth, following the Jacobin denunciation of inequality and the disloyal attitude of the rich to the Revolution. They had argued for communal property, operated by directly elected committees paid the same wages as the workers. Work was to be compulsory and only workers could vote. This state was to be achieved by a revolutionary dictatorship of the proletariat. Babeuf was executed for conspiracy to overthrow the régime, but his views remained underground, and sprang to the surface after the Revolution of 1830, which brought the bourgeois Louis-Philippe to the throne.

Saint-Simon and Charles Fourier took a less revolutionary line. Saint-Simon (1760–1825) was an aristocrat, who enlarged his future by speculation during the Revolution. He fought for the American revolutionaries and supported progressive causes. He sought to make a major intellectual contribution along the lines of the Encyclopaedists and his ambition was to found a universal science of mankind which would embrace all existing sciences and enable mankind collectively to plan its own future. To Saint-Simon, therefore, may be traced the socialist preoccupation with the social sciences. The social sciences were founded largely in the nineteenth century to provide a science of society as valid and universal as physics and chemistry; their laws had therefore to be universal – a tradition which Marx inherited (though rejecting its visionary overtones). Proudhon was a pragmatic realist, preferring the known organic basis of social life – the family – to misty pseudo-scientific generalizations. Saint-Simon, out of his conception of universal history, foresaw the overthrow of the industrialist class by the workers; and the industrialists were (like Robert Owen) to operate their industries as trustees of the people. Here, again, Proudhon was profoundly opposed to Saint-Simon's paternalism. Included in this paternalism, in Proudhon's view, was the whole conception of planning the future of society and curtailing productive forces in the 'general interest' of the 'general will' as a force independent of men's own wills, which Rousseau had long since argued was the deepest force in society. The view that ultimately everybody would pull together in the same direction offended Proudhon's sense of the continual struggle in society.

Fourier, who was vastly opposed to Saint-Simon's vague and windy generalizations, came from a middle-class family (which was almost ruined by the Revolution) and, like Proudhon, from Besançon. He was not a Utopian, in the sense that he held that human nature was unchangeable and therefore could not be improved, but he thought that, given the right social organization, men could cooperate in ways which led to harmony rather than to strife. He regarded bourgeois society as a way of life which wasted men's time in trivial and worthless occupations – especially buying and selling – and he wanted them to eat splendid food, and drink good wine, which they themselves had grown in decent conditions. Like Morris and Ruskin he wanted to see honest craftsmanship the basis of a way of life, and consequently he sought to establish communities where people lived rewarding lives, following a diversity of healthy jobs – growing food, weaving, carpentering – and finding their chief enjoyment in honest work. He envisaged a kind of kibbutz – a *phalanstère* (from the Greek phalanx $\Phi\acute{\alpha}\lambda\alpha\gamma\xi$) – where families would have their own rooms but where communal facilities would be available. Incomes would not be equal but they would be far less unequal than in existing society.

Fourier's ideas were practised in a few countries, chiefly in North America, but his influence was profound, since he drew attention to the need to construct a society which met the emotional needs of the individual, especially his need for happy and satisfying work. It was in France, where society had never lost its peasant roots and where satisfaction of general needs was most adequately achieved, that his ideas became firmly rooted. Proudhon, certainly, though rejecting Fourierism, by elevating the family to the centre of his thought, emphasized precisely this aspect of full satisfaction of emotional needs. Proudhon argued that if the credit system could be got right, so that the economy functioned automatically, an anarchic system based on the family would be successful, and that such a society would not only not be repressive, it would be positively liberating of joy and satisfaction.

To Marx this was anathema. Initially he curried favour with Proudhon, whose awareness of the complexity and contradictions of life was Hegelian. Hegel, the great German philosopher, saw life as a system of opposites whose conflicts led to constructive progress. When Marx found that Proudhon was unable to help him, that he was not only not a Hegelian but was opposed to abstract systems, Marx attacked him violently. Proudhon believed there was no one way to salvation; that, given freedom, especially freedom from property (except purely personal possessions), because 'property is theft', the family structure could create a diversity which would be part of the richness of living. Marx thought exactly the opposite. He believed in laws of historical necessity, where people did not have freedom, but did what historical forces told them. Marx, infuriated by Proudhon, developed his own ideas in *The Poverty of Philosophy*, which was the basis of his dialectical materialism. Proudhon may have been unsympathetic, but his ideas were concerned with a central question – how to make life, including work, satisfying, and how to ensure diversity. Marx had other goals in mind. He wanted to discover the laws of society and to overthrow capitalism.

Marxist thought has been one of the most powerful forces in the world. It is 'scientific' – we shall see in what sense – and it is successful because half the world owes allegiance to it. How did it come to be so powerful?

Marx
Karl Marx was, in his personal life, one of the most disagreeable and distasteful great men of his time, much given to rage and anger, to intense self-pity, avid for praise, hostile to friends, allies, companions, constant only in deceit, and odiously vain. A Jew, he was a frenzied anti-semite; a scholar, his scatological abuse of rivals was pathological; a socialist, he despised the workers and hardly had a comrade in his life. His only redeeming feature was his love for his elder daughter, Jenny. But he was a genius. His early work is obscure and almost unreadable; but with the *Communist Manifesto*, published in 1848, and *Capital* (of which the first volume was completed and published in his lifetime) Marx established two claims to fame. The first was a revolutionary, political vision of the overthrow of

capitalism and its replacement by an egalitarian society, and the second was a view of the historical process which put capitalism and industrialism into perspective and suggested the mechanism by which it had come to power and the mechanism by which it would be overthrown.

Marx will not be understood unless it is realized that his own revolutionary influence was at most concerned with a tiny group – perhaps ultimately a thousand people in his own lifetime – of those entirely without power, with about as much immediate impact on nineteenth-century history as nudists or observers of flying saucers have had on the world since 1945. While the forces of industrialism swept the world, while revolution broke out all over Europe in 1848, and the French Commune came to power in 1871, Marx was on the periphery. His work was entirely theoretical, though he manoeuvred himself into office in the First International – the first revolutionary international socialist movement – and destroyed it. Marx was the opposite of Napoleon, who established a system of law and thought as a result of practical revolution and conquest: Marx thought, and others subsequently practised. Moreover, in many respects, their practice was in direct contradiction to Marx's own predictions and recommendations. His texts were to be gone through, as the Bible is gone through, for aphorisms and judgements that could be wrenched out of context and used as justifications for what was being done.

The texture of Marx's thought was violent and apocalyptic. He continually expected the downfall of capitalism in the most violent revolution. He was extraordinarily authoritarian, both in personal affairs and in his view of the world order. He expected the intolerant governments of Europe to be replaced by the dictatorship of the proletariat. (In fact the governments were extremely tolerant and he operated with only occasional brushes with the authorities, despite his desperate attempts to overthrow them.) Thus, in interpreting Marxist doctrine, it must always be seen through a prism of authoritarian violence.

According to Marx, the economy had progressed from slave societies to feudalism, an agricultural economy, and from there to capitalism. In each society was to be found a class in control of the *new* economic forces. In the case of feudalism this was the capitalist bourgeoisie. It was their job to overthrow feudalism and to endow humanity with industrial capital. But to operate capitalism they had to have propertyless workers – the proletariat, from whose labour the surplus was extracted to accumulate the capital. But the proletariat, increasingly impoverished, would be unable to purchase the goods that capitalism provided, and as a result, the machine would fall into crisis, and – politically – the proletariat would rise. It would overthrow the capitalist class with all its paraphernalia of social and political machinery and thus under the guidance of well-informed leaders the dictatorship of the proletariat would be established.

There are two major points about Marx's thought which are of supreme importance for the present discussion. Firstly, how did he think capitalism worked and what were the main points of his diagnosis which socialists could use for analysing (and attacking) capitalism? The second is, what was his vision of socialism and how did it differ from what democratic socialists (as distinct from communists) would call socialism?

Capitalism operated by the division of society into two main classes who were at war – the capitalists and the proletariat. The capitalists accumulated capital, by buying and selling commodities at prices exceeding their cost. Their profit represented the surplus value over the wages paid to the workers. The value of goods corresponded to the amount of socially useful labour embodied in them; and the socially useful labour value was determined by the objective technical considerations prevailing. The workers were increasing in number the whole time; as they competed for employment, their pay tended continually to fall below subsistence level. The fact that it did so meant that the entire working class lived at (or just beyond) the verge of starvation. The capitalists, seeking profit, would find that, beyond a certain point, the rate of profit fell during successive crises of overproduction, and they would therefore seek overseas and colonial markets where profit rates were higher. Colonial powers would go to war with each other for markets (this was a view that Lenin developed) and to this international chaos would be added the internal chaos as the capitalists sought to oppress and exploit the workers ever more intensively, and as the workers sought to organize against the capitalists. Capitalism was double-edged, so to speak. Fighting against feudal societies, as in Russia, it was a progressive force; fighting against the militant and organized workers, it was a reactionary force.

The superstructure of the state reflected the underlying class relationships, which were deeply embedded in economic reality. It followed, therefore, that the role of the bourgeois state was to aid the capitalists in their exploitation; and that the notion of a state as having regard to the welfare of its members, or of the law being 'fair', was an idealistic fallacy.

The areas of dispute with Marx are obvious. First, economics did not explain everything: quite often politics (especially nationalism) determined economics. The state could be used to improve the conditions of the workers, and its development as a force for social improvement was a major contribution of the nineteenth century to social life. The rate of profit was not continually declining. Though there were frequent financial crises, which were accompanied by falling prices and widespread unemployment, there were also frequent booms, with rising prices and full employment. The general trend of real wages, after 1850, was upwards, and the general immiseration of the proletariat was not brought about. Above all, the militant working class did not organize itself for the overthrow of capitalism. Most workers voted for bourgeois liberal or conservative policies, and the active revolutionary socialist and communist movement was always a minority, able to seize power only at moments of social breakdown, usually in time of wartime disruption.

The diagnosis of capitalism, then, was a brilliant construction which bore an ever-diminishing relation to reality. Yet at times of social and economic crisis Marx's apocalyptic analysis seemed, superficially at least, to bear relation to what was happening. His emphasis on unemployment, on the key role of profit, on the state's domination by the bourgeoisie, and his dark view of the world, corresponded sufficiently to an atmosphere of repression and violence, as in Russia in 1917 or Europe in 1931, to enable the communists to use Marx for their diagnosis of underlying reality, which the periodic good times seemed to mask. And, oddly enough, Marx's description of capitalism remained for a long time the accepted mode of interpreting capitalism even by those who repudiated his conclusions. This is because his emphasis on economics and on the class struggle undoubtedly struck a chord of reality, compared with the superficiality of most capitalist apologetics.

Marx's diagnosis of socialist society was necessarily sketchy. He emphasized the dictatorship of the proletariat, the absence of conflict in a socialist society, the elimination of alienation between the worker and his work when all production was for use and when the principle of 'from each according to his ability and to each according to his need' was applied. Democratic socialists, on the other hand, rejected any form of dictatorship; they saw conflict surviving in a socialist society, and it was unclear as to what alienation exactly applied, for socialist societies were always unclear about the nature of authority in work, and the nature of payments for work, in an egalitarian society. Marx envisaged that under socialism the state would 'wither away' and a situation of gentle, cordial abundance would ensue, where non-perspiring peasants would gather the fruits of the earth with quiet dignity, as in some pre-Raphaelite painting. The harsh reality of Siberian prison-camps, show trials, and atomic spies was hardly a prelude to this roseate idyll.

Marx's vision – both his dark vision of capitalism and his bright vision of socialism – dominated socialist thought. All socialist thought other than Marxist had to be defined in relationship to it. Socialism, when Marx died, was a fringe theory held only by cranks; within a couple of decades it was far from that.

5 High capitalism

New lands

The early capital funds for the industrial revolution had been built up by trade, partly on the slave trade. The spread of steam-age capitalism involved more than trade. Permanent settlement took place, and the subjugation of coloured races. The Californian gold boom of the 1850s was followed by the rapid filling-up of the almost unpopulated spaces between the Ohio and the west coast; by 1910 'the Frontier' had come to an end, after three centuries. Australia, Canada, South Africa and New Zealand were other 'empty' lands which found people, partly on the basis of a new agricultural pattern and partly on a new basis of mineral exploitation. As England, and to some extent the rest of Europe, industrialized, so markets were created for North American grain, for meat, for wool, for dairy products – all of which were produced by the new lands. So, too, were minerals – gold, silver, copper, iron ore – which increasingly came from non-European sources.

South Africa was the country where a relatively populated area was colonized by the Europeans, and the Negroes driven northwards or brought into servitude. A similar pattern had prevailed in North America, where the American Indians were victims of genocide. But in tropical countries, some of which were fairly heavily populated, whites settled in only small numbers and colonialism meant trading and military outposts, from which plantation agriculture, under white ownership, spread through the hinterland. From the 1860s onwards the colonization of Africa began. India had been absorbed by the British crown, which replaced the East India Company after the

Mutiny of 1857. The French and the Dutch also conquered empires in Asia. By the end of the nineteenth century large parts of China lay under European semi-suzerainty.

The pattern of the 'new' world, then, was of large, English-speaking and sparsely populated countries, like America and Australia; Latin America, settled by Spaniards and Portuguese, sometimes intermarried with Negroes and Indians, organized in nominally independent states but dominated by European capitalists; Africa, divided between Britain, France and Germany, with a European-settled southern tip but for the most part consisting of European-dominated black colonies. Russia pushed across Asia to Japan, which remained one of the few states not dominated by Europeans. Only the Ottoman Empire stretched across Asia Minor, open to European penetration but not colonized till after the First World War.

This system of world domination, in which all the leading capitalist states took part – America in Cuba and the Philippines, Italy in North Africa and Ethiopia, Britain in Asia and Africa, France in Asia and Africa, Germany in Africa and the Pacific – was imperialism, and capitalist imperialism was the name given to the period of high capitalism, the latter half of the nineteenth century.

What was the basis of imperialism? It was a dispersal of white people, some to settle permanently and to found new nations, like America and Australia, others to rule where on the whole they would not settle, as in India. It was a great dispersal of capital, to open up sources of raw material and food for the capitalist countries. According to the socialists this was because the profit rate was declining in the capitalist countries and the margin for exploitation was greater in the tropical lands. This is doubtful. Great profits were made overseas but they arose from the physically advantageous conditions of production in countries like America, where wages were far higher than in Europe. Apart from mineral exploitation, the profits from tropical crops were not extraordinary and the main area of capital flow was not the tropics but the temperate zones.

Undoubtedly, traders, settlers, missionaries and military expeditions tended to accompany one another, and as the capitalist states became efficiently organized so they began formally to draw boundaries round their colonies. After a time, in the 1880s, the 'unclaimed' lands began to run out and a competitive rivalry between European states began to assert itself, between Britain and France and between Britain and Germany, to add to the rivalries that had always existed between the powers with regard to the Ottoman Empire and was coming to exist with regard to the division of control over China. The rivalries of European states, which had persisted since the seventeenth century, underwent a change to rivalry in foreign lands, as the British and the French had struggled over America, Canada and India. The difference this time was the bitterness of the rivalry and the totality of the involvement, to which was added a real fear that industrial advantage would be lost. Objectively this was absurd: Sweden, Switzerland and (effectively) America flourished without colonies. It was mercantilism revived: if trade were not conducted between the colonial power and its colonies, there would be a loss. This was a view that was reinforced by socialist views of the nature of empire. In truth, it was state rivalry and state competition seeking new forms. It was this rivalry which led, directly, to the First World War; it was that war which ended capitalism as it had flourished largely without serious challenge.

The opening of the Suez Canal in 1869 by de Lesseps (and its subsequent purchase by Disraeli for the British government) and the building of the Panama Canal which opened in 1914 indicated how travel times to the Pacific and Indian Oceans were reduced by the steamship; and indicated as well how fast traffic was growing between the colonies and metropolitan centres. By 1900 over half the food consumed in Great Britain came from overseas, including such perishable commodities as meat, vegetables and dairy products. The development of refrigeration helped to bring food to Britain, as did the increase of speed of ships and trains. But the import of food was only one aspect of an increase in world trade which took many forms. Much of the transporting of goods was a two-way traffic, of raw materials from the colonies to metropolitan centres and a reverse flow of trade in manufactured goods from the metropolitan countries to the colonies. Increasingly, however, the trade pattern shifted to trade between industrial countries. As Germany and America became big manufacturing centres, so their exports went not only to the primary producing areas but also to England, France and Russia. The pattern of trade thus produced was a complex system, involving many-sided transactions. Many of these transactions were financed from London, which became an international financial centre in a new sense. A ship taking Japanese goods to America, American goods to Chile, and Chilean nitrates to Germany, might be chartered from London, insured in London and have its cargoes paid for by bills drawn in London.

Thus the great growth in world trade in the years 1870 to 1914 was accompanied by a complex international financial nexus which extended the role of bankers and financiers to an extent that the classical economists had not been prepared to imagine. The simple operation of the gold standard was now masked by a flow of international monetary transactions in credit terms which were only very loosely connected to the flow of gold and bullion on which, nominally, the gold standard rested. This was a paradox which ultimately led to the collapse of international trade in the 1920s and 1930s. It was in the later nineteenth century that almost the entire world had moved on to the gold standard, often with serious internal opposition (as in the United States) to the severe monetary discipline that was implied by a gold standard mechanism operated through central banks, which came to dominate the domestic banking system in all the important countries. The gold standard required a severe discipline, but the growth of a world credit system took the world more and more away from gold as a medium of exchange.

It was the drawing of the whole world into a nexus of trade relationships, based upon a common monetary and credit system, between 1870 and 1914, then, that represented the apogee of high capitalism. After the First World War, Russia withdrew from the system and tariff barriers began to go up. With the virtual collapse of the gold standard in 1931, the elaborate structure of free trade and free monetary movements formally ended. Thus within twenty years, from 1911 to 1931, the system passed from its zenith to very nearly the opposite, and the financiers who were the heroes of one era became the villains of the next.

The positive achievements of this trading system were many.

The first was internationalism, which allowed a free flow of men, ideas, capital and trade on a scale never before or since equalled. Even Russia, which every true liberal regarded with horror, allowed virtually unlimited travel by foreigners; and the beginnings of capitalist enterprise in Kharkov, Kiev, Moscow and St Petersburg received continuous stimulation from the inflow of capital (especially French capital) which occurred after 1870, as did the exploitation of oil in the Caucasus and coalmining in the Ukraine and elsewhere.

The rise in trade certainly raised living standards in 'European' countries, wherever the white races were to be found. It did not do so generally for the other races, partly because their populations began to increase as fast as their national incomes. Indeed, some of this impact of world trade on developing nations was disgusting, both in terms of colonial violence and oppression (as in the Congo) and in terms of the disintegration of hitherto viable cultures, as in the Pacific and south-east Asia.

Nevertheless, the spread of trade also encouraged the development of local industries, often based on the local extractive or agricultural industry. India, for example, began a substantial cotton manufacturing industry (which was destined to knock out the British cotton industry) and an iron and steel industry. The 'white' colonies of Canada and Australia especially also began to industrialize. In this respect they were copying the European countries that had begun to overtake Britain and inevitably they began to chafe at the notion that their role was eternally to provide raw materials for Europe to manufacture. This chain of reasoning led, via nationalism, to tariffs and trade barriers which, in the case of those colonies which were not self-governed, were impossible to impose, and this became a powerful source of trouble. Irish nationalism, which became the model for nationalism elsewhere, derived a large degree of its impetus from the desire to make Ireland fiscally autonomous of Britain and to erect barriers to shelter infant Irish industry (dismantled after the Union in 1800) against British competition. That this argument was based on a false view of events before and after the Union, and that the Irish standard of living in fact rapidly improved after 1850 as a result of free trade, is irrelevant to the nature of nationalism.

Once nationalism had begun to assert itself it was to be a potent force in dissolving free trade.

Nationalism and tariffs got powerful boosts during periods of trade depression, which occurred with increasing severity and were internationally felt as economies were so closely linked by trade. Primary production prices always fell during a slump, with disastrous consequences for primary producing countries, while the effects of the slump were somewhat mitigated in the industrial countries by cheaper food. It was a series of slumps, following the collapse of the international monetary mechanism in the First World War, that effectively ended high capitalism, the period when trade and travel were largely free of restriction and the capitalist system was nowhere seriously challenged. It was to be followed by modern consumer capitalism based on mass-produced goods.

Over twenty million people emigrated from Europe to North America, Australasia and southern Africa between 1850 and 1900, and by the outbreak of the First World War in 1914 the total had reached over forty million. This is one of the great migrations in history, probably the largest that has ever occurred. It was made possible by cheap transport, settled government, and a liberal view of population movement which was, in turn, based upon increasing prosperity in the host countries. Outside the United States most immigrants came from Britain and Ireland, except for Latin America, which received Spaniards and Portuguese, and North Africa which the French colonized. The United States received wave after wave – Irish, Germans, Scandinavians, Italians, Poles and Russians (especially Jews), and, finally, Greeks. All were received in America and, after dreadful suffering and generally vain attempts to maintain their own culture (as the French and Scottish migrants to Canada successfully did), went into the 'melting pot' of American culture.

America and other host countries continually drew highly skilled craftsmen from Europe, as well as engineers and other professional people to help manage the capital investment which was built with European money. But, after the Irish emigration in the famine, most American immigrants were poor and unskilled. The great achievement of American education and industry was that within two generations the majority of these settlers became educated and highly qualified members of the labour force, while their relatives who stayed behind made far less significant advances. It was the rapid improvement in the quality of the labour force which, together with the rise in the capital stock, explains the continued distance between American and European output per head. Initially it had been higher in America because the English-Americans were on the whole highly qualified and were working with plenty of capital in a rich natural environment. As poorly qualified immigrants arrived it became essential to raise their standards quickly; it was for this reason (among others) that America's open education structure developed so fast. In Europe, on the other hand, the education system remained élitist, even where – as in Germany – it had a very strong technical and vocational bias; in Russia and much of southern Europe the education system in rural areas was vestigial.

Nothing changed so much in capitalism as the reduction in these vast migrations after 1920. Even the colonial peoples had participated – Indians had gone to the West Indies and South Africa, Chinese had crossed the Pacific. But for the most part these migrations were confined to European stock. After 1920, Europe became far less significant as a source of new people in the mass, though the flight of Jewish intellectuals from Germany in the 1930s added a new dimension to the cultural injection.

The background, then, of free trade and great migrations of peoples, was based on an outflow from Europe, and an inflow to Europe of food and raw materials. This movement represented the creation of a new world-wide culture, based in Europe but in which America began to play a significant part. After the mid-nineteenth-century scientific achievements of Darwin and Liebig, there were two major developments. Pure science, based mainly at this period in Germany and Britain, developed an irresistible impetus of its own which led to ever more 'break-throughs' – ranging from Clerk Maxwell to Mendel, from Thomson to Pasteur. Science advanced boldly into physics, bacteriology, biology, statistics, and a host of new disciplines. Thus as universities were developed throughout the world – increasingly on the German model of the professor with his group of research students – scientific communication became a central feature of intellectual life, provoking discovery after discovery in an endless series of chain reactions.

Secondly, however, the new scientific knowledge became increasingly applicable to practical affairs. Pasteur, for example, was able to fight phylloxera, which was devastating French vineyards, and silkworm disease, which was affecting the Lyons silk trade, as well as helping brewers achieve a reliable product. The consequences of this for the acceleration of technological advance were notable; by 1900 the basis for modern 'scientific' industry already existed. Artificial fibres, new materials, electricity, the internal combustion engine, modern medicine, new agricultural techniques, were all developed as a result of science, reversing the order of events in which technology had posed intellectual conundrums which the scientists then attempted to resolve.

The impact of these ideas, together with the ideas of Marx, Comte, Mill and Darwin, on the conception of the world held by ordinary people, was profound. Though church-going continued to be a normal acceptable practice in Christian countries (except for the working class, whom the churches left on one side), the intellectual leaders of the capitalist world either overtly or covertly gave it up. When an idea is no longer entertained by serious people, when only politicians and the bourgeoisie hold to it, the position cannot be maintained. The central decline of religious beliefs, and their replacement by a belief in scientific progress, is one more distinguishing feature of high capitalism. This, and the rise of irrational nationalism, created the world where capitalism was severely challenged and in some places overthrown.

Bourgeois culture

Despite the formal allegiance of all the white races to Christianity, high capitalism was the first secular and rationalist culture. It was also the first international culture in the sense that (despite the importance of English) no common language dominated the area in which it prevailed. Capitalism was a secular, polycentric culture, its eyes firmly set on this world and its own physical environment. Science was of growing importance in the *weltanschauung* and was related to rationalism, though it was by no means the same thing. (Voltaire was no scientist, and many scientists were exceedingly credulous outside their own fields.)

Within bourgeois culture there were always 'opposition' forces harking back to a non-rational era. The Romantics, the Gothic novelists, the Victorian architects (the Houses of Parliament in London are a supreme example), all resented the counting, canting tone of a society revolving round money. But the dominant tone was realism.

It is always dangerous and nearly always wrong to argue from economics and society to the arts; but it does look as though the main trends in art have some relation to the ideas that are prevalent among dominant groups. For one thing, the market determines some at least of what will be produced.

Bourgeois culture was affected by the fact that more people owned more objects than ever before. The world filled up with people, and cities became full of artefacts. Many of these artefacts were manufactured and therefore set a new context within which the arts were carried on. The individual artist was increasingly an untypical member of society, producing objects for which there was no immediate resemblance in the objects that were not defined as art. Artistic objects ceased to have any connection with use and became reproductions – not of another world, of gods and goddesses, but of this world. Bourgeois art had a *motif* of realism even when it dwelt on historical or mythical figures. From portrait painters like Rembrandt through landscape painters like Constable, to pre-Raphaelite and high academy art of the late nineteenth century, there is a steady progression towards a conventional view of reality, seen through optimistic eyes. But then realism took a new turn, towards what came to be called sordid reality: so Goya's preoccupation with dark reality in his scenes of the Napoleonic War found successors less in Delacroix's battle scenes than in the painters of the humble, and of poverty and distress, like Courbet and Daumier.

Art took a second turn. Following Turner, the impressionists in the later nineteenth century affirmed that reality was what was seen, not what was conventionally thought to be seen. The impressionists and the post-impressionists carried realism to its logical conclusion of the visual rendering of sense data.

It is unwise to draw parallels between painting and writing, just as it is dangerous to regard either as having any direct relation to social relationships and conditions. But bourgeois culture's most characteristic products were reporting in newspapers, and the novel, rendering an imagined reality. The great mid-nineteenth century novelists – Balzac, Dickens, Flaubert – were all dedicated to intimately detailed descriptions of contemporary scenes. Here again there was a shift to 'sordid reality' – Zola being the supreme example – and to the detailed descriptions of minute by minute, second by second experience, internalized by Proust and Joyce in the twentieth century.

Eddies and flows occurred; poetry certainly followed no similar pattern, though the theatre became increasingly naturalistic.

The highlighting of certain features of artistic activity enables some distinctive aspects of art under capitalism to be brought out. Art entered the market-place. Artists became a consciously separate group of individual entrepreneurs, not a caste as in other societies, nor a group whose activities were related to other essential activities in society (like magic or religion).

The separation of artists and writers from any but a decorative role led many of them to adopt a critical or moralistic position which was profoundly opposed to some or all of the characteristics of capitalism. Though many of the most successful artists, financially, identified themselves wholly with the successful bourgeoisie, some of the most highly regarded artists – the writers' writers, the painters' painters – became the major source of articulate criticism of society as it was.

The artist as Job, crying woe on society, was not unknown, but it had never before become a dominant feature of an artist's position in society. As the Church sank into disuse, as the working class failed to seize for itself the role that Marx had predicted for it, the main sources of opposition inside capitalism were the artists, writers, historians, social thinkers and 'intellectuals' whose ideas spread the more rapidly for the resentment they aroused.

There was scarcely a major artist whose work was not at one time or another looked upon with derision by some of the well-to-do bourgeoisie. The fact that many of these artists became rich, or (like Proust) came from rich families, or (like Joyce) were supported by the rich, and that the bourgeoisie bought their books and pictures, was forgotten, but the derision was remembered. The capitalist as philistine is a description that has stuck. It is not wholly fair.

That this description of the capitalist was unjust may be clearly seen from the high point of capitalist society, which achieved a degree of civilization that bears comparison with Greece of the golden age, or the age of Shakespeare. The last years of Napoleon III and the Third Republic up to 1914 – the years which embrace *la belle époque* – represent the consummation of capitalist society.

Great painters, great writers, great musicians, great scientists and great humanists congregated in Paris. They could also be found in Vienna, in London, and (to a lesser extent) in more remote capitals, but Paris was acknowledged to be the capital of civilization, just as London was the financial capital. To look at Paris of the *belle époque* is to look, therefore, at capitalism's claim to be a great as well as a potent civilization.

It was, for more people than ever before, a comfortable and safe city. The domestic arts, which now included central heating, lifts, flats, gas and electric lighting, gas cooking, and fairly efficient sewage and sanitary arrangements, enabled a society to flourish which encouraged good eating, good drinking and good talking. Apart from the submerged tenth – the distressing but almost unseen poor, who were witness to the other side of the story – the Parisians lived well. Comfort and safety, accompanied by improved medical care and a steadily increasing number of technically based amenities, provided the environment where cooking and drinking were raised to the level of art. From the point of view of domestic life, it would be hard to find a more congenial civilization.

It was one where personal freedom flourished: not only the formal freedom to come and go without let or hindrance (not unimportant for an international capital full of foreigners) but also the personal freedom given to individuals in a big city to choose their own way of life. This freedom from conventional pressures – sexual, moral, social – was the more piquant since it took place in a society where the tight nuclear bourgeois family was at its most characteristic (and probably at its happiest). The texture of the culture was exceptionally rich, as the language shows.

What, then, brought *la belle époque* to an end? Militarism and nationalism, to begin with. The period saw two disastrous wars against Prussia – 1870 and 1914 – in which France suffered losses of men, loss of nerve, and loss of treasure (though it recovered from its economic losses with extraordinary rapidity). Prussia played Sparta's role to the French Athens. Prussian militarism was not only a desperate external enemy; its habits proved contagious and the French found some of their number prepared to copy the enemy.

Next, internal disruption caused by the gross neglect of the poor gave the achievements of French bourgeois society a hypocritical aspect. More and more of the articulate lined themselves up with the dispossessed, having come to regard the structure of the Third Republic as a façade erected by the middle class to expropriate the poor. With the distresses caused by the wars, the opposition developed a socialist ethos based on genuine social protest; and as the Soviet Union came into existence a model existed – based in part on the old and close links between French culture and Russia and partly on Marxism – opposed to the Third Republic.

Third, there was the rise of illiberal absolutism, partly in response and opposition to socialism. It showed itself in various ways: a credulous and nasty Catholicism of a Jansenist type, anti-semitism, admiration for the inviolability of the army, and, above all, a loss of confidence in political and bourgeois institutions.

At this stage – and what is cause and what is effect it would be dangerous to say – art turned to abstraction and writing moved into a phase either of committed Marxism or of dissociated consciousness. The Third Republic lived on after 1918 as a consciously hollow shell – its frock-coated politicians openly despised, its bourgeois comfort rejected, the bourgeoisie loathing the opposition and the opposition loathing the bourgeoisie. When Prussia struck again, in 1940, the bourgeoisie turned openly fascist and the intellectuals and some of the workers joined the resistance as communists. The compact of enjoyment, the treaty of comfort, known as the *belle époque*, which had allowed bohemianism to flourish, broke into open class war.

The great boom

The advance of technology, revealed in an increasing flow of improved goods selling at lower prices, ensured the bourgeois comfort of Paris, Vienna, New York, London and the other great capitalist cities. Indeed it was the spread of markets, and the growing prosperity of the lower-middle and upper-middle working classes all over the capitalist world, that formed the basis of the great boom. Paradoxically, however, the boom coincided with a period which came to be known as the great depression, for the lower prices of goods were due partly to lower costs but also partly to depressed profit levels. It was the response to lower profit levels which accelerated the tendencies towards large monopolistic and cartelized organizations, seeking to keep the profit rate up, and which also provided much of the impetus for the export of capital from the industrialized coincided with a period which came to be known as 'the great depression', for the lower prices of goods were due partly to

The factor of the fall in costs was due in part to improved communications and to a dramatic fall in transport costs. That brought down the cost of food. But changes in manufacturing techniques were also important. Veblen discussed 'the technology of physics and chemistry' because, for the first time, science led technology, rather than technological advance providing problems for science to solve. The widening of the market, caused by the falling transport costs and also by rising incomes, enabled mass production techniques to be adopted. These mass production techniques involved massive investments in capital-intensive equipment, which in turn required big companies to operate them, with sophisticated and complex managerial systems. It was in this field especially that the Germans and above all the Americans were able to overtake the British, to become the industrial giants of the early twentieth century.

The developments on which the mass production age rested were, first, cheap steel. Bessemer, Siemens and Gilchrist were examples of scientifically trained technologists who between them reduced the cost of steel by a factor of ten or more. The rise of a cheap steel industry led to the growth of a machine-tool industry, which could manufacture steel into machinery, on a large scale, by the use of interchangeable parts, and which was capable of a high degree of precision. The machine-tool industry, from the time of Eli Whitney on, became an American speciality, owing its origin to the need to produce many thousands of rifles for the conquest of the west and for the American Civil War.

Henry Ford, who began to turn out motor cars in large numbers just before the First World War, used cheap steel and machine-tools on an assembly line. But the assembly line was first used for meat packing in Cincinnati, about eighty years earlier. By Henry Ford's time it was a procedure that had been widely adopted in American industry.

To operate the new processes electricity was a great help, since it eliminated the complex arrangements for belts, pulleys and shafts that were entailed by steam power. Here again, America and to a lesser extent Germany dominated the world.

So the effect of all these changes was dramatic. It reduced costs of production in all metal-using industries where bulk markets could be brought into existence. It reduced costs in all industries that used machinery. It shifted the balance of world economic power away from Britain towards America and Germany, and also began to shift the weight of industrialism away from textiles and coal to steel and electricity. And it boosted the engineering industry, and the importance of science, technology, and the highly skilled workers.

Applied to transport, for example, the speed and cheapness of the railway and the steamship were profoundly affected. Frozen meat was transported across America and across the Atlantic in refrigerated vans and ships.

Farming in the United States began to be mechanized on a large scale. Elsewhere, especially in Britain, the fall in farm prices and the rise in incomes produced a notable shift towards horticulture and animal products. Agriculture, too, began to see the application of natural science on a wider basis than ever before.

The great boom, then, was a mass production boom, based on steel and electricity, with consequences for almost all other industries, including agriculture. The invention of the internal combustion engine, the arrival of the motor car, and the growth of the oil industry, completed the boom. Modern consumer capitalism had arrived.

For the ambitious entrepreneur, the host of small but increasingly prosperous consumers represented the newly wealthy lower-middle and upper-working classes of the 1890s and early 1900s, a market with several characteristics that were notably different from those which had gone before.

One characteristic was that market forces were mediated through a complex retailing and wholesaling structure, in which department stores, chain stores and mail-order houses began to play a significant part. Thus the retail structure itself began to determine the manufacturers' production pattern. The manufacturer, interested in steady runs, began to integrate forward into the retail market. An interesting example was the English brewers' purchase of public houses in the 1880s and 1890s, where survival as a brewer depended upon control of a retail market whose extent was limited by the number of drink licences extended by magistrates.

Manufacturers were interested in long runs of their products, which meant standardization, which meant a development of advertising to create a steady market for the standardized product. The retailer, far from being a man who consulted his customers' tastes and then ordered for them, was a man who tried to convince his customers that the manufacturer's products were what they wanted. Consumers' tastes and needs were now manipulated and even invented. This represented a striking break with the system about which Adam Smith had written and about which the neo-classical economists were writing, in which 'consumer sovereignty' dominated the productive process and directed the pattern of output.

The third shift in the market was towards manufactures. The rise in consumers' incomes and the fall in agricultural prices meant that proportionately less was spent on food, liberating more and more purchasing power for manufactured goods of all kinds. The improvement in domestic comfort – better houses, better lit and better heated – meant that more time was spent at home, especially as the hours of labour were falling rapidly.

Better education led to more sophisticated tastes. As a result there was a shift towards more books, more newspapers, more furniture, more equipment of all kinds.

More was spent on travel, on holidays, and on entertainment. The market was therefore established for wide-scale provision of service trades of all kinds, and the extension of retailing was one indication of this.

Society, as it existed in the industrialized countries in 1914, had in it the very rich – a small but obvious class, with huge houses, special trains, racing stables, steam yachts – and the very poor, a large but unseen class; but the prevailing tone was set by the middle and upper working classes. They had servants (a skivvy in an artisan's house, several of them in a middle-class house); they had a growing quantity of manufactured goods; and they had political weight. It was they who lived a life that was recognizably modern: their hours of work were short, they had Sunday and possibly part of Saturday off, their children went on to a secondary school, they read daily newspapers and took regular holidays, and many of them practised birth control. The 'emancipation' of women had begun. The world of H. G. Wells, of the silent movies, of the early Gide had arrived.

The emphasis on consumption rather than on work carried with it a profound cultural and economic transformation. The function of capitalism had been to accumulate the means of production by keeping the standards of consumption down while an increasing part of the national income went into the construction of capital goods. Mass production meant that the trickle of factory-made consumer goods now became a torrent. Food was processed and manufactured; household goods and clothes – virtually every commodity – was enmeshed in the mass production process. This meant that an ever wider range of industry was dependent for its existence on constantly expanding markets, which enabled costs to fall as the economies of scale were reaped: the consumer market had to be created. The direct end of capitalism now became one of creating enough consumption to absorb the ever growing production.

The increasing severity of cycles of economic activity meant that in some years there was a serious slackening of activity and acute unemployment. It was then, as mentioned earlier, that the paradox of crises of under-consumption, of poverty in the midst of plenty, became apparent for the first time. For if it were true that technology, by mass production, could steadily produce goods at an ever decreasing cost, then it must follow that it was technologically possible to produce enough goods to give to the working class, and the 'submerged tenth', a more middle-class standard of living. The rise in the real incomes of the artisans in steady employment (a rapidly increasing class) created expectations in the less prosperous groups which could not then be fulfilled. The immediate power of mass production to solve all production problems was exaggerated, though its long-run potentiality was not.

Allied to the submerged industrial proletariat, also excluded from these benefits, were the remnants of domestic labour and the agricultural workers and small peasants. These people thought of themselves as the victims of the mass production system, and mass production came to carry with it the revolutionary consequence that it both raised expectations as to its technological power, and provoked fear and distrust, since it seemed to impoverish those who were outside its scope; periodically, too, those who worked in its factories were thrown out of work.

A consumer society, then, laid emphasis on a steady, rising level of demand, manipulated by manufacturers and mediated through retailers. It generated exaggerated fears and hopes. And it raised the question: who was to consume its products and who was to control its power to create abundance? At the same time it created organizational forms and managerial skills which threatened the logic of free competitive capitalism. How could the doctrine of consumer sovereignty survive advertising, which treated the consumer as a victim? How could free trade coincide with a desire for orderly, steady markets? How could poverty be reconciled with the means of achieving plenty? And, ultimately, mass production, which virtually began with the manufacturing of rifles for the first modern war – the American Civil War – created the means of mass slaughter, in the European war of 1914–18, the war which signalled the arrival of modern mass consumption.

Mass manufacturing and the great monopolies

While individual businessmen were the dominant form of capitalist enterprise throughout the nineteenth century, the railway joint stock companies formed the model on which mass manufacturing industry came to be based. In the relationship there were stockholders, usually a transient body of people buying and selling on the stock exchange; directors, increasingly a managerial body; workers; and customers. But the early joint stock companies were usually dominated by one man or by a family who had a large block of shares. It was men of this type who created great commercial monopolies, or combined with other industrialists to form combines and cartels. They came to have increasing political power, and were to be increasingly identified by socialists and social populists as the source of evil in all capitalism, trampling on workers and consumers alike in order to amass great fortunes.

The early monopolies and cartels arose out of severe cutthroat competition. Vanderbilt, Jay Gould and Jim Fisk, American railway kings in the area between Chicago and New York, engaged in a ferocious war to reduce freight costs. In 1877 they joined in a pool, raised rates and shared revenues. Cartels developed in electrical goods, in meat-packing, in tobacco and in other trades. The pool, which could be broken, was succeeded by the trust, which had legal force. Standard Oil was the major example of a trust; and it enriched the ruthless Rockefeller family, who have been expiating their guilt ever since by philanthropy and by seeking and even occasionally filling public office. Oil was a rapidly developing industry, first for kerosene for lamps and cooking and then with gasoline for cars. Profits were enormous; and the power to create a monopoly, based on difficulties of freight and limited access to the oil fields, was enormous.

So rapid was the growth of trusts and so ruthless their business methods that the United States Congress passed the Sherman Anti-Trust Law (1890) which prohibited combinations in restraint of trade. The law was virtually a dead letter but it signified the apprehension which monopolists caused even in legislatures where they had great influence. The Act was followed by more trusts, and a growth of mergers: Carnegie's US Steel Corporation, Duke's American Tobacco Company, and many other great combines, often in the new and growing industries, where large amounts of capital were required and where big plants operated under conditions of decreasing costs. The big financiers aided the process of amalgamation, especially when mergers were involved. By 1904, it has been estimated, forty per cent of the American manufacturing capital was controlled by mergers and trusts with a capital value of $1 million or more. The world of 'big business' had arrived, with one big company, or at most two or three, dominating an industry, setting prices and determining the pattern of consumption.

In Germany the cartel was the dominant arrangement in big business. The coal cartel, formed in 1893 into the Rhenish-Westphalian Coal Syndicate, ended competition in the German coal industry by setting prices and regulating production. It did so behind a tariff barrier.

The *Stahlwerksverband* (steel union) did the same for steel; another cartel limited competition among potash producers; and a further series of cartels led to IG Farben's dominance of the chemical industry, and AEG and Siemen's control of the electrical goods industry. These giant concerns, like that of the arms manufacturer Krupp, had big banking interests behind them.

Monopolies and mergers were less prominent in Britain than in America and Germany for two reasons: Britain stuck remorselessly to free trade, so that there was always the possibility of foreign competition, and Britain was relatively backward in the developing industries like electricity and steel since so much of its capital was invested in the older staple industries which were still extremely competitive. Nevertheless, Lever Brothers in soap, the Salt Union and the railway companies provided examples of big businesses which exercised near-monopoly powers.

The monopolies were intended to safeguard profits, which they did – when they were successful. They were also intended to stabilize output and safeguard regularity of employment, but the evidence is that they did not do so: if anything they were a de-stabilizing influence. What they did do was to substitute for the power of market competition by price, the rivalry of product development. If one firm controlled the railway industry, there was an incentive to develop motor cars as the alternative means of transport, rather than to build a second railway. The great companies which were dominant in America and Germany by 1900 became major sources of technical innovation, in rivalry with each other, especially in third markets. Technical innovation depended to a great extent on the corporation.

This was inevitable. The very size of the enterprises associated with heavy technological investment required massive organizational forms. They employed thousands of workers and commanded thousands of dollars of capital. To control these enterprises complex managerial skills were necessary.

The development of the giant corporation, increasingly international in scope, raised acute problems of control. Most of the shareholders were virtually anonymous; and the men who directed the enterprises – Krupp, Rockefeller, Lever, Vanderbilt – were powerful in a way that no capitalist had been before.

Some of them – Lever for example – controlled tracts of Africa, where they virtually ran the government. Others – Krupp was the supreme instance – made the arms for the growing military forces of the world. Inevitably, the expansion of capitalism through imperialism was interpreted as a thinly veiled attempt on their part to use their power in the state to enrich themselves by conquest. Inevitably too they were accused of fomenting war, or fear of war, to enlarge the markets for their own wares. The old aristocracy was involved with the big businessmen in every way it could find – investment, marriage, assimilation. It even overcame its anti-semitism if the profits were large enough. It was not known in detail but well enough known in general that monopoly capitalism represented a coalition between those with political authority and the rich industrialists. Thus the new technology erected industrial empires which yielded a vast output of consumer products. But it raised acute problems of control. Lenin and others saw in monopoly capitalism the coalition of business interests, faced with falling profit rates, to exploit the colonies and to repress the proletariat, whose growing demands for some of the proceeds of capitalism threatened the industrialists' existence. The picture may have been highly coloured, even wrong, but it had some verisimilitude.

The trade unions

As business coalesced, the workers founded their own groups. Faced with monopoly buyers of labour, it seemed inevitable that the sellers of labour would also seek to become monopolists of what they had to sell.

The early trade unions were British, and were limited in objectives, weakly organized and primarily political. Robert Owen's Grand National Consolidated Trades Union of the 1820s is an example of an unfocused union, with no staying power and chiefly concerned with constitutional reform. In the 1850s a number of craft unions were formed in Britain – like the Amalgamated Society of Engineers – which negotiated wages and conditions for skilled workers and provided social security benefits for their members. They were in many respects analogous to professional bodies. They were small, relatively rich, and well organized, but the mass of individual workers were outside their scope.

In France some of the workers were loosely organized in political revolutionary groups but there was no parallel development of trade unions in the British sense. In America the early unions were broken in the 1830s, as the Owen union in Britain had been; and in the 1850s a craft union movement spread which was parallel to that in Britain.

Unions, then, which had been illegal in the early days of capitalism, were now tolerated, but they confined themselves to the skilled and more prosperous workers.

In the 1880s and 1890s the trade union movement spread to the ordinary industrial workers. In 1867 the British Trades Union Congress was formed; in 1869 the American Knights of Labor. Both marked a step forward in class consciousness among the working class and both were followed by a marked rise in union activity.

This rise was followed by severe industrial unrest, and in America especially by employers' attempts to break the unions. In America the Knights of Labor fell apart (as an organization they were too big, with objectives which were vague and apocalyptic) and in 1886 the American Federation of Labor was formed, on an almost exclusively craft basis. The craft unions in Britain in the 1850s and 1860s, and the American Federation of Labor, accepted the framework of capitalist society and negotiated on a limited basis for small (but genuine) improvements in conditions.

The new industrial unions in Britain in the 1890s marked a transition to a completely different basis of trade unionism. First, they encompassed the unskilled workers; secondly, they provided few, if any, social security benefits for their members; thirdly they were militant; and fourthly, they believed in the formation of a trade union political movement, which was rapidly to become an explicitly working-class socialist party. In Britain this movement took place against a background of growing political and legal freedom for trade union activity. In France (after the legalization of trade unions in 1888), the movement was weakly organized and more explicitly socialist and syndicalist than the British movement. Elsewhere, as in Germany, the socialist commitment was strongly Marxist, but when after 1890 the German trade union movement was legalized, its weight moved the socialist movement to the right and Bernstein's revisionism (far more akin to Fabian socialism than to Marxism) became the official doctrine. The German unions, in contrast to the British, were big and were earlier politically influential, though in a context where state absolutism limited the potentialities of their power.

Thus, the growth of capitalist enterprise called forth organizations of working people. These organizations spread their activities from negotiation with the employers to outright opposition to the system in which they were all involved. Members of trade unions were still a minority of the working class. Rural workers and peasants were unorganized, as were women (especially domestic servants, who formed up to one-tenth of the urban labour force in western Europe) and the casual transient members of the working class amongst whom poverty was endemic. The trade union movement, therefore, was not a movement of the really poor but of those who were above the poverty level, and it was strongest among those groups who came nearest to the lower-middle class in incomes, aspirations and outlook. Their concerns were with the detailed negotiation of conditions affecting their work and with wider political participation for the working class. The industrial leaders tended to be politically cautious, even conservative, because their main activities were negotiations with employers; to gain one cent or a few pennies an hour meant a great deal for their members and provided the justification for the continuation of the union. The political leaders, on the other hand, tended to be secularists, rationalists, conservatives – serious, puritanical figures, with a small following and a 'scientific' creed and outlook. They were part of the growing army of the intelligentsia, those rootless, fanatical 'half-educated' (according to the bourgeois classical canons of the time) men who sought the overthrow of society.

In America the trade unions were small and their influence among the working class negligible: the American dream still held sway, and the continuous influx of immigrants enabled employers to dismiss 'trouble-makers'. In Britain the trade unions were influential industrially, but the socialist movement was relatively unimportant. The unions and the politicians came together, forming a pragmatic social democratic party to represent the working class – inside the capitalist order. Thus social democracy became principally defined as an attempt by politicians, supported by the unions, to ameliorate capitalism. Before 1914, however, the emphasis was mainly upon trade union activity to improve wages and conditions.

In Europe, on the other hand, the socialist parties were more powerful electorally, whilst the unions were less influential in industry. Socialism in Germany and France especially was more ideological, concentrating on the overthrow of capitalism, and it drew upon the revolutionary tradition of 1789, when the French Revolution had overthrown the monarchy and engulfed Europe in revolutionary war. The ideological hard edge of continental socialism meant, too, that doctrinal disputes frequently divided parties, leading to schism, purges and disorder.

Thus socialism had two faces – one seeking amelioration, the other seeking revolution. The capitalists detested and feared them both; and the socialists themselves often had pragmatic solutions and revolutionary rhetoric combined in uneasy compromise.

The bourgeois state

Most social amelioration, whether it called itself socialist or not, depended on state machinery for its implementation. Gladstone had stripped down the state to its bare essentials. It kept order, kept a minimum army and navy for foreign affairs to be conducted, and it had a residual Poor Law. It would have been hard to discover anything else that the government did. By 1914 the state's functions were greater than ever before and its role more significant that it had been since Tudor times. What caused this transformation?

First, growing technological development in war *matériel* meant that armies and navies were considerably more expensive than they had been, and on top of this, growing international rivalry led to an increase in the requisite armed forces. The American Civil War and the Franco-Prussian War both marked significant advances in fire power. As a result, by 1914 the cost of armaments was substantial: rifles, machine guns, steel battleships, big guns and the very earliest aircraft were all bought in substantial quantities. France, Germany and Russia had large conscript armies, while Britain and America had small professional forces. Thus the revolution in steel manufacture and in machine tools raised the cost of war preparations to unprecedented heights.

A change of an equally profound character occurred in the Poor Law – the invention of social security. Most countries had spent a little on education in the nineteenth century; by 1900 compulsory primary education was universal in all industrialized states (it had been earliest in Germany and the northern United States and latest in England). Secondary and higher (especially technical) education was beginning to spread and significantly to affect the quality of the labour force and the rate of technical progress. Education thus formed a significant part of public outlays.

Bismarck started in Prussia a system of compulsory health, old age and unemployment insurance, making that country – despite its authoritarian political character – a greatly envied nation by the militant working classes elsewhere. Britain followed in 1911 with the Lloyd George schemes for sickness and unemployment insurance, and old age pensions were introduced in 1908. Thus the stage was set in the industrialized world for a significant step forward in social security.

The causes of this were manifold. Society was more prosperous and the claim of the poor to share in the prosperity was becoming increasingly hard to resist. The growing trend of cyclical unemployment threw groups of workers out of employment through no fault of their own. The decline of the extended family left the old socially independent and therefore needing independent financial support. Medical advances raised the cost of medical care. Above all, the Germans had never accepted the basic tenets of laissez-faire and had never thought that the growth of social vigour and economic welfare depended upon the virtual absence of social services for the poor. On the contrary, the Prussians took the view that it was the state's duty to protect its people and to encourage their physical and mental development by whatever means came to hand, and those means certainly included the use of a highly developed state bureaucratic apparatus.

A third aspect of the modern state was a growing intervention in industry and commerce. In Germany many of the railways were publicly owned. In America there were laws against monopolies and trusts. Workmen's safety acts, factory acts, acts against adulteration of food: a whole host of laws giving powers of intervention in the working of the economy were passed. And they were much more ably enforced, as there had also been over the last decade or so a notable advance in the efficiency with which the state was conducted. There were technically qualified inspectors in many fields and the officials in Britain and Germany were impartial and incorrupt. Taxes were collected, even in France and Russia, and the growing use of the typewriter and the telephone made rapid communication possible. Thus the bourgeois state by 1914 was bigger and more efficient than would once have been dreamed possible.

This professional bureaucracy also faced in most advanced countries a government of semi-professional politicians, no longer wholly drawn from the aristocracy and relying now upon a mass male electorate. The extension of the franchise had been achieved in the last half of the nineteenth century in America, France, Britain, Prussia, Italy and – to some degree – in Russia. This meant that the character of politics had changed.

Politicians depended for office on the response of a mass electorate, many influenced by the press, and consisting partly of workers organized in trade unions and in Europe already to some degree committed to socialist ideas. It followed, therefore, that there was pressure to define politics as the use of the new bureaucratic machine to satisfy the demands of the poor. This led to a concept of radical imperialism – a concept which powerfully influenced Germany and Britain and – to a lesser extent – France and America.

The radical politicians supported imperialism for a mixture of motives. One was patriotism. Another was a desire for cheap raw materials to reduce costs and prices. A third was to find places for the poor to emigrate to. But imperialism, combined with social reform at home, became immensely popular. It led to the growth of the state's power by increasing expenditure both on armaments and on welfare services. The poor, far from being internationalist, were excessively patriotic. It was their patriotism as well as their manifest needs for state help that provided the basis for the modern state.

When Edward VII succeeded his mother, Queen Victoria, to the British throne in 1901, the classic phase of capitalism was drawing to a close. Britain, which had been the centre of capitalism, was already declining. It had missed the greater part of the new technological revolution which was transforming America and Germany, mainly because its inadequate education and training system did not provide the necessary technologists to initiate change, and also because there was a severe lack of capital prepared to risk new ventures. Edwardian capitalists wanted something safe, preferably abroad, to put their money in.

Britain was engaged in an imperialist war in South Africa, against the Boers, in order to gain control of the Rand gold mines. It nearly lost the war. The Germans and the French were also engaged in imperialist expansion, which nearly led to war in 1911 over Agadir. The Russians and the Austrians were near to conflict over the Balkans. The Russians were defeated by the Japanese in a naval war in 1904. The atmosphere was becoming increasingly warlike.

The doctrine of free trade and laissez-faire was on the retreat. Germany and America were building tariff walls. Government intervention in commerce and industry was growing. Industrial competition in international trade increasingly took the form of competition aided and abetted by government support. The most clear example of this was in subsidies to shipping, and in colonial rivalry, but in many fields of activity it was possible to perceive a rivalry of governments as well as a commercial rivalry between countries.

The 'social question' came increasingly before the public. Poverty was diagnosed, by Charles Booth in London, by Rowntree in York, and by professional social workers elsewhere. The Webbs, and Bismarck, proposed machinery for its treatment. Unemployment was a social disease which defied treatment, but it was apparent that capitalism unaided would not be able to cope with it. The condition of women was a matter of intense social conflict, and in all countries women were seeking education, civil rights and the vote. Thus the Liberal government of 1906 in Britain faced serious social problems, which it attempted to deal with by social insurance legislation and other social legislation for health and welfare. It faced and failed to deal with the women's suffrage issue. It faced and failed to deal with increasing industrial strife, with strikes and with lockouts.

And, on top of all this, nationalism was becoming a central question of the age. The unification of Italy had become a great liberal issue in the mid-nineteenth century. The unification of Germany under the Empire had been widely welcomed. In the early twentieth century the Irish, the Hungarians, the Czechs, the Serbians, the Poles and many other nationalities began an agitation for national self-government which raised new issues. Liberal-minded supported movements for independence. But the nationalists themselves were backward-looking, supporters of tariffs, anti-industrialism, sometimes revivers of dead languages (like Irish), and militaristic.

The Edwardians tried to keep afloat on this sea of troubles, which all the time was becoming increasingly stormy. They increased taxes to pay for more arms and for more social security but did not seek to reduce the great wealth of the rich. They tried to give home rule to Ireland, and they did give it to the Boers in South Africa, but they did not assuage nationalist passions, which were increased as victory grew nearer. In Germany, nationalism became increasingly identified with the notion of military grandeur. In France, French nationalists and Catholic reactionaries looked forward to a military revenge for the humiliations of 1870 and 1871. Even America, under Teddy Roosevelt, became an imperialist, nationalist power, as de Tocqueville had predicted it would. The age of democracy became the age of nationalism.

As George Dangerfield argued – brilliantly – the glittering façade of Edwardian society suddenly cracked. The European aristocracy had married the American plutocracy, and it kept up a hideously vulgar and expensive life. The King of England, the Emperor of Germany, the Czar of Russia and the other royalties, were all related to each other. The appearance of a unified, stable, international society, presiding over an economy with a rapidly advancing technology, was maintained. But nationalism threatened the empires; democracy threatened the aristocracy; unemployment and strikes threatened the economy; and socialism challenged the capitalist assumptions on which it all rested.

After King Edward's death the new reign saw a period which was manifestly drifting into war, and in which Irish nationalism, women's suffrage and the rise of the Labour Party showed, almost conclusively, that the attempt by the Liberals to modify the laissez-faire capitalist system by extending the suffrage, giving limited self-government to national minorities, and extending the social security system, was doomed to failure. There was an air of increasing violence and social tension that showed itself in social relations and in art. Freud, with his hypothesis of the unconscious, Trotter on the herd instinct, Graham Wallas on human nature in politics, the early D. H. Lawrence, Guillaume Apollinaire, the Cubists, all showed an increasing distaste for the superficial rationality, the simpleminded notions of cause and effect, which were the hallmarks of Liberalism. It seemed that the world was full of dark forces which the rational, liberal-minded businessman was illequipped to understand and wholly unable to appreciate. Of these forces, it was to be seen, the most devastating was nationalism, and the war to which it gave rise.

The First World War

The First World War brought capitalism almost to its knees. It broke out, it seemed, almost by accident, and once having begun it was waged with a cold ferocity which confirmed all the fears of dark forces in man's soul and showed up liberal internationalism as a sham. An even greater surprise was that almost all the socialist movements proved as nationalistic as the bourgeois political parties.

The war disrupted international trade. It bankrupted Britain, hitherto the prime source of capital for many countries. It led to currency inflations. It led to massive government intervention in industry and trade, culminating in food rationing, import restrictions and government control of whole industries for war production purposes. It thus achieved, in four short years, many of the measures for which socialists had been arguing for years. Almost by stealth as it were, the ideas and programmes of forty years became accepted fact.

The destruction of property was small. But the loss of life was enormous and has never been accurately assessed. It was sufficient to weaken France for a generation.

The chief effects of the war, however, were political. Four empires collapsed – Germany, Austria-Hungary, Russia and the Ottoman Empire. Two major industrial powers – France and Great Britain – were gravely weakened. Three of the empires were succeeded by many weak nationalist states: Czechoslovakia, Poland, Iraq, Transjordan, Hungary, Estonia, Latvia and Lithuania were only some. This gave rise to grave political instability and led to further nationalist demands which were eventually to dissolve the British and French empires.

In Russia the régime collapsed in 1917. The decision of the liberal successor to continue the war with Germany led to a further collapse of the régime in November 1917 (on the unreformed calendar, October) and to a successful *coup d'état* by Lenin and the Bolsheviks, who declared peace with Germany. A major civil war followed, which the Bolsheviks won. This led to the expropriation of most private capital, including foreign capital. In one of the major states of the world capitalism had been overthrown.

In Germany the collapse of 1918 was followed by a revolution, and a situation developed in Berlin in which it seemed that in Prussia, too, the communists might take power. A counter-revolutionary rising succeeded in preventing this, and a social-democratic republican régime was established. This Republic, called the Weimar Republic after the town where it was set up, began life under the twin handicaps of a military defeat which was attributed to internal subversion, and a severe food shortage which was due to a continuation of the naval blockade of German ports after the armistice was signed. For fifteen years the Republic staggered from crisis to crisis, unable to pay its debts, surviving a massive inflation, a further foreign occupation and massive unemployment, until it was finally brought down by a majority vote for Hitler and the Nazis in 1933.

In France the Third Republic looked at times as though it would be overthrown, but it continued, though gravely weakened internally by the rise of left-wing and right-wing parties who rejected (for opposite reasons) its ethical and political basis.

The United States saw two opposite consequences of the war. The first was that it became manifestly the richest and most powerful country in the world. Power moved from the City of London and the continental bourses to Wall Street. The boost to demand offered by the war resulted in a great burst of investment which continued through the 1920s, especially in the new technological industries, automobiles, engineering goods of all kinds, chemicals and synthetic fibres. But, at the same time that Wall Street became the financial capital of the world, the United States recoiled from the political involvement which was entailed by world power. The American Senate refused to ratify the Treaty of Versailles and the United States effectively withdrew into isolation.

The consequences of this withdrawal were catastrophic. Laissez-faire capitalism had flourished during a period which was predominantly peaceful. The peace had been kept by the balance of power and the effective naval dominance of Britain. Economic growth had been ensured by the gold standard, which in turn was maintained by the continuous outflow of capital from Britain and other European financial centres to support new ventures overseas. America, the centre of financial and political power, refused both these roles. In this situation, France and Britain behaved with growing foolishness.

The First World War revealed a political bankruptcy which amounted to an intellectual weakness of an extraordinary kind. It seemed as though capitalism must have grown old, tired and timid in the face of new ideas. The continent which had produced Napoleon and Wellington now threw up a group of generals of limited intelligence and sympathy, whose one idea was a static war in which millions of conscripts were slaughtered. The continent which had produced Pitt and Talleyrand, Disraeli and Bismarck, Cavour and Metternich, now produced people like the drunken Asquith who, having blundered into war, could not end it, and when it finally petered out, like Lloyd George had no idea how to settle it. Faced with financial problems, unemployment and serious social unrest, all that the businessmen could think about was Bolshevism.

The feeble wits of the governing class had become manifest before the war and could in no way be attributed to the loss of able young men during the war. It was an unwillingness to accept a world which had changed that was to render them impotent before the world's financial problems and the rise of authoritarian régimes.

The First World War then, apart from the immense suffering that it caused, led to a complete recasting of international politics. It accelerated technological change especially as it affected the automobile, aviation, wireless, and chemicals. It led to social upheavals that ranged from a new political and social status for women in the West, to a Bolshevik dictatorship in Russia. It accelerated the nationalist movements throughout the world; after seven centuries, the Irish, on Britain's doorstep, became virtually independent. Above all, the First World War completely upset the monetary apple-cart. In face of the consequences of this upset, socialism became the number one question of the day: if capitalism did not work – if there was inflation, unemployment, bankruptcy – would socialism do any better?

The disruption of world trade

How was the monetary apple-cart upset? First, by government intervention in a growing number of money and commodity markets throughout the advanced countries, which meant that the network of communications that had been established informally over the years was broken or disturbed, with consequences that revealed themselves in shortages, sudden price alterations and all the signs of a severely maladjusted system.

Next, by a flow of gold and currency reserves from the European combatants – especially Britain – to America and the neutral countries, the basis for the gold standard was destroyed. European currencies were separated from their gold basis and (as had been seen in Britain after the Napoleonic Wars) the return to gold was certain to involve serious deflation.

The exporting trades of Europe were diverted mainly to home production, and consequently many overseas countries received a boost to their own industrial development which ended forever the neat reciprocal flow of manufactured goods and raw materials; future trade patterns would have to be far more complex. Thus not only did Britain especially lose markets, it also gained competitors in the old staple trades on which its prosperity had been based.

In addition to the loss of currency and reserves, the European countries became saddled with external and internal debts. The external debts, owed chiefly to the United States, were intended to be repaid by Germany, but Germany's economy, disrupted by the war and particularly by the loss of large parts of its coalfields owing to territorial adjustments, was unable to meet the cost of reparations to the victors. In addition, the victors, facing unemployment, were unwilling to receive the goods with which Germany would have had to finance its reparations (which would have meant a continuing German surplus on current account). To replace the outflow of British and (to a lesser extent) French capital, there was a chronic inter-governmental indebtedness, which required each country to earn a surplus on its balance of payments. This could only have been financed by a massive outflow of capital from the United States, which would in turn have required a massive United States trade deficit based upon a large and steadily growing propensity to import. This, of course, was impossible both because the United States had no tradition of importing and also because the United States' tariff situation was such as severely to discourage imports. Thus there was a fundamental imbalance in world trade patterns.

In addition to the problem of external debt, each country in the war was faced with the problem of managing the public finances. Germany financed only 6 per cent of its war effort by taxation, the rest having been raised by borrowing – and the price level rose by 250 per cent between 1914 and 1918. The situation was as grave in France and almost as bad in Britain. Britain, determined to return to Ricardian orthodoxy, attempted to service its national debt through a budgetary surplus, causing the chronic deflation of the interwar years. In Germany, the borrowing by the government which had financed the war was continued in the peace to service the debt. As a result, there was a continuous printing of bank notes which led to a continuous and accelerating fall in the value of money.

Thus, internally, a major industrial nation experienced the inflation that had been experienced in France during the Revolution. The fear of inflation haunted Europe. It caused a continuous fall in the value of the mark on world markets, leading to still further international troubles, but above all to the expropriation of virtually all fixed-interest saving and the ruin of the older members of the middle class. At the same time businessmen were converted into 'profiteers', people who lived on profits from inflation rather than on the profits of production. The detestation of the militant working class and the dispossessed intellectual middle class for the capitalist system was enhanced by this experience, especially when, in the deflationary situation which followed the return of monetary stability, the horrors of unemployment succeeded the miseries of inflation. The humiliation of Germany, until 1917 a nation full of patriotic imperialist fervour, was very genuine, and formed a basis for the Nazi appeal for national regeneration by clearing out profiteers – whom they identified as Jews.

In the midst of this mess, the rapid advances in technology continued, partly accentuated by the growing prosperity of large groups of Americans, who created a market for consumers' electrical goods, for automobiles, and for the light engineering products of the rapidly growing mass production industries. Not only was Europe badly suited to adopt this technology, since its chaotic monetary and fiscal system prevented the steady development of rising demand for new products, but Europe's heavy investment in older industries left it with an apparently chronic problem of overcapacity.

Britain suffered most because its industrial capital was the oldest. British output records in many trades – coal, ship-building, textiles – were achieved in 1913. Thereafter there was a decline, which was directly due to the growing difficulties of international trade but which was also indirectly due to Britain's growing obsolescence in capital equipment.

Thus, the radical effect of the war was the disruption of the international pattern of trade and of the monetary mechanism. But there were two other major consequences. The first was the growing difficulty of emigration from Europe to America: the American immigration laws stopped the great tidal waves of emigrants from crossing the Atlantic and there was no longer a European safety valve. There were still big population movements but they were the result of persecution, like that of the Greeks in Smyrna, or the Armenians, and the victims moved to neighbouring European countries.

This growing illiberalism was connected with an extension of governmental powers which coincided, however, with an increasing fragility of constitutional institutions. Russia, Turkey, Germany, Austria, and the successor states, all suffered civil war or near civil war after their change of régimes. In some cases there were military *coups d'état*. Even Italy, for so long the hope of liberals, suffered the indignity of becoming the first fascist country, in 1922, and Mussolini, himself a direct product of the social distress caused by the war, became the archetypal European dictator. The liberal era of capitalism was, it seemed, over, wrecked in those trenches which its third-rate generals had caused to be dug.

6 Socialism in practice and theory

The communist revolution

The supreme event in socialist history was the Russian Revolution of October 1917 which brought the Bolsheviks into power. The Russian secret police were proved right after all: the tiny clique of Marxist revolutionaries, riven by schism, reading manifestoes to each other in the Parc des Martyrs in bourgeois Geneva, were the most dangerous men of the century. Lenin was one of the most *difficile* men imaginable, continually splitting the communist movement (which was tiny) by metaphysical distinctions that only de Valera (in another context) could rival. He continually declared his minority a majority, until he convinced people it was.

Whether or not he was sent to Russia in 1917 by the Germans, his arrival in St Petersburg was the most devastating blow Imperial Russia ever received. Within six months he had successfully engineered a *coup d'état*. A year later and Trotsky had organized the Red Army. In the midst of intolerable suffering, the Bolsheviks clung to power and extended the power of the state throughout Russia. Despite foreign intervention, the White Army of Czarists was defeated; the Poles were thrown back from much of the Ukraine; and the Communist Party established itself throughout Russia, except for the Baltic states which were taken from it by the Treaty of Versailles.

After the Revolution socialism was to be defined in terms of the split between it and communism, and though at times the two were drawn together, for the greater part of the years after 1917 the two movements were irrevocably opposed ideologically and practically. To the communists the socialists were capitalist lackeys. To the socialists the communists were un-principled tyrants. In the process democratic socialism lost the greater part of its Marxist roots, though it made periodic attempts to keep them alive. Its search for a set of principles is its chief intellectual endeavour.

In 1917 the socialists were in alliance, generally speaking, with their governments in Britain, France, Germany and Italy. In all countries a minority of the socialist movement was pacifist, a smaller minority revolutionary. The world was sick of war. Social conditions were deteriorating. The senseless slaughter of soldiers was terrible. Nowhere was it worse than in the Russia of the Czars, where socialism was forbidden and hence conspiratorial.

The Russian socialist movement was split into several parts. On one wing were social democrats in the Russian Parliament. On the other were 'maximalists' or terrorists. In between were the Mensheviks and Bolsheviks. Certain key issues came up. One was whether to regard peasants as 'proletarian'. It was apparent that peasant support was essential for a successful revolution. The Bolsheviks, necessarily, were hostile to peasant proprietorship, though Lenin was prepared to regard the Kulaks as incipient capitalists and the others as incipient workers. The Mensheviks were prepared to have a mass party of workers and peasants, which implied a major role for the peasants, but Stalin and Lenin were united in believing that the proletarians must have the leading role and that the Bolsheviks must lead the proletarians. Stalin also argued for permanent revolution – against the concept that once a liberal régime was established revolutionary activity would cease to continue. The Bolsheviks also argued that the way to consolidate the Revolution was by establishing control of revolutionary bodies like the soviets of workers, peasants, and soldiers and sailors, of which the St Petersburg Soviet had been a model. It had been, under Trotsky, a kind of nucleus of a possible provisional government rather than a source of revolution itself; the idea was to allow the revolutionary situation to evolve, and to manoeuvre the soviets into the key points of control.

The Russian socialists, then, were divided before 1917 into three main groups, though there were many more small factions. One group wanted to collaborate with the liberals, achieve the revolution, and then support the liberals until industrialization had been carried on long enough to create the conditions in which socialists could win an election. The Mensheviks took this point of view, except that they would not have collaborated with the liberals after the revolution. The Bolsheviks, under Lenin's guidance, advocated support for the liberals in the bourgeois revolution, followed by a false period of collaboration, after which they would stab the liberals in the back and establish the dictatorship of the proletariat.

This was the course which was followed in 1917. There were two revolutions. The first brought the liberals to power under Kerensky. Lenin was rushed back to Russia by the Germans. He arrived in St Petersburg and brought the Bolsheviks to support the new régime. Then his party seized power in October (old calendar – November new style). Kerensky, his government undermined from within, had made the fatal mistake of not ending the war with Germany. The armed forces rose against their officers, public order broke down, and the Bolsheviks seized power. They promptly inaugurated the second revolution by establishing the dictatorship of the proletariat, ending the war with Germany, and calling in the workers of the world to rise with them. In 1918 it looked for a while as though in Germany and Austria-Hungary this call would be listened to, and that the workers would rise, but in both Berlin and Budapest the risings were brutally repressed and no general revolt took place.

Lenin, Stalin and Trotsky, and their collaborators, found themselves in a strange situation. The first Russian Revolution of 1917 had overthrown absolutism, the second had overthrown the liberals. But it was not followed by world revolution. Instead Russia suffered from civil war and foreign invasion until 1922. The dictatorship of the Bolshevik Party was established, but its establishment was accompanied by an almost complete collapse of civil order and of the economy. Paradoxically, Trotsky's organization of the Red Army was the first triumph of the communist revolution; the other expected results obstinately refused to appear.

Lenin was helped by Kerensky's lack of ruthlessness. Kerensky refused to sue for peace, so that he lost the war and could not cope with the consequences. Had he denounced the allies and gone over to the German side, not only would the Germans have won the war but Russia would have been saved for liberalism. Kerensky also refused to accept the seizure of land by the peasants. He wanted to compensate the landlords. All he succeeded in doing was getting most of them shot, except for those who escaped to drive taxis in Paris.

Lenin ended the war and shot the landlords. It was scarcely surprising that the rest of Europe trembled in its shoes. The spectacle of the successors of Cromwell and the French Revolution weeping for the death of the Romanov–Hanoverian Czar, Nicholas II, was as ironical as it was indicative of the loss of nerve that the capitalists had suffered.

Lenin broke all the rules. Communism did not come to power where industrial monopoly-capitalism had failed but in the country where it would next have been tried. (The closing of Russia to capitalist investment was a potent force in reducing the scope for profitable outlays of savings and so accentuated the deflationary conditions in the West.) The Revolution was carried through against the opposition of the peasants, and Lenin mobilized the industrial workers during the period of war communism to fight them – an enemy identified in Marxist theory as the bourgeoisie. By 1921 the economy had virtually collapsed and the workers were fed only by the forcible seizure of food from the countryside. Then anarchy and distress added to the horror with which communism was regarded in western Europe. The failure of communist revolutions in Berlin and in Hungary ensured that a world-wide revolutionary movement could not centre on the industrialized countries; if communism were to succeed, it had to survive in Russia.

In order to do that the economy was revived by passing, in seven years (1921 to 1928), through a period which resembled in some respects a crash course in the revival of capitalism. The New Economic Policy restored the market, which brought food into the towns and revived the small capitalist enterprises which had been multiplying rapidly in the early years of the twentieth century. The big enterprises were nationalized but even they were sometimes leased to capitalists. Foreign capital was briefly encouraged. The production levels of 1913 were never restored until after 1950 but the economy revived enough to give some hope of rapid economic growth.

Lenin acted pragmatically, as had always been his way. The Bolsheviks organized a Third International (the Comintern) to work for world revolution and to organize support for the Russian Bolsheviks. Lenin also sought to establish some sort of relations with the bourgeois countries. Internally, he sought to conciliate the peasants. As the economic breakdown grew desperate, he restored a degree of capitalism to the agricultural system. When Stalin overthrew Trotsky, in the late 1920s, the capitalist experiment was drawn to a close and, with collectivization, the conciliation of the peasants was ended. But up till the time of Lenin's death in 1924, and for some years subsequently, the Soviet Union was progressing, under the dictatorship of the proletariat, through a not wholly unconvincing parody of the capitalist stage of development.

Not since the heroic days of the French Revolution had the leaders of so great a nation sought so deliberately to reconstruct a society; and the Russian leaders were striving to do more than the French had attempted a hundred years before, because they were reconstructing the economy as well as the political structure of society. The impact of the Bolshevik Revolution was, inevitably, profound.

In the first place, it removed socialism from the status of a hypothetical fear that afflicted statesmen and businessmen in their cups to an ever-present reality. The Russia of the Czars had seemed ramshackle, but its very size and backwardness had seemed to give it a certain massive security. It was Russia, after all, that had brought Napoleon to his knees. Thus to normal conservative, constitutional people, Bolshevism became a very genuine threat; and all socialists were to be regarded, henceforth, as tarred with the same brush. The behaviour of the Bolsheviks, too, was repellent. Not only had the violence of the revolution and the civil war been as repellent as violent revolutions and civil wars usually are, but the Bolsheviks had broken a great many of the more usual conventions governing the treatment of the defeated. Executions, expropriation and dispossession of the entire bourgeoisie on a massive scale seemed to be both their declared object and their actual practice. In addition, the Bolsheviks specialized in conspiracy and in deceit. They had plotted to achieve power and having got into office they had plotted and deceived their collaborators. They boasted of deceit. It was part of their plan. Whether in fact they were actually worse in this respect than any other group of politicians is a moot point; their honesty in admitting it was, of course, unforgivable.

Thus socialists who embraced liberal values were bound to be almost as horrified by the Bolsheviks as the capitalists were; and in addition they were to feel especially badly about the deceit and betrayal. On the other hand, by whatever mechanism and however bad the means, a socialist state was being created. Socialists were bound to admire this. And some of them were, perhaps inevitably, certainly understandably, to find excuses for what was done. Russia stood alone. It was surrounded by enemies. The communists had inherited an extremely backward economy and a tyrannical form of government. However illiberal the régime, at least the poor were being looked after. The long catalogue of excuses covered every evil, up to and beyond the millions who were executed and starved by Stalin's régime, and almost every socialist who denounced the Russian leaders for their evil ways felt in some degree guilty and disloyal for doing so. But the differences went back to the earliest foundations of communist policy by Marx, and its reformation by Lenin. Stalin was in their tradition. And democratic socialists had continually to recall that they were not. The difficulty of doing so was twofold: capitalism turned nasty, in Germany and Italy, and the non-Marxist socialists had only the weakest of doctrinal bases to oppose, on the one hand, capitalism and, on the other hand, Lenin and Stalin. It is the search for this doctrine, and for a compromise between collaboration with the communists, on the one hand, and the need to oppose the capitalist régimes that had gone wrong on the other (which meant an alliance with the communists), that led to desperate twists and turns. Because the social democrats basically wanted to ameliorate capitalism, it was necessary to show that it could be ameliorated. But where it had turned bad it had to be opposed. So the social democrats could be labelled as collaborators with communists, or as capitalist lackeys. And they had no strong theory of their own to oppose both communists and capitalists.

The Communist Party took control of the state and ruthlessly destroyed its opponents. It used this power, first, to make a great leap forward in education, at all levels, and secondly to introduce electric power on a wide scale. The decision was also taken to plan the economy centrally. After Lenin's death and the struggle for the succession, Stalin seized power and in 1928 inaugurated the era of five-year plans, which accomplished the industrialization of the Soviet Union by ruthlessly driving down consumption standards and using the surplus to build industrial plant. At the same time a proletariat was created by collectivizing the farms and driving many of the peasants off the land. Agricultural output fell catastrophically; a terrible famine raged in the Ukraine and millions of people were executed or sent to labour camps, but industrialization was successfully carried through.

The significance of this experience was that communism survived. Despite the abundant evidence of starvation, suffering and persecution, when western capitalism was going through its worst years, in the 1930s, socialists and communists were able to point to the Soviet Union and say that a post-capitalist society was functioning. Capitalism was no longer the 'natural' form of society: it was one of two forms. The suffering was either ignored (Russia was more than ever a society where secrecy was universal), or explained as the parallel to the sufferings of the industrial revolution – only that in 1840 it had been the English working class who had been the victims, while in Russia it was the working class who were benefiting and the 'useless' classes who were suffering. And, certainly, if that comparison was regarded as valid, the Soviet emphasis on education and social welfare represented a positive advance in civilization.

When widespread unemployment chronically afflicted Britain, America and Germany, Russia apparently had none. Against this economic suffering, and the manifest benefits of communism, was political liberty a serious counterweight? It would be wrong to present this view too starkly: the majority of people in the capitalist countries remained anti-communist and, except occasionally, anti-socialist. But capitalism was now on trial as it had not been before. And the accusers were theorists, chiefly socialist theorists.

German socialism

Soviet Marxism was not the only model of socialism. In three major countries – Germany, France and Great Britain – there were alternatives on offer. Germany was Marx's own country and offered the most serious interpretation of his ideas.

Edward Bernstein (1850–1932) was an important figure in German socialism, which was the most advanced in Europe in the late nineteenth century. Proscribed by the Anti-Socialist laws in Bismarck's Prussia, the Social Democratic Party had still, despite Bismarck, managed to get members elected to the Reichstag and to the various Landtags, even though party meetings were forbidden. By 1887 almost ten per cent of German voters were voting Social Democrat and when the laws expired, in 1890, they polled twenty per cent. The parliamentary freedom of Germany enabled Members of Parliament to speak and vote freely, so that though the party was forbidden the right to engage in propaganda in the country, its Members of Parliament could argue on its behalf and fight elections. It seems, then, that the Anti-Socialist laws (like other oppression in pre-1917 Europe) were relatively mild by modern standards.

That being the case, it is apparent that by 1890 socialism had made little headway. In most big countries – Britain and the United States for example – it was not represented electorally at all. The socialist movement was a collection of small cliques with no effect on practical affairs. When the interminable wrangles of the Second International occurred, the disputes were about metaphysics rather than about practical realities. In France there were socialist deputies; but they were radicals rather than socialists, and in any case the French socialist tradition (based on Proudhon) was hardly recognized as socialist by the Marxists and post-Marxists. In a political sense, therefore, socialism hardly existed: far from being a spectre haunting Europe, as the *Communist Manifesto* put it, it was scarcely more than a bump in the night. For the bourgeois, socialists were but one of numerous minor groups of terrorists, assassins and trouble-makers, usually living in exile. Among these groups of outcasts socialism steadily gained ground as an intellectual force, but only alongside the other ideas – like that of nationalism – which in particular countries (Ireland or Hungary for example) were far more important. As it advanced, it added to itself disparate notions from these other groups. In Ireland, where nationalist feelings were strong after Parnell's organization of the Irish Party, socialism had a strong nationalist context, as it did in India. Where they were weak, as in England, the ideas associated with socialism included pantheism, vegetarianism and the occult (all three embodied in the person of Mrs Annie Besant, the eccentric British theosophist). Thus socialism became a protean doctrine adding to itself other dissatisfactions with the world as it was. But it is important to remember that in the eyes of the world socialists were cranks.

The major step forward was to capture working-class institutions. As industrialism spread, there was a great growth of trade unions, co-operatives, working men's clubs, and other organizations whose membership was primarily or wholly working-class. At no time in the nineteenth century did any of these organizations embody the whole of the working class: the trade union movement, especially, was based mainly on the more prosperous skilled artisans and barely touched the unskilled working class. The greater number of trade unionists and their leaders were conservative in religion, politics and ideas; but a growing group of younger members became socialists, atheists and advocates of other radical ideas. They too were often displaced intellectuals – self-educated men who fitted ill into existing society and therefore sought to change it. To them socialist doctrine offered an explanation of the alienation they felt and of the misery and unfairness they saw around them, and often suffered themselves, and the socialist movement, by offering a key role to the militant working class (that is, to them) offered them a practical and exciting way of changing things radically for the better. An alliance of socialist middle-class intellectuals and intellectual working-class trade unionists therefore offered a really effective possibility of action. The spread of universal male adult suffrage enabled this action to be channelled into parliamentary activity. The formation of working-class parties, like the German Social Democratic Party and the British Labour Representation Committee (the forerunner of the Labour Party) followed. Though they were working-class in orientation, their leadership was often middle-class and the greater part of the programme was drawn up by intellectuals, with special sops offered to individual working-class interests.

Thus, though the socialists were to claim to be a working-class party, they were in fact an uneasy coalition of ambitious working-class leaders and middle-class people wishing to do good to the working class.

The German socialist dilemma was this. Proscribed by the Anti-Socialist laws, with only parliamentary activity possible, the socialists almost automatically classed themselves as a revolutionary party, determined to overthrow the Federal and the Prussian state and replace it with other political institutions. After its return to legality there was the possibility of achieving socialist aims within the constitution, provided that the Reichstag (for which universal manhood suffrage had existed since 1867) could achieve control over the executive, which was quite independent of the legislature and derived its authority from the kaiser. The situation within the states themselves varied, but in general the legislative control of the executive was absent. Yet, should it be achieved, the socialists could combine with the liberals to out-vote the conservative parties. Cooperation with the liberals had been anathema to Marx, and on most domestic issues the socialists and the liberals were poles apart, the latter believing in extreme laissez-faire and opposed to welfare measures; but on constitutional issues their positions were close. The socialist Gotha programme of 1875 envisaged such collaboration, and Marx had violently opposed it. Were socialists, then, opposed to the German constitution as such, and were they still a revolutionary party? If they were not, could they collaborate with the liberals? There was also the additional point, that the German Empire was militaristic; its first action, on its formation in 1870, was to wage war on France and annex Alsace-Lorraine; and the socialists were internationalists. If they attacked militarism, they attacked the Reich; and if they attacked the Reich, they were revolutionary.

The argument centred primarily on three figures – Liebknecht, Kautsky, and Bernstein. Liebknecht, a Marxist follower, originally held firmly to the belief that the socialists were a revolutionary party; but by 1891, at the Erfurt Congress, he had so modified his position as to accept the possibility of successfully achieving socialism by parliamentary means. At this, the left-wing socialists promptly left the Social Democratic Party, which now embarked on a programme demanding parliamentary reform (the secret ballot, biennial elections, women's suffrage), and the responsibility of the executive to the legislature and to the electorate. In the 1890s the great issue was whether or not to collaborate with the liberals to achieve social and industrial reform; and the liberals tacked about, at one time working with the socialists and at other times combining with other parties against them. By 1900 the socialists had finally decided that collaboration with the liberals was essential.

Kautsky, on the other hand, violently attacked the Social Democrats, in particular over their policy of coming to terms with the peasants and adopting an agricultural policy. According to Kautsky (and Marx) the peasants were not proletarians but reactionaries, and by aligning itself with them the Social Democratic Party abandoned socialism.

Kautsky, Marxist though he was, differed from Lenin and Trotsky in that he thought socialism could be introduced piecemeal and peacefully. But he did believe that the growing centralization of industrial power which was apparent under capitalism would continue under socialism and that it would entail a highly planned, centralized, socialist state. This was in great contrast to the libertarian vision that informed Proudhon and Owen and (in some moods) most other socialists, even the Marxists; and it was a vision that Bernstein was a 'revisionist', that is to say, he said he was a Marxist who, while accepting the central doctrine, wanted to drop its politically unnecessary and offensive irrelevancies. He wanted the Social Democratic Party to be the party of immediate social reform – improving labour conditions, removing taxes from goods largely bought by the poor, regulating monopolies and trusts – and the party which took the economy piecemeal into public ownership. This implied that the state was not necessarily an instrument of class oppression, and that it was possible to use it for social transformation. For Bernstein the vision of socialism achieved in its entirety at one blow was Utopian. The way ahead lay through detailed reforms, as Engels had argued in his last work. (This was Bernstein's claim to be in the orthodox Marxist tradition.) Evolution rather than revolution was his watchword.

There is no doubt that Bernstein, in adopting an almost Fabian view of the possibilities of peaceful evolution, was radically breaking with continental traditions. He held that capitalism was not in the last stages of collapse; to German socialists this was heresy, for they believed in a catastrophic Day of Judgement. His reason for this break was philosophical, for he rejected historical determinism: inevitability had no place in a true social philosophy. Social and political forces could overcome economic forces. It was this assertion that marked a clear break with Marxist philosophy, properly understood, however much Bernstein might claim to the contrary. For socialism was not 'inevitable' now: its coming depended upon successful political action. And successful political action entailed the widespread acceptance, not of proletarian consciousness, but of a concept of the 'common interest', 'the public good', which would overcome individual and private interest and conflicts. Socialism must also be built on the achievements of liberalism and incorporate them within itself:

It is true that the great liberal movement of modern times arose for the advantage of the capitalist bourgeoisie first of all, and the parties which assumed the names of liberals were, or became in due course, simple guardians of capitalism. Naturally, only opposition can reign between these parties and social democracy. But with respect to liberalism as a great historical movement, socialism is its legitimate heir, not only in chronological sequence, but also in its spiritual qualities . . . .

Having accepted, that is, liberal institutions, Bernstein went on to accept the German state. Socialists must be patient. They must accept the duties and rights of citizenship, including the responsibilities of the defence of their own countries. For Bernstein, therefore, social democracy was one party among others – a socialist, democratic party of reform, but a party within the gradually improving social framework of the nation-state.

The Party Congress rejected Bernstein. He was not expelled, however, because it was obvious that there was widespread support for his views. And, in practice, the party adopted his programme while retaining Marx's theory. It was an odd position, and was shown to be such by the First World War and the revolution that followed it.

After 1900, the German Social Democratic Party was in an odd position. Despite the fact that the government was autocratic, in practice it found itself unable to govern without

parliamentary assent; and if the Social Democrats allied themselves with other opposition parties they could out-vote the
government supporters. But they were unable to ally themselves with these parties because to do so would imply assent to
the basic principles of the régime, which they refused to give.
They were poised, therefore, for inaction, so long as they had no
independent parliamentary majority. To keep the party
together, doctrine had to be kept pure. To get votes, the programme had to be heavily pragmatic and revisionist. In this
way, the Social Democrats won more votes, and by 1912 they
were the biggest opposition party, but still they could do little
practical work, except that by the size of their vote they could
keep the pace for social reform quicker in Germany than in most
other countries, as the other parties and the government sought
to outbid them.

In understanding German social democracy it must be recalled that Germany's neighbour was Russia, a backward feudal
tyranny of whose aggression all Germans were afraid, and therefore a strong army was a necessity; that Germany was in many
respects a progressive and enlightened state, and that German
socialists could assume that in many respects it was benevol-
ently paternal; that southern Germany and east Prussia were
backward and rural, while the Social Democrats were urban
and sophisticated; and that Germany was autocratic, and liberalism exceptionally weak. In such circumstances a successful
Social Democratic Party was bound to be patriotic, autocratic,
and given to making intermittent gestures of meaningless affec-
tion to the backward peasantry.

The international context in which socialism was developing
had changed rapidly. When Marx disrupted the First International in 1872, socialists were a small group of people, chiefly
refugees, at work in a few countries. The Second International
brought together growing socialist parties from many
countries. As industrialism spread round the world, working-
class organizations developed – trade unions, co-operative
societies, political parties – all of which took on their own local
colouring. These organizations all to a greater or lesser extent
had a socialist tint; so that socialism became a generic term
covering organizations and opinions from the palest pink to the
deepest red. But it is important to understand that the split

between communists – meaning Marxists – and the socialists –
meaning Fabian, Bernstein-type revisionists – had not yet
formally occurred. Though the socialist movement was continually splitting and re-grouping, and people expelled each
other from their ephemeral organizations with unfailing zest
and regularity, it had a vague ideological unity in that its basis
lay in Marx and Engels.

The world Marx had known was, however, gone. The international industrial system had been created; the proletariat was
not immiserated; and the modern nation-state had been
created. Western Europe and North America practically dominated the whole world. The peaceful atmosphere of the
nineteenth century was breaking up and an arms race to
accumulate modern weapons was accelerating. Socialism,
politically speaking, embraced constitutional reformist parties
like the Labour Party in Britain, the Social Democratic Party in
Germany, and the Socialists in Scandinavia, on the one hand,
and the revolutionary conspirators on the other hand. Among
the industrial powers Russia was the only repressive autocracy;
she alone, therefore, generated serious revolutionaries. The
revolutionaries elsewhere, like Zapata in Mexico, were of the
old-fashioned kind, though often they acquired a smattering of
socialist jargon. Yet while the Russians were virtually the only
serious socialist conspirators (with practical experience in the
revolution of 1905), the German party, as well as most other
continental parties, officially held to the revolutionary doctrine,
derived from Marx, that in the crisis of capitalism they would
take over the state, representing the intelligent, conscious vanguard of the working class. Apart from the Russian rising of
1905, the debate about revolution and its place in socialist
thinking was highly abstract and remote. In practice, though
rejecting Bernstein's revisionism, German social democracy
was revisionist. The British Labour Party, under Fabian influence, was openly so. It seemed that revisionism was the order of
the day.

The First World War, the Russian Revolutions of 1917 and
the revolutions in Germany, Hungary, Ireland and other
countries, that accompanied and followed the armistice of 11
November 1918, turned the debate from an abstract one to
reality; they turned petty squabbles into life-and-death

struggles; and they finally achieved the split between Marxist communists and social democrats.

It was Lenin who formalized Marxist revolutionary doctrine, who was rushed to Russia after the first Revolution in 1917, who overthrew the liberal régime of Kerensky and achieved a communist dictatorship in Russia. With his collaborator Trotsky, who organized the Red Army, he overcame foreign intervention, won the civil war, and established the dictatorship of the Communist Party – or of the proletariat – in Russia. Lenin played little part in the Second International, which was mainly a meeting place for socialists – meaning by that social democrats – who were seeking to play the parliamentary game to achieve power. Such a game could not be played in Russia. Lenin, therefore, embodied the Marxist tradition of a conspiratorial overthrow of an established régime, though the régime he overthrew was not capitalist but feudal. Lenin and Trotsky justified the establishment of communism in Russia by the expectation that there would be a general world revolution; it was an accident of chronology that it occurred first in Russia. For them the First World War was the long expected crisis of capitalism, while the German revolution which overthrew the kaiser in November 1918 was the beginning of the capitalist collapse.

The theory of this collapse was developed by Rosa Luxemburg, a Polish Jew, born in 1870, who joined the revolutionary organization 'Proletariat' at the age of sixteen. Poland, divided among the powers, was continually striving for nationhood, and Proletariat was organizing the workers in Warsaw and other industrial towns against the Russians. In 1888 she fled to Switzerland, where she became a Marxist, and came to represent Polish socialists at the Socialist Congress of 1893. She moved to France, then became a German by marriage, and from 1900 onwards she worked in Germany. As a socialist theorist, Rosa Luxemburg was a major figure. First, in the growing identification of socialist and nationalist movements, she became a staunch internationalist. The international working class claimed deeper loyalty, it seemed to her, than fatherlands, and in view of the subsequent development of national socialism, this was of supreme importance. These views split the Polish socialists, most of whom were nationalists.

Secondly, out of the experience of the underground Polish movement, Luxemburg insisted that the Marxist parties, while seeking the dictatorship of the proletariat, should be democratic within themselves and in close touch with the masses. Lenin was strongly opposed to this: he believed in complete control of the party from the top, and this was always the practice in Russia after the revolution. Thus, had Luxemburg's views come to dominate the socialist movement, the communist development might have taken a different course.

Luxemburg's main claim to fame was her reinterpretation of Marx's laws of capitalist development. She argued that capitalist development was spreading throughout the world, bringing the underdeveloped countries into its net, and that it was this continuous expansion that kept the rate of profit up and allowed wages to rise rather than fall. Obviously there was a limit, which would be achieved when there were no fresh lands to conquer. This thesis later seemed extremely apposite as an explanation of the great depression of 1929–34, when the so-called 'stagnation thesis' was widely held by economists, that the slump was due to a lack of profitable opportunities for investment. Luxemburg had also argued that the struggle for markets and for opportunities for profitable investment would lead to wars. It was in these coming wars that she saw the opportunities for mass unrest, and for the party to seize control. Thus, in her thinking, she was a revisionist as far as democracy went, but she rejected the relatively naïve optimism of the revisionists about the peaceful transition to socialism. Her theoretical work, too, on the economics of socialism was subsequently to be of great significance.

War broke out in August 1914. Despite passionate appeals, all socialist parties rallied to their national causes. Honourable men in all countries stuck to the internationalist line – Ramsay MacDonald in Britain, Luxemburg and Kautsky in Germany – and were repudiated. But the horrors of the war, the 1917 Revolution, and the squalor of the peace confirmed, it seemed, the Marxist diagnosis.

The collapse of the German and Austro-Hungarian Empires was less dramatic than the collapse of Czarist Russia. The emperors of Germany and Austria went into exile and acceptable republics succeeded them, which were able (under protest) to sign the Versailles Treaty, giving Alsace and Lorraine to France and parts of Prussia to Poland. Austria and Hungary were separated; Czechoslovakia was created and given Austrian land with a substantial German-speaking minority. Trieste was given to Italy, and Yugoslavia was created by adding Montenegro and Croatia to Serbia. Thus the Balkanization of Europe was a corollary of the dismemberment of Austria-Hungary.

Rosa Luxemburg and Karl Liebknecht had published *War and the Proletariat* in 1915; in it they had advocated the continuation of the class struggle and just such a territorial settlement. When the war ended, therefore, it seemed as though in some respects the territorial settlement of Versailles was compatible with socialist aims. But these aims were to have been achieved by a rising of the international working class; they were in practice brought about by the collapse of the German economy, revolt in the army and the victory of Allies. Meanwhile, the working-class Revolution had taken place in Russia, over which Germany had first achieved victory, followed by the humiliating treaty of Brest-Litovsk, and against which the Allies were now sending an expeditionary force to help the counter-revolution. Thus, the risings of the German workers, though leading to peace, seemed to have led to a peace based on defeat. There had been strikes in April 1917, which had helped to bring the German economy down; in early 1918 they recurred; the Spartacists (the left-wing socialists) were behind them. The defeat had occurred suddenly – a retreat in France, a government crisis in September 1918, the appointment of Prince Max of Baden as chancellor on 3 October, a mutiny at Kiel, and a revolt throughout Germany. Thus it was the revolt which immediately preceded the armistice of 11 November 1918. Friedrich Ebert, the right-wing socialist leader, succeeded Prince Max on 7 November, Kurt Eisner formed a socialist government in Bavaria. The kaiser was deemed to have abdicated and he fled to Holland; abdication was forced through to forestall Liebknecht's declaration of a Soviet republic; Ebert wished to preserve the monarchy but the Republic was declared by Scheidemann in order to ensure a non-Soviet republic.

The Republic was treated by the Allies as the successor to the kaiser: it was the Republic which accepted the armistice and signed the Treaty of Versailles. It was the Republic which guided the country through the horrors of the immediate post-war period, in which the Rhineland was occupied and the blockade was continued. Mass unemployment and great hunger were its immediate companions, defeat its midwife, and a savage peace treaty its immediate consequence. Ebert's government was formed from the socialist parties that had split earlier. Its job was to take over the régimes – both imperial and princely – which had collapsed. The socialists had three possible policies. First, to convoke a constituent assembly, which was the policy of the majority socialists; secondly, to establish a socialist republic, *de facto*, which was the independent socialist policy; and thirdly, to establish a Soviet republic, based on councils of workers and soldiers and sailors, which was the policy of the Spartacists. Ebert was a leader of the majority: Liebknecht and Luxemburg were leaders of the Spartacists. In the event, the majority opinion was accepted and elections were held.

The Spartacists had the precedent of the Bolsheviks for a second revolution to overthrow the first. But the German working class, which had flocked to join trade unions, was not revolutionary in this sense. The Spartacists, however, expected that the revolution proper – Marx's revolution – would occur in Germany, inevitably and rightly; and so they set out to make it. Without mass support they failed, hopelessly. They had some armed support, notably the marine division, which occupied the Chancellery. On 24 December 1918 the army bombarded the marines; but then a truce was arranged. The Spartacists declared themselves a communist party and sought to declare a Soviet republic, occupying police headquarters in Berlin, and the office of the socialist newspaper *Vorwaerts*. Noske, the Minister of Defence, organized a Free Corps, or militia, which destroyed the revolutionaries, murdering Liebknecht and Luxemburg, and Luxemburg's lover, Jogiches.

In so doing, Ebert and Noske saved the democratic Republic but they destroyed the left. The communists thus became the open and bitter opponents of the social democrats, and the Free Corps became a model for the Storm Troopers. The socialists lost the election of January 1919, though they were the largest party, with 11½ million votes out of 30 million. A coalition was formed, of Democrats, the Catholic centre and the Social Democratic Party. In Bavaria Kurt Eisner, the moderate socialist prime minister, was assassinated. A soviet which tried to take over was dispersed, after a small bloodbath, followed by executions of well-known socialists. Thereafter Munich was a stronghold of the militant right. More fighting broke out in Berlin and over a thousand people were killed by the republican forces.

The Weimar Constitution attempted to conciliate the left by giving workers representation in the directing bodies of enterprises and in joint economic councils at all levels. The works councils in factories were organized, but not those at government level, nor was the coal industry nationalized, as was expected. The situation was terrible: the blockade continued; starvation was widespread. Ebert's government had to sign the Versailles Treaty. Thus the Weimar Republic became the republic of traitors which Hitler was to overthrow thirteen years later. The Treaty was followed by a rising of the army against the government – the Kapp putsch – and the government fled to Stuttgart from Berlin. A general strike defeated the putsch. A new government was formed with a Catholic, Hermann Müller, as chancellor. Kapp and his allies were pardoned, and the army, restored to its allegiance, was sent to arrest the members of the soviets set up during the strike. This led to the overthrow of the 'Red' Ruhr. Thus, by 1920, the socialists in government had an uneasy relationship with the army; because of proportional representation they were unlikely ever to get a parliamentary majority; they had alienated most of the active left; and they were detested by the patriots.

The troubles in the rest of Germany continued. Béla Kun, the Hungarian leader, arrived to organize revolt; he was sent by the Comintern. The risings occurred and were suppressed, and the communists lost much of their support. But they continued to take the view that a revolution was imminent. When, therefore, the communists sought to collaborate with the socialists, it was on the clear understanding that this was a temporary situation, waiting for the revolution. The Social Democrats were in a coalition with the Catholic Centre Party, and held office in some of the states. After more violence, including the murder of Walter Rathenau, a Law for the Protection of the Republic was enacted. The Comintern instructed the communists not to support demonstrations in defiance of the law but to concentrate on penetrating the trade unions. The Social Democrats, on the other hand, were committed to the Republic. It followed once more, therefore, that the Social Democrats were aligned with the bourgeois parties. A right-wing government followed, headed by Wilhelm Cuno. The government was unable and unwilling to disarm – if only because of fears of violent revolution. It therefore followed that they broke the disarmament clauses of the Treaty of Versailles. The French occupied the Ruhr. Inflation followed the government's payment of subsidies to the workers who indulged in passive resistance to the French. The collapse of the mark ruined the smaller middle-class and bigger working-class groups. Thus, by the end of 1923, the communists and the right were united in regarding the Weimar Republic with profound distaste. The right – with its Free Corps and Black Reichswehr – was more para-military: the left was more conspiratorial. Though the Social Democrats detested Cuno's government, they were bound to defend the Republic; and as the attacks on it mounted they were put in an impossible situation. In ten years Germany had fallen from the most powerful nation in Europe to ruin and the Social Democrats had always been on the 'wrong' side. It was a situation fraught with tragedy and irony, which developed an inevitability of horror upon horror.

After Cuno fell, the Social Democrats entered the Stresemann coalition, to restore the mark, with the aid of Hjalmar Schacht, the President of the Reichsbank. An attempt was made to restore the economy. Once more the Social Democrats suffered. The communists determined to support them; their leader, Brandler, joined the socialist government of Saxony, which was then deposed by the Reichswehr, as was the socialist government of Thuringia. In Bavaria, the right-wing government was put under military control by Stresemann, whereupon the Nazi Party, founded by Adolf Hitler in Munich in 1921, led a rising. The rising was suppressed and Hitler was interned in a fortress. This act of strength was followed by an improvement in German affairs. Inflation was stopped; the Dawes Plan stabilized the external value of the mark by meeting debt repayments; the French left the Ruhr; and employment rose. The Social Democrats had left office. Ebert, the president, died, and the election of 1925 showed that the republican parties – the right, the centre, the socialists – had over 22½ million votes, while the Communist Party had only 2 million and the Nazis about a quarter of a million. In 1925, therefore, the election of 1924, which had given 3¾ million votes to the Communists and 2 million votes to the Nazis, was partially annulled; stabilization was working. After this came the presidential election in which Hindenburg was put forward as a right-wing candidate, narrowly defeating the Centre Party's Wilhelm Marx. Hindenburg's election was crucial. He detested the Republic; and he was growing senile. In any crisis, therefore, he would back the Republic's enemies.

Nevertheless, by 1928, when another election was held, although the Nazis and the Communists gained votes, the Nationalists lost them, and the Social Democratic Party made a notable advance. It entered a coalition government with its leader, Müller, as chancellor, and other socialists in key ministries, like those of the Interior and of Finance. Yet, as in Britain, the socialist Finance Minister, Hilfarding, was a prisoner of the orthodoxies of public finance and of banking; he had no alternative to offer. None, indeed, existed. Hilfarding resigned in 1929 but his successor had no alternative either.

Once more the paradox of social democracy revealed itself. Committed to democracy, a victory in an election meant the victory of social democracy. Yet, in office, nothing happened. Nothing happened because they had no other policy to offer than to govern well and humanely. But when the bottom falls out of the economy, that means running the labour exchange with a smile. The smile becomes a leer. The government falls.

Stresemann, the Centre Party leader, died in February 1930, as unemployment worsened. The Müller cabinet lost a vote of confidence in the Reichstag in March and was replaced by Bruning of the Centre Party. As unemployment rose, the fears of the German people of a repetition of 1923 became palpable. Support for the Nazis and the Communists rose.

It was at this time that the Communists took the decision that the Nazis would prepare the way for communism, and rounded on the Social Democrats. In the face of these blows, and with unemployment amounting to many billions, the Social Democratic Party collapsed. In 1932 the Nazis polled over 13 million votes in the first election, and nearly 12 million in the second; by February 1933, when Hitler was already chancellor, they polled over 17 million.

The Nazi Party had three great factors in its favour. It was patriotic: it repudiated the Treaty of Versailles, the traitors, the Jews, the pacifists – everybody who was against the German Reich of 1914. It intended to use the power of the state ruthlessly to eliminate unemployment and to maintain the value of the mark. In this it had the support of Hjalmar Schacht. And, thirdly, it had well organized Storm Troops and Brownshirts, able to defeat the Communists. The first meant that it had the support – or at least the willing abdication – of the army and the police. The second meant that it had the support of the working class and the petty bourgeoisie. The third terrorized the Communists who, for once, were beaten at their own game.

The Nazis came to power in a coalition with Von Papen, but after the election of March 1933 they assumed total control. The trade unions were dissolved and replaced by a Labour Front. The Social Democratic Party was dissolved in June 1933. Some of its leaders fled abroad, others were imprisoned. Many workers joined the Nazi Party while the Communist Party was declared illegal, and carried on its activities from Moscow.

The rise of the Nazis ended German social democracy as it had been known for over fifty years. They created a new kind of state – an industrial state, with full employment, based on terror abroad and at home. Its title – the National Socialist Party – was no accident. In many respects it was a socialist party. Unlike the communists, however, it did not expropriate the private owners. Unlike the socialists, it was anti-international. The Social Democrats, even after the Nazi victory, behaved true to form. They voted for Hitler's foreign policy in the Reichstag; they resigned from the Socialist International when it denounced the Nazis. German Nazism owed something to German social democracy. Nazism was cruel where the Social Democrats were ineffectual; it was efficient where they were incapable of rule; but both parties were nationalist. The big differences were in the attitude to the Weimar Republic, which was partly a Social Democratic creation, and to the Jews, from which group many Social Democratic leaders were drawn.

After 1933 German social democracy was dead. Its revival waited for fifteen years. But the example of its death was a signal to social democrats elsewhere of what fate held in store for them.

British socialism

British socialism had many strands. There was, for example, Robert Owen, with his co-operatives, his community, his paternalism and his trade union. In the 1850s and 1860s British trade unions organized the skilled workers; their leaders were of great respectability, and with the extension of the franchise to most urban males in 1867, some of the trade union leaders became interested in parliamentary representation, an interest which was given a further fillip as the liberals and conservatives gradually began to encourage working-class participation in government, especially at local levels. Other working-class organizations also grew rapidly, especially the co-operatives. So an important strand in British socialism was a growing working-class experience in taking part in public life, and a wish to do so on an increasing scale.

The intellectual tone moved away from extreme laissez-faire as the nineteenth century progressed. There were some Christians who called themselves socialists and who thought that the message of the Church and of its founder was strongly hostile to the ethics of capitalism. Christian socialists like F. D. Maurice were few, but they were the tip of an iceberg of moral disapproval of many aspects of capitalism and of industrialism.

There was an aesthetic revolt against industrialism which took the form of an interest in and a revival of medievalism – the revival of Gothic architecture, for example, or William Morris's handcraft workshops – and a revival of the concept of an organic community, based on shared values and experience, to replace the cash nexus and the destructive competition of capitalism. This aesthetic revolt was of supreme importance. Nowhere had the impact of industrialism been more distasteful than in England – a small, beautifully landscaped island over which hideous urban sprawl, squalor and debasement had spread like a sore, until it had become unbearable to civilized and sensitive people. The tradition of wholesome craftsmanship had been broken, to be replaced by the endless repetitiveness of mechanization. It is no exaggeration to say that in some – perhaps most – respects industrialism was a cultural disaster. The countries that best survived the disaster – Scandinavia, France and Italy – escaped early industrialism.

Of fundamental importance among the influences on British socialism was the impact of the Utilitarians and John Stuart Mill. The Utilitarians, inspired by the writings of Jeremy Bentham, believed that happiness could be quantified and that society should be based on the principle of 'the greatest happiness of the greatest number'. John Stuart Mill, with his deep-rooted concern for individual freedom, developed this doctrine in his own highly distinctive way. He too believed in the greatest happiness of the greatest number (he was – consistent with such a belief – a prominent feminist) but he was also concerned with the quality of that happiness. As a young man he went through a spiritual crisis, a sort of nervous breakdown, which was one of the most memorable illnesses in intellectual history. Reacting to his austere, rational upbringing, his emotions rebelled. He felt empty, hollow. If all his schemes for improving man's lot were carried out, would he be happy? The answer was that he would not. His reaction was important, for he did not abandon his radical ways and utilitarian thought, becoming a Roman Catholic or a Hindu. He kept to rational paths, but saw that, for him, true happiness consisted in altruism and the enjoyment of the creative arts. The creativity of the artist, that is, had a validity of its own. It was this deepening and strengthening of his character that gave to his thought a characteristic note which was to become the hallmark of English socialism. Allied to detailed bureaucratic plans for social and industrial improvement, he expressed a concern for the organic life of the community and for its creativity that was entirely lacking in the advocates of laissez-faire and the Marxists. Mill, in his essays on Bentham and Coleridge, put his own position as a judicious mixture of the two, with a strong emotional leaning to Coleridge, but in fact, if anything, his instincts were to lead him in a socialist rather than a conservative direction. To make bureaucracy non-philistine was a characteristic hope of British socialists.

Thus 'socialism' in Britain was a mixture of Marxism, Utilitarianism, Owenism, and Utopianism, of Christianity, of trade unions, of aesthetic disgust with industrialism, and also (it being England) sheer eccentricity. The socialist movement was extremely small until the First World War. The original working-class Members of Parliament were working men elected with Liberal support ('Lib-Labs'); it was only after the New Unionism of the 1890s had spread trade unionism to the unskilled workers that the working-class Members of Parliament, like Keir Hardie, became Labour members who were socialists. The characteristic English socialist doctrine was Fabianism.

The Fabian Society was founded in 1884 as an offshoot of the Fellowship of the New Life, whose very name suggests the cranky nature of the group. The Fabian Society's key members were Sidney and Beatrice Webb, Bernard Shaw and – for a while – H. G. Wells. Their doctrines were an amalgam of other doctrines, drawn partly from Ricardian economics, partly from John Stuart Mill, partly from Marx and partly from the accepted doctrines of liberal England.

The Fabians were first and foremost a constitutional, anti-revolutionary body. Their view was that the permeation of existing institutions and political parties at national and local levels with their ideas would speed up a process of change whose direction was in most respects inevitable. Capitalism was becoming larger and larger in scale, and more efficient in the process. As it did so, inevitably the municipalities – which provided an increasing range of services, from water to gas, from education to tramways – would take over the main work of production. A system of social security and medical care would eliminate poverty; a systematic programme of public investment would eliminate unemployment. Capitalism, in their view, suffered from lack of planning and from inefficiency. They adopted Ricardo's notion of rent, as a surplus over the costs of production paid to the landlord, and (following Marshall) applied it to all unearned income, including profit and interest. The income of the rentier was rent. If the ownership of property were collectivized, the rent could be used partly for collective purposes (education, parks etc.) and partly to reduce prices. Their main policies, therefore, were for the municipalization of power, and its democratization, which they regarded as an inevitable corollary of the ever increasing size of industrial units. The impracticality of this scheme was that the municipalities were quite unprepared to assume this role; and the Fabians only thought of it because the process of local government reform in England coincided with the early years of their activity, when some of them were serving on local government bodies. The municipalization doctrine was replaced, subsequently, by the doctrine of nationalization – partly because of continental experience (many continental railway systems were nationalized) and partly because of the obvious strength of the central government compared with the municipalities.

Politically the Fabians could be described as radical imperialists. In the South African war of 1899–1902, when Britain went to war with the two small Boer republics, and British opinion was split, liberals and radicals supported the Boers, the Fabians supported imperialism. It was the function of advanced industrial countries to bring the benefits of industrialism and urban systems of government to benighted peoples. This view caused uproar. It seemed cynical, bureaucratic and technocratic. Ironically, three-quarters of a century later, in the case of Rhodesia, the left of the day took the Fabian line. Within this intellectual context of growing industrialism, the Fabians were radicals: they wanted to take up all social institutions by the roots, examine them, scrap them if they were weeds, and, if they were capable of growth, prune and replant them. Ultimately their philosophy became the dominant philosophy of the Labour Party, spreading to large numbers of people who would not have thought of themselves as socialists but as pragmatists.

What, then, did their philosophy consist of? It was a belief in the power of the social sciences to analyse social situations in great detail, to predict their future courses, and to suggest remedies and changes. In the Fabian view these sciences were neutral politically – economics was economics, sociology was sociology – but an honest examination of the evidence would convince people that socialism was not only inevitable but reasonable. The London School of Economics which the

Webbs established was not a school for socialist propaganda – indeed most of its staff were never socialists – but the Webbs thought that by giving a boost to the study of the social sciences, a shift to socialist policy recommendations would be inevitable as social scientists were called in to examine social problems and suggest remedies.

Beatrice Webb's own experience on the Royal Commission on the Poor Laws confirmed this judgement. She was a well-born, rich daughter of a businessman called Potter, who took up social work and married beneath her class – a clerk of extraordinary ability and industry, Sidney Webb. Together they used her money to study social institutions – trade unions, co-operatives, local government – in great detail. When a Royal Commission on the Poor Laws was appointed Beatrice was made a member and undertook a series of massive investigations into the causes of poverty, and recommended, in a Minority Report, a series of major innovations in social administration – including a public health service, old age pensions, social security based on national taxation, public creation of employment, and a comprehensive range of local social services for the care of the sick, the disabled, the old, children and the unemployed, available as of right for all who needed them.

The Webbs, therefore, were pioneers of what came to be called 'the welfare state', which comprised a comprehensive range of public social services and became a characteristic achievement of socialism. They recommended such measures as a result of what they called 'scientific' investigation of social phenomena. 'Scientific' was a word used not in a Marxist sense but in a bourgeois sense – that all men of good will, using the same techniques honestly, would reach the same conclusions on the basis of the same agreed evidence. The Fabians, therefore, appeared deluded to the Marxists who saw science, just as much as religion, as a manifestation of economic reality, and who considered that the function of bourgeois science was to rationalize – not to explain – the exploitation of the workers by the capitalist.

Allied to the Fabian belief in science was a strong, pragmatic approach to social and political institutions and problems. Pragmatism was a virtue much cherished by the British, though to continental observers it represented intellectual incoherence and muddle in practical affairs. In the socialist context it meant that, like Bernstein, the Fabians were prepared to achieve social reform by any (legal) means, even if it meant supporting conservatives against liberals, radicals, or even (on occasion) socialists. It also meant that for Fabians the ideological issues were of far less importance than the building of bureaucratic machinery for social improvement.

The Fabians were bureaucrats. They believed that if the administrative arrangements were got right, all would be well. Most problems were matters of professional judgement, so that if it was made possible for people to give dispassionate professional judgements, the best would be achieved. Thus they wanted to ensure that doctors were free from financial pressures when they treated patients, and when they certified to the public authorities whether their patients were well or ill, and so qualified for benefit. The Webbs wanted teachers, engineers, housing officials to make social judgements in an atmosphere free from political pressure, or pressures to do anything other than what their professional judgement told them. This attitude was, of course, eminently reasonable; it appealed strongly to the rapidly growing class of professional people; and it was profoundly paternalist. The Webbs were, for example, deeply hostile to syndicalism and to anarchy.

The Fabian attitude to democracy was complex. On the one hand, they wished to subordinate almost all aspects of social life to elected representative bodies. The early agitation of the Fabians was concerned with suffrage and electoral reform. But the power of the elected representatives was in fact to be limited in two ways: first, the actual administration of affairs was to be by professionals, exercising (within a broad policy framework) their own independent professional judgement, and second, the elected representatives would share with each other and with their professional advisers certain basic assumptions about the way that the world should be governed. In the Fabian philosophy the world was without tensions, conflict or strife: a cool scientific approach would solve all problems.

It is an attractive view, very much in the utilitarian manner, but it is a curiously empty one. And it certainly bore little resemblance to the apocalyptic strife of the twentieth century.

When Beatrice and Sidney Webb's ashes were deposited in Westminster Abbey, in the presence of a Labour prime minister, the social life of Britain was in large part their creation. But the world of wars, of revolutions and of deep dissension was far from their way of thought, and it may be that such a world represented, ultimately, the reality that socialism was concerned with. That, at least, was the Marxist view.

The two major advocates of socialism in Britain (and, as a result, in the English-speaking world) were both writers – Shaw and Wells. Bernard Shaw (1856–1950) became the enemy of cant and the advocate of honest personal relationships, and he took an uncompromising radical line in sexual and moral matters. Nineteenth-century radicalism was largely concerned with two things – moral questions (including the truth or otherwise of Christianity) and the franchise. On the first of these – moral and personal issues – Shaw stood out as a friend and ally of any progressive cause that could be found. This is important for an understanding of the nature of socialism. Respectable nineteenth-century opinion imposed a code of accepted behaviour which was formidable in the extent and rigidity of its tenets. Though many people broke the code they did so in secret, and when they were publicly discovered they were disgraced. In 1895 Wilde was convicted of homosexuality and sentenced to imprisonment. In 1892 Parnell was found to have committed adultery; he was destroyed as leader of the Irish Party. Even in libertarian France, President Faure's dramatic death, still embracing his mistress while *rigor mortis* set in, until her terrified screams brought assistance to release her, was hidden, and an official, all-male deathbed scene was drawn. To transgress the letter of the law was to invite disgrace, as George Eliot found when she lived respectably but 'in sin' with G. H. Lewes. Yet to live by the spirit of the moral law – to love, to be true, to be frank, to be upright – brought no reward. It was to support the spirit of love, truth and freedom that the artists and moralists rose in revolt against the prevailing moral laws of the time.

Shaw's was one of the most eloquent expressions of the revulsion. He championed Wagner and the new music. He was passionately in favour of Ibsen as the new social-realist dramatist, dealing with adultery, venereal disease and domestic tyranny rather than drawing-room comedy. He was a convinced atheist. He was a feminist regarding the 'degradation' of women as a result of their propertylessness, and the exploitative relationships that were inevitable in a commercial society, so that marriage was a contract between unequals. (He himself married, well into middle-age, a millionairess.) He thundered about domestic tyranny, of youth over age. He was a vegetarian, an opponent of blood sports, an advocate of reformed spelling, a dress reformer – in fact, for every received opinion Shaw provided an alternative, generally one tending in the opposite direction. He put forward a new decalogue – including the aphorism 'Do not do unto others as you would be done by, their tastes may be different' – and, though people did not necessarily agree with him, they slowly ceased to hold the opinions that formerly prevailed.

His plays showed his opinions forcefully, and his prefaces related them to an analysis of capitalism which suggested that it was caused by inadvertance, and was inefficient rather than vicious. He showed respectable capitalists drawing their dividends from slum property; prostitution as an inevitable corollary of late marriage (postponed for property reasons); moral uplift as no substitute for social services; and class as mainly a matter of accent and attitude and not based on innate characteristics. The implications were clear. Capitalism made people hypocritical because it had to defend its inefficiencies by a mask of lies. Tear away the tissues of lies and the inefficiency would be exposed; expose the inefficiency and people would move voluntarily to a more rational society.

The other popularizer of socialism, H. G. Wells (1866–1946), had three characteristics, besides the facility and abundance that marks the successful and usually the distinguished author. He was a Utopian – greatly gifted in fantasy about the future. He was a realistic wry novelist about the comico-tragic failures of shopkeepers and small bourgeois. And he was, above all, a scientist. Wells was trained as a scientist, and he greatly admired scientific achievement. His criticism of the world in which he grew up was that it ignored and despised science, rejecting the fact that it could – and would – transform the world, and man, and man's view of the world. The way that science would effect this transformation was through new social arrangements. Science applied to major problems required large-scale organizations, and that pointed to the nationalization of industry. It implied, too, that power should be given to the technically qualified, not to gentlemen amateurs who happened to be nominated by the private owners of capital who had inherited their authority.

Wells' fundamental belief in science and technology was the hallmark of a certain kind of socialism which became very influential. The impression was held by growing numbers of people that man's disinterested intelligence could unravel the secrets of the universe. The scientists were thought to be *ex` hypothesi* disinterested: as they toiled away in their white coats they were the models of the New Men and the New Women – uninterested in wealth or ostentatious display, frank, open, comradely, interested in things for themselves rather than for their own glory. This idealization of scientists was set against a picture of the typical muddled capitalist, his fingers continually in the till, spending his time obstructing the march of progress and looking down on the low-born but high-minded scientist. Remove the capitalist and his politician lackeys, organize government on a rational basis, create a world authority, and the power of science would be unleashed. Mankind would be ennobled by scientific education and fed, housed and clothed by the new technology. Whizzed from country to country, or from planet to planet, by nuclear energy, a new race would inherit the universe.

The obvious fallacies in this line of reasoning do not need to be pointed out: Wells recognized most of them himself early in the First World War. What does need to be emphasized is the attractiveness of the doctrine, and it was attractive because large parts of it were true. In all countries, among young intellectuals and semi-intellectuals, the victory of scientific rationalism was won. God did not exist. T. H. Huxley was right. Science was on its way to a completely rational understanding of the world and the way in which it functioned – both physically and socially. Rarely has the conviction that the physical and social sciences would transform the world been as strong as it was in the first ten years of the twentieth century. And it was this feeling that Wells captured.

Wells' world was miles away from Marxism and it was

scientific in a sense that Marxism never was. It was a world dominated by social evolution, not by revolution. The great sweep of evolution, from the microbe to the universe, made the class war seem an irrelevance. Convert people to science, he argued, and you convert them to socialism; 'make socialists and you will achieve socialism'. If mankind could see straight it would alter things. Wells was a practical-minded visionary and a great popular educator. Through his influence, especially on school teachers, whole generations of people grew up in Britain to whom socialism was the rational way to organize a modern society. Class conflict never accorded with their own experience of the world.

The socialist movement that Wells, Shaw and the Webbs helped to create was always small. Between 1900 and 1914 a growing number of Labour Members of Parliament were elected, but they remained a small group, far less important than the Irish Party, for example. Yet, despite this small band of parliamentarians, there were dramatic developments in the political and social world. The first was the election in 1906 of a large Liberal majority which remained in office until 1916, and in the coalition government until 1922. Almost immediately there was a series of clashes with the House of Lords, which drove the Liberal Party in a more radical direction but also made it seem ineffectual. People increasingly turned against the Liberals because they seemed unable to implement their radical ideas. On several issues – Irish nationalism, women's suffrage and defence – they seemed unable to put a foot right. Increasingly, to be radical on these sorts of issues was to be on the left to the Liberal Party.

The Liberals enacted a considerable amount of welfare legislation, yet once more they lagged behind the advance of ideas and continued, by failing to adopt Beatrice Webb's Minority Report on the Poor Laws, to be put in a posture of conservatism, despite Lloyd George's histrionics. Only on the issue of progressive taxation, when Lloyd George's budget was unconstitutionally and unprecedently rejected by the House of Lords, was the Liberal Party able to capture the left-wing imagination. Even there, everything was soon lost by the atmosphere of financial scandal that hovered over Lloyd George, and of philandering drunkenness that emanated from Asquith. When the Liberals finally blundered, almost totally unprepared, into the First World War, no reasonably intelligent radical could conceivably have any enthusiasm for them. The support of the militant working class had already been lost. Between 1900 and 1914 prices rose and real wages in some trades fell. Trade union militancy mounted. This drove more and more trade unionists into active membership of Labour organizations and to seek independent Labour (and socialist) representation in Parliament.

When war broke out, therefore, the Liberal Party had lost all respectability in radical eyes. When Lloyd George joined the Conservative-dominated coalition as prime minister in 1916, he split the Liberal Party into the 'squiffies' (appropriately named after Asquith) and the Lloyd George-ites. The socialist movement was ready to replace the Liberal Party, not only as the working man's party but as the party of the radical, thoughtful, 'new' people. But, first, it was gravely afflicted by the issue of pacifism and internationalism. Socialists held that war was a manifestation of the capitalist struggle for power, and that – as Marx put it – the working class had no country. The majority of French socialists had always indignantly repudiated internationalism if it involved a renunciation of patriotism, and on the outbreak of war it was shown that this was true of a majority of socialists in every country. Only exceptional spirits like Ramsay MacDonald stood out and, in standing out, they brought obloquy on the socialist movement. Public opinion throughout the world turned chauvinist and reactionary. Yet, when opinion swung back after the war was over, socialism reaped the benefit. Less than five years after the Peace Treaty, MacDonald was socialist prime minister of the British Empire. The opportunity came to him, as it had come to Lloyd George, to betray his principles. Like Lloyd George, he did so, immediately.

7 Capitalism on the defensive

Capitalism after the First World War

Technological development continued its headlong progress. The 1920s saw a boom in the United States. The car, electrical goods like refrigerators, cookers, radios, improved housing, aircraft, telephones – the whole complex world of durable consumer goods – all became part of everyday life for ordinary middle-class Americans. It was at this period that virtually universal secondary education was introduced; that the film industry became the great entertainment industry; that mass production of high quality cheap clothes became common; that the five and ten cent retail store became a model for retailing; and that America – as the movies revealed it – became the model for the desirable way of life. Even communist Russia set itself the task of catching up with America, and by America it increasingly meant Hollywood.

The biggest 'new' industry in America in the 1920s was housebuilding, and all the other construction work associated with it. The boom occurred in Britain in the 1930s. This movement into housing affected the whole nature of American and British civilization, which became increasingly suburban and home-centred. Taken with the emancipation of women, birth control, and nuclear families, the pattern of life perceptibly changed, now radically differing from the way of life of the poor (and, in America, especially the Negroes) with their extended kinship system, high birth-rate, and densely urban style of life. Allied with this shift to the suburbs was the extra mobility generated by the automobile. By 1928 four million cars and lorries were being produced annually in the United States.

This meant a boom for the automobile firms and their suppliers, a boom in road construction and a boom in oil supplies. The internal combustion engine formed the basis, too, of a revolution in agriculture, with the tractor; and a revolution in the art of war, with the aircraft and new long-distance ships and submarines operating on diesel oil.

Electricity was the other boom industry of the interwar years. Except during the worst years of the slump, electricity generation continued to grow, as did all the industries which were related to electricity. There was a perceptible shift to light engineering, to chemical-based industries (including the beginnings of plastics), and to all new consumer goods.

The basis for this 'revolution' in industrial structure was the pronounced shift in the demand pattern. The rising middle class, without capital, was spending its increasing income on the goods and services which made use of the new technology. Paradoxically, throughout the depressed interwar years, technology leaped ahead. This meant that productivity rose in the new industries, and as it did the numbers of people employed per unit of output decreased, thus intensifying the problem of unemployment. Electricity generation, for example, was a far less labour-intensive industry than coalmining had been. The chief characteristic of the new industries was that they were labour-saving. They also tended to be located near the great suburban consumer areas which provided their markets – New York, California, London, Paris – rather than in the old industrial areas. This meant an internal migration of population, which intensified the depression of the badly hit coalfield-based industries.

The new industries tended to be controlled by large corporations, and were heavily dependent upon substantial advertising. The workers in these industries were only slightly affected by the trade union organizations that had developed in coal, steel, railways and the other older industries. Typically, a new factory employed a transient force of unskilled and semi-skilled workers (many of them women), with a much higher proportion of skilled engineers, technologists, research workers and sales people.

The major new industry, quantitatively speaking, was distribution and the service trades – retailing, hairdressing, laundries and dry-cleaning – because as less of the consumers' dollar was spent on essentials (like food), more was spent on personal entertainment and the consumer satisfactions that sophisticated retailing existed to foster and meet.

The new industries marked, then, a clear break with the heavy industry phase of capitalism (the period which the Soviet Union was entering) and entry into a period of a consumer-oriented society, based on the satisfaction of non-essential needs, where advertising and fashion played a part out of all proportion to the role they had previously known.

Had demand been higher during the period 1920 to 1940, and had unemployment been avoided, there is little doubt that the growth of the new industries and service trades would have been far quicker. The period from 1950 to 1967 in Europe indicated what could happen under full employment, for the rate of accretion in the national incomes of western Europe was faster than that of America between 1920 and 1940, yet America in 1920 and Europe in 1950 were not too dissimilar in industrial structure. Thus between 1920 and 1940 it might have been expected that the relative growth of the automobile industry, of home construction, of consumer durables and of service trades could have been faster, and (the other side of the coin) the contraction of the older industries more rapid. By contrast during the 1950s and 1960s European railways, coalfields and cotton textile industries were drastically run down. They were, too, between 1920 and 1940; but their former employees remained idle for the most part, and governments went to great lengths to try to reconstruct the industries, to protect their markets, and to bolster them in every way possible. In this process they were most unsuccessful and their lack of success was another nail in the coffin of liberal, democratic government. For if government could not achieve even the limited ends that it set itself, what could it do?

The decline of the heavy industries and the rise of the light industries had two consequences which were of immense importance. The first was the development of credit institutions for consumers, which was one of the main bases on which the new industries stood. Mortgage corporations and building societies for new housing, hire purchase and consumer credit for durable consumer goods and cars – all this meant a great growth of credit institutions. These institutions led the way in the erection of a structure of credit which collapsed in the great depression, but which (once revived) formed the basis of the post-Second World War capitalist era.

Secondly, and connected with the credit developments (which lend credence to the view that bankers were at the heart of the mismanagement of capitalism), the shift to light from heavy industry implied, for many critics, a basic frivolity in capitalism. While the many went hungry, the affluent bought 'toy' machines; in Russia, on the other hand, steel works, dams and electricity plants were the order of the day. When the Second World War demanded more heavy industrial output, the frivolities of capitalism were to be blamed for a state of military unpreparedness against fascism and Nazism. This was an unfair charge, but for many people, by 1940, nothing that capitalism did could be right.

From 1920 onwards the scientist-technologist assumed a key role in economic and social change. In medicine, for example, the pharmacological advances, based on biochemistry, meant a steadily accelerating rate of improvement in medical sciences, progressing through sulphonamides and penicillin to the powerful drugs for treating mental illness and other serious diseases. Parallel advances occurred in anaesthesia, surgery and almost all other aspects of medical practice. The consequences for society were obvious – a continuous rise in the cost of medical care, a fall in the death rate, a diminution in the number of crippling diseases.

Medical science is a good instance of a general tendency for scientific advances to be transferred into the economy by technology with much less of a time lag than formerly. The advances in energy generation, culminating in modern power, make another example, as do aviation and chemico-plastic processes.

The growth of the physical sciences had three interesting characteristics. First, their discoveries were neutral with respect to the form of the society that adopted them. Capitalism had come into existence to accumulate capital, ultimately in the form of steam engines or their equivalent. Other forms of society had found it difficult to accumulate useful capital without adopting capitalist modes of operation. Science showed

itself fruitful under communism and capitalism, and it doubt-
less would have been so under Nazism had so many distinguished scientists not been Jewish.

Secondly, to an increasing extent the scientific and technical
procedures which led to significant advances were supported by
government. A government enclave, as it were, produced the
basis for economic and social progress. A special example of this
was the fact that the Second World War, and the succeeding
Cold War, led to significant advances in fields primarily
relevant to defence, but which came rapidly to have peaceful
applications: radar, micro-circuitry, nuclear power, computers
were but some of the fields that owed most, if not all, of their
major development to defence appropriations. Thus the state,
whether in capitalist America, social-democratic Britain, or
communist Russia, adopted an almost wholly new role in
society. It would be almost impossible to think of a privately
financed rate of scientific and technical advance which would
come anywhere near that achieved with state support. According to neo-classical capitalist criteria, this devotion of resources
to technological advance was a misappropriation of resources,
since it rendered obsolete capital that was fully able to function
adequately to meet consumer needs, and it was certainly argu-
able that the world would have been capable of giving its people
a higher standard of living if it had not devoted so much of its
surplus to scientific and technological development.

But that argument was strikingly irrelevant, because the
third feature of scientific advance that was especially note-
worthy was that it had become a headlong process, with a logic
of its own; one discovery led to another; one hypothesis
confirmed raised doubts about another hypothesis; and the
insistent demand of science and technology for more resources
could no more be resisted than could the demand of the nation-
state for armaments. There was a long series of major scientific
discoveries, many of which had direct and indirect technological implications.

There were also major innovations in the fields of management and industrial organization which were in their own way
just as significant. The growing use of 'scientific' management
techniques, derived from the social and behavioural sciences,
was allied to the spread of mechanical aids – culminating in the

computer – which enabled management and organization to become a procedure far less dependent upon whim and genius, and far more 'rational'. It was this 'rationality' that gave big corporations and state bodies a significant advantage which overcame the inherent infeasibilities of large-scale organization. Capitalist competitive economic theory had been based upon the fact that for most purposes a small organization was more successful than a big one, and that the consequent diffusion of power among many units was both economically and politically desirable. It became obvious that economically this was no longer so. The economic justification of the small-scale unit had largely gone in many fields; and the political justification, far from being rooted in economic reality, now seemed a romantic one.

The slump

On 'Black Tuesday', 29 October 1929, the American boom ended in a Stock Market collapse, when the ill-regulated credit system seized up. The confidence of investors in the situation suddenly drained away and share prices collapsed. Probably nearly $30 billion of paper value were lost in two weeks or so, and many rich and middle-class people were ruined.

Why did this loss of confidence occur? Partly because the upward speculation was bound to come to an end, as prices had got quite out of hand (they reached a spectacular height on 3 September 1929). Underlying the end of upward speculation was a realization that profits were ceasing to rise; this was because investment was becoming less profitable, as the market for the goods that the investment was producing had suddenly ceased to grow.

Businessmen were slow to realize that this was the cause, and buoyed up by spectacular technological inventions which were continuing to appear, they assured the government and the public that record sales were in the offing. When the sales were not made, the shock to confidence was even greater. The first trades to be depressed were the investment goods trades, when a few businessmen prudently postponed extending their plants and installing new machinery. Credit began to dry up. And as that happened, the sales of consumer goods began to plummet.

Unemployment rose rapidly: it doubled in a year. By 1931 it stood at about eight million; eventually it reached well over thirteen million. Between 1929 and 1937 the national income was halved; industrial production was halved; and investment became negative: capital, far from being extended, was not even replaced.

The process of downturn was cumulative. Stock Exchange prices fell repeatedly. That helped to knock the bottom out of credit institutions, and so did the collapse of their debtors. Farmers, for example, faced with astonishing falls in the prices of farm products, found themselves quite unable to pay their mortgages and the interest on their bank loans. Thousands of banks and credit institutions in the rural states went bankrupt – as did several of the states themselves – and this in turn spread to the cities, where many mortgage companies and consumer credit institutions were also faced with similar problems.

The effects in America were dramatic. But the slump spread throughout the world, bringing down the depression in Europe to new and catastrophic depths. In the brief stabilization period of 1927 to 1928 the gold standard had been restored in full force. This stabilized exchange rates in terms of gold and meant that when a deficit occurred in a country's balance of payments, and gold began to flow out, deflationary action had to be taken by cutting the money supply, and internal prices had to fall. But internal prices proved exceptionally sticky, as Britain discovered upon returning to the gold standard in 1925 under Mr Churchill, when it attempted to cut coal miners' wages, leading to the General Strike and a lockout and to apparently interminable labour troubles. When the American collapse began, international trade took a turn for the worse and deflationary policies were intensified throughout Europe. The first major casualties were the overseas primary producing countries, as primary products (food and raw materials) dropped to catastrophically low prices. The primary producers severely reduced their purchases of European goods. At the same time, the American banking collapses cut off the supply of American money which had come across the Atlantic to Europe for investment.

The European countries most badly affected were the heavily agricultural countries of central Europe, whose bankers were chiefly in Berlin and Vienna. Berlin and Vienna were major financial centres but, in turn, their credits came from London, Paris and New York. Thus when financiers in central Europe were badly affected, their difficulties were transmitted immediately to London and New York.

1930 was a year of relative calm, while things got steadily worse. The 1929 panic passed. Bankruptcies mounted, unemployment rose, investment plans were cancelled, and trade fell. More and more countries adopted policies to restrict international trade. More and more firms joined defensive alliances, cartels, groups, mergers and monopolies to try to preserve themselves in a world of falling demand, falling prices and vanishing profits.

In May 1931 the central European bankruptcies caused a crisis in Vienna – a city already gravely weakened by the dismemberment of the Empire of which it had been the capital. The biggest bank, the Creditanstalt, collapsed. As a result, Germany, to which Vienna was closely linked, experienced a further collapse. The Stock Exchange closed in Berlin, and the discount rate rose to fifteen per cent. By July Germany had ceased to make foreign payments, and what it owed in London and elsewhere became a sheer loss on the books of its creditors. This caused a run on the London credit institutions and gold began to flow out of Britain at an astonishing rate.

Britain, where industrialism had begun, suffered continuous unemployment between 1920 and 1940; its statistical measurement is disputed but it hardly fell below 12 per cent of the labour force and on occasion probably rose to something like 25 per cent. In Germany, as well as the inflation, unemployment again never fell below 11 per cent and on occasion rose to over 40 per cent of the labour force. According to Svennilson, about one-quarter of the potential European labour force was out of work in the years between the wars. In 1932 and 1933 one-third of the labour force in America was unemployed.

Unemployment represented a chronic incapacity of the capitalist economy to use its productive resources to achieve high consumption, because those terrible years of unemployment were accompanied by dreadful poverty. One-third of the British working-class families were clinically undernourished.

Agricultural incomes throughout the world collapsed and there was widespread underemployment and suffering in the great primary producing countries like Canada and Australia, and in the peasant economies of Europe.

What caused the unemployment? Why was it not remedied? The most obvious cause in Britain, and to some extent in Germany, was the decline of the old staple industries like coal, shipbuilding, cotton textiles – the first industries to be revolutionized by capitalist technology. This unemployment tended to be heavily localized in the coalfields – especially, in Britain, in Northumberland and Durham, south Wales, Scotland and Lancashire.

But, more generally, as profits fell and confidence in the future sank ever lower, the level of investment was far below what it could potentially have been. Thus unemployment was severe in the investment goods trades – steel and engineering especially – with consequent effects on the demand for raw materials, particularly coal.

As the slump worsened, the Labour government in London, under Ramsay MacDonald, had no idea of what was happening. A committee it had appointed now reported that the loss of confidence was due to high government spending (which was partly and superficially true). The party was deeply split on this issue, and disillusion had rotted its heart, as MacDonald had failed to deal with the economic problem and, notably, unemployment, which was growing weekly more intense. MacDonald went to the king and formed a national government, a Conservative-dominated coalition, the rump of the Labour Party going into opposition. MacDonald's government was set up to save the gold standard; within three weeks the gold standard was abandoned. The international credit system collapsed. In the general election the Labour Party was virtually annihilated.

The collapse of the Labour government had widespread consequences. For all its faults – and its merits could be written in large characters on the back of a postage stamp – it was a social democratic government, drawing its support from trade unionists and non-communist intellectuals. It was revealed to be ineffectual in the face of international monetary convulsions, and to be completely devoid of intellectual resources. When the neo-classical economists trotted out their dogma that the only way to cure unemployment was to cut wages, the Labour Party intellectually accepted the arguments; even its honest leaders (who were few enough) like Hugh Dalton had no effective policies to propose which differed, in essence, from those of the bankers. Thus, by the collapse of the Labour Party in 1931, social democracy was widely discredited and there was a retreat either to authoritarian solutions (whether communist or fascist) or to ineffectual liberalism, vaguely waiting for the economic storm to pass.

Oddly enough, after the collapse of the gold standard in September 1931, Britain managed to insulate itself from the worst of the storm, largely because the national finances were exceptionally well managed by Neville Chamberlain. This did not mean that things got better; they did not, however, get very much worse. Unemployment remained in the millions. In Germany and America, however, things went from bad to worse. The flight into gold continued. Credit declined rapidly. Unemployment mounted. Government crisis succeeded government crisis on the continent, while in America it seemed as though the very constitution itself was irrelevant to the crisis through which the nation was passing. President Hoover, who said in 1930 that 'prosperity is just around the corner', was utterly powerless.

France and America, which stuck to gold, suffered the worst loss of exports in 1932, and the loss of gold that America suffered caused still more credit contraction and further collapses. By the time that Franklin Delano Roosevelt was inaugurated president in March 1933, the economic system had virtually come to a stop. The banks were shut. Roosevelt promptly broke the link between the dollar and gold. This marked, for all practical purposes, the end of the gold standard. It also marked the beginning of the New Deal and of the United States' recovery.

The slump, then, marked the end of many stages of capitalism. It meant an increasing disillusion with democratic, liberal politics, and a growing attraction to authoritarian régimes of the left and of the right. It meant an abandonment of free trade and the gold standard. Great Britain's reversal of policy was the most dramatic. For a century Britain had been the central advocate of free trade, and its nineteenth-century prosperity and political reputation had been indissolubly linked to free trade. By the events of 1931 Great Britain not only cut the link with gold, but it went over to tariffs, and (to a marginal extent) to exchange controls. Germany, which had always been a protectionist country, went over to exchange controls – or autarchy – rejecting international trade entirely, save as a means of obtaining products that could not be produced at home. The concept of international specialization was rejected and as an inevitable corollary the search began for territories which could be militarily conquered and which could supply what Germany could not produce.

The disillusion produced by the slump also marked the end of the belief that the system could work spontaneously. From the spokesmen for the unemployed to the manufacturers, the call for government intervention was almost universal and was irresistible. No government, whatever its dogmas, could sit by and watch its economy be paralysed. The trouble was to know what to do. Lloyd George and Keynes moved to the concept of deficit financing – that government should take up the slack in the economy and put the unemployed to work on useful projects. The Swedish government, advised by its excellent economists, managed by monetary and fiscal policy to insulate Sweden from the worst of the depression and to embark on a programme of social amelioration. Roosevelt tried a pragmatic policy: he attempted to guarantee agricultural incomes, to develop industrial combines, to raise prices, to increase relief payments. The bankers reconstructed a system of international payments based on mutually acceptable exchange levels, and reserves held in the major currencies (the dollar, the franc and the pound). The American banking system was reconstructed.

Out of this chaos of ideas and initiatives two things stood out. One was that totalitarian countries somehow seemed to come through. The other was that Roosevelt's New Deal seemed to begin to work. Thereafter it was a contest between the New Deal and totalitarianism, between the techniques of social democracy and the mystique of fascism, to see which system could lead to permanent economic recovery.

The Cambridge economists

It may seem curious to regard the Cambridge economists, Marshall, Pigou, and Keynes, as key figures in the development of democratic socialism, yet the modification of laissez-faire and acceptance of a mixed economy owe a great deal to their work. Moreover, with the abandonment of Marxism as an ideological basis for socialism, its claim to be based upon a 'scientific' analysis of society meant that it relied increasingly upon the social sciences for its understanding of the forces that were to transform capitalism into socialism. Since economics was the leading social science, and since socialism almost from its inception had held that changes in the economy were basic to all social change, it followed that it was the development of economics which was to exercise the most important influence on socialist thought and on socialist practice.

Of all the great schools of economics, Cambridge was to be the most influential. The Austrian economists were for the most part identified with a sophisticated defence of extreme liberalism, characterized by Von Mises and Hayek. The Marxist school degenerated, with few exceptions, into an apologia for Stalinism. Pareto provided an ideological content for fascism. Marshall, however, the true originator of the Cambridge school, carried on the utilitarian tradition of pragmatic solutions to social questions which he had got from Sidgwick, the Cambridge Utilitarian, and his colleagues.

Alfred Marshall (1842–1924) regarded the economic system as a self-regulating process of tremendous complexity. But, being a man of infinite caution with considerable leanings towards 'socialism' (in the sense that he wished to take steps towards improving social welfare by public action), he never produced a theory of the economy which held that the economy could only work on laissez-faire principles, and on no others, nor did he ever produce a capitalist manifesto.

So blandly did he present his views that when Sidney Webb read the *Principles* (at a sitting) he said 'nothing new'. Yet, in fact, an explanation of the economic system had been produced which was new, because it explained why the system worked reasonably well and why dramatic changes were unlikely to improve it, but which was completely compatible with a considerable degree of public ownership of industry, progressive taxation, and with a considerable extension of social welfare provision. Of course Marshall was concerned that the mainspring of economic progress – the willingness to invest and to take risks in order to achieve a higher income in the future – should not be broken, and in his view it was probably the case that this was the main justification for private ownership of capital as a means of achieving the accumulation of capital. To this extent Marshall represented an intellectual assault on Marxism, whose economic analysis rested on Ricardo.

But Marshall's system (at least as it was widely interpreted, for Marshall's thought was so complex that he carefully covered most eventualities), was unacceptable on two counts. First, it seemed to offer a justification for the existing distribution of income, by relating incomes to productive efforts, or to the rewards for savings, suggesting that a more egalitarian distribution could only be achieved by a steady improvement of the productive skills of the labour force and by the accumulation of savings on their part. This was quite unacceptable to socialist opinion, which saw the existing extreme inequality as a major reason for abandoning capitalism and saw no reason why rapid change should not be brought about.

The second weakness of Marshall's thought was that it provided no general explanation of the periodic crises of unemployment that afflicted the capitalist world. Even those who accepted Marshall's view that the rate of economic progress in the nineteenth century had been, by historical standards, exceptionally rapid, were bound to admit (as he did himself) that the periods at which hundreds of thousands of men and women were thrown out of work, and they and their families reduced to destitution, were (to say the least) severe blemishes on the face of capitalism. And, as the twentieth century opened, the periodic crises became, as it were, permanent: a continual pool of unemployment was created. In Marx's system this was the reserve army of the unemployed whose function it was continually to bid down wage rates to subsistence level. But in fact wages were not beaten down to subsistence level. It looked as though a less sinister, more ordinary explanation of the phenomenon was necessary.

These two limitations of Marshall's work were tackled by his pupils Pigou and Keynes. Pigou's contribution to socialist thought was to develop a technique for assessing the differences between private and public benefits. First he developed Marshall's concept of the diminishing marginal utility of money – that, beyond a point, each additional unit of money yielded a diminishing amount of satisfaction – to give credence to the notion that money taken away from the rich and given to the poor would add to the sum total of satisfaction, since the money taken away from the rich would have a low marginal utility, while the money given to the poor would have a high marginal utility. This argument for progressive taxation (and ultimately for equal incomes), was based upon a series of post-utilitarian assumptions about the possibility of comparing dispositions towards happiness (and also upon some more technical considerations). But it represented a breakthrough because, henceforth, in the social sciences the onus was on the supporters of inequality to defend their position. When the findings of sociology (in the British tradition) were added to this economic reasoning, the weight of the social sciences was turned in the socialist direction. Marx had claimed that socialism was a scientific theory. Now it seemed that social scientists were themselves claiming that science (of course in a different sense from the word used by Marx) made socialism inevitable as a way of running society efficiently. This was a major intellectual development.

Pigou's other ideas were equally important. One was his distinction between private costs and public costs, and private benefits and social benefits. A man could operate a noisome factory to his private profit, but the smell would add to his neighbours' costs by way of increased discomfort; and similarly a service – say a railway – could be provided at a private loss while yielding a public benefit. When Pigou also demonstrated that industries with large fixed equipment would usually make a loss under competitive conditions and competitive pricing policies, there was a cogent argument for nationalization on technical economic grounds. Many socialists – Dalton, Gaitskell, Crosland – were to base most of their economic arguments for socialism on the reasoning developed by Pigou.

Keynes accepted the Marshall–Pigou scheme of reasoning. It is important to emphasize that this was a liberal view of the economy. None of the three was a socialist. But the arguments shifted radically from an acceptance and justification of laissez-faire as the proper way to organize an economy, to arguments in favour of predominantly private control of business on the pragmatic ground that, despite their shortcomings, businessmen were likely to make fewer mistakes than civil servants and politicians.

John Maynard Keynes was a Cambridge mathematician and economist, a pupil of Marshall and Pigou, the great neo-classical economists. He was a member of a distinguished group of philosophers, writers and artists (Russell, Wittgenstein, Virginia Woolf, Lytton Strachey), the lover of Duncan Grant the painter, and the husband of Lopokova the ballerina. He dabbled in government, was an amateur of the arts, and was a brilliant journalist. He wrote some of the most distinguished economics of the century and some of the best prose. His worst book, *The General Theory of Employment, Interest and Money*, became the bible of the new society.

The thesis that Keynes propounded, from his book on the Versailles Peace Treaty which ended the First World War – *The Economic Consequences of the Peace* – to his last essays on world monetary questions, in 1945, was in essence this. Capitalism was not an ideal system. It would be a mistake to raise to the level of eternal moral principle the doctrines which enabled it to operate successfully. What capitalism had done was to provide the means by which scientific and technological progress could be incorporated into machinery, equipment, and capital goods of all kinds. The ends to which this productive capacity could be put were a different consideration. Abundance was techni-cally feasible, within a reasonable span of time, and at that point the real issues of what life was to be lived for would be discuss-able, because the struggle for existence would be at an end.

As a matter of pragmatism, it had seemed that private initia-tive was the most successful system for achieving high economic and technical progress. As a further matter of pragmatism, free trade, generally speaking, also was the most successful way of arranging the international order. All previous systems – feud-alism, slavery – had been inefficient, and Keynes regarded the totalitarian systems of communism and fascism as hopelessly inefficient and inflexible. Thus, at the level of tactical decision, as it were, Keynes held that decentralization, by response to the price system, worked best, and that centralization did not really work save in grave emergencies where one end was dominant. Since the economic problem was to reconcile diverse ends, centralization could not last long. But government had a strategic role. Left to itself, capitalism had reached the stage where it was in danger of chronic deflation, partly because of the way the international monetary system worked, but also because the most urgent of man's needs were satisfied in the industrial countries, and people tended to save extra income, thus not spending enough to create the demand to keep the advanced technological resources of modern capitalism fully employed. The government's task was to generate this demand, by deficit finance, and (on an international level) for all governments to continue to take a collective policy to make international trade once more what it had been in the nineteenth century, a force for economic expansion. It was this strategic role of government that marked Keynes' second major break with capitalist philosophy. Not only was market economics not a moral principle, but a pragmatic one; government was important as a strategist rather than as a policeman.

His third break with the past was his view of personal liberty. Keynes was a libertarian (of a somewhat stuffy Cambridge kind) in sex, art, morals and politics. In his view, capitalism had interfered less with people than any other system, past or present, for ordering society. It therefore was to be commended as a system that accorded with a moral absolute, that people should be allowed to go to heaven or hell in their own way, because only in that way could they achieve the harmonious personal relationships, and the cultivation of taste, which formed the basis of true civilization. For the purpose of economic activity was the good life. The good life consisted of making love to beautiful people, talking to intelligent people, reading books, seeing plays and painting pictures, in a free society. To do this, affluence had to be available for all. Keynes, as the apostle of hedonistic affluence, could not have been more in conflict with the puritan philosophers on whom the capitalism system had rested its case. Their defence of capitalism was that it maximized savings: Keynes', that it taught people how to spend them happily. Their defence of capitalism was that it encouraged people to work: Keynes looked forward to the only work that was done being done for pleasure. They regarded discipline and morality as synonymous. Keynes was a moral anarchist.

Thus the entire philosophic defence of a free society moved on to a different ground. Keynes held that society could be so arranged that people could be free and prosperous. The New Deal and the postwar North Atlantic economy proved that this was so. Keynes argued that totalitarianism was both inefficient economically, and, once adopted, very difficult to shake off. Soviet Russia showed this to be the case. Keynes argued that in a free society the government's role was limited to seeing that the economy functioned and to providing welfare services; beyond that, business would solve the economic problems.

This hypothesis was never to be tested. The whole of Keynes' case – which reads like a philosophical justification of much of Roosevelt's New Deal – was swept aside by the Second World War and the Cold War. A new society came into existence which was based, in part at least, upon war. Keynes' techniques allowed the western allies – Britain and America – to survive the war (though the war was almost certainly won by communism); but the world that followed was one that was of a very different character from what might have been expected. For not only did communism survive, but it spread to China. Communist doctrine proved extremely attractive to the poor countries of Latin America, Africa and Asia. America and its allies undertook vast expenditure on arms. Governments regulated their economies to a degree that would have seemed impossible in the 1930s. Above all, scientific endeavour, subordinated to the arms race, transformed the world. Keynes was proved right that governments could avoid the curse of unemployment. But the society which was created – scientific armaments, for embattled alliances, in a framework of social democracy – was utterly unlike the good life of artistic endeavour that Keynes had hoped for.

The politics of the depression
The difficulty of governing a country is partly in the realm of theory – how to understand what is happening – and partly in the realm of practice: people are weak and foolish.

Labour drew its main support from areas where there was often deep suffering; and the split between the prosperous south (where the greater part of the middle class lived) and the north, was acute. The situation, in fact, resembled the position in the old United Kingdom, when the condition of Ireland was incomprehensible to the English and Scots. The immediate postwar depression of 1920–1 revealed the weakness of the British economy, which first led to severe problems in the coalfields. The British export markets had been partly lost as a result of the disruptions of world trade caused by the war; their net surplus position in foreign trade had been jeopardized by the liquidation of a number of investments and the blows given to the export trade, while the instability of the exchanges caused growing problems. The trade unions in coal mining and other heavy industries, and in the railways – that is, most of the leading manual workers' unions – were involved in growing militancy, strikes and lockouts. The Triple Alliance – coal-miners, railwaymen and transport workers – lived in uneasy harmony, seeking to support each other without jeopardizing their own individual interests. But the threat of a general strike of all trade unionists was genuine enough; it had nearly been carried out in 1914, again in 1919, and it remained a constant menace.

The Labour Party in Parliament was predominantly a trade union party, though its leader, J. R. MacDonald was an intellectual. Its main role was to press for social reforms, especially in the fields of social insurance and working conditions, and to support the trade union movement. Therefore, fear of the Labour Party, on the part of the capitalist class, was partly a fear of its trade union militants, for the weapon of the general strike had been discussed for nearly a century as the weapon for the inauguration of socialism. Yet trade union militants in fact thought of the general strike as a means of enforcing, by a general stoppage, the wage demands (either for more money, or for the restoration of a cut in wages) of one particular, threatened group. Nothing could have been further from their immediate thoughts than the overthrow of capitalism: their concern (legitimately and understandably) was with pennies an hour. The other fear of socialism stemmed from what was happening in Russia. The socialist movement had been all-embracing, so it was not wholly unreasonable to assume, as middle-class people did, that the comrades in Britain who sang the Red Flag at Labour Party meetings had something in common with the comrades in Moscow who sang the Internationale at Communist Party meetings. In fact the two groups had about as much in common as Jesuits and Plymouth Brethren – both Christians in their fashion. The Moscow communists had now organized the Third International, which was busily penetrating the Labour Party; and the Labour Party was fighting back, though not, alas, penetrating the Third International.

When Ramsay MacDonald became prime minister his first aim was to find enough 'experienced' people to be ministers and he therefore recruited a number of office-hungry Liberals. He also sought to give the impression that Labour was respectable enough to govern a great empire, and the governing class responded, much as they would have politely applauded a band of naked but loyal Africans rendering, by grunts and groans, a version of the national anthem. For any legislative enactment, Labour depended on Liberal support. For any radical measure the House of Lords had a two-year delaying power. It was therefore impossible for the government to be in any major sense radical. But it also suffered from the disadvantage that had it been in a position to do anything, it would not have had the least idea what to do.

The Labour Party had adopted a new constitution at the end of the war which declared it a socialist party. Proposals had been adopted for the nationalization of the coal mines and the railways, and of a few other industries, but there was no possible executive mechanism for implementing them. At that time it was thought that an industry, once purchased by the government (for expropriation was ruled out) would be run like a government department – the Post Office, say – directly responsible to a minister who would in turn be responsible to Parliament. A growing body of younger opinion was frightened of the bureaucratization involved in this notion and took a syndicalist line. Others still were Marxists and repudiated the notion that the state could run industry in a capitalist society. When socialism came, the state (that is the coercive powers of the state) would 'wither away' and industry would run itself.

Meanwhile, the Labour government enjoyed office. Virtually

its only intellectual apart from Sidney Webb was the prime minister, an amiable man, greatly taken with office and its fruits. The cabinet put on its top hats, went off to the social and business engagements that cabinet ministers had usually kept, and let the country drift along. And even if they had wanted to nationalize coal, or had been able to do so, what good it would have done the coalminers was not clear as the export market for coal was continually declining.

On the main issues of the day the Labour Party not only had no ideas but no viable ideas existed. Unemployment was a problem. There was no economist of serious standing in the world who believed that it could be cured except by cutting wages, or by cutting prices, or both. There was a tremendous amount of poverty. No serious economist in the world believed that public expenditure could rise significantly without cutting savings, depressing investment, and causing more misery. There was a crisis in international trade. Keynes argued that German reparations and the bad alignment of parities were the root causes of the trouble, but (even if he had been right) he was regarded as an eccentric. Nor, it must be pointed out, were the Marxist theorists in better case. All their predictions were hopelessly wrong and Russia was staggering from crisis to crisis, held together (as it had always been held together) by tyranny. It was later to be shown that unorthodox action was possible – Hitler in Germany, Roosevelt in America, and Stalin in Russia – but the first and the last of these used measures so barbarous that they were wholly repugnant to all men of sense and goodwill who knew what was going on. Indeed trade union missions to Russia almost inevitably came back disenchanted, except with particular instances (health services, for example).

The Labour government fell in 1924, partly helped on its way by a series of stories that it was sympathetic to communism and that the communists were plotting to overthrow the constitution. There is no doubt that they were so plotting, but not only was their plotting ineffectual, it was mainly directed against the Labour Party. The Conservatives returned to office under Baldwin. The industrial situation continued to deteriorate. The mining industry fell into increasing difficulties as German coal, which had been stopped after the occupation of the Ruhr by the French, came on the market again and British exports fell further. The mine owners sought to cut mine workers' wages and a Royal Commission was appointed, which, to a great degree, supported such action in its report. The miners were locked out when they refused to accept the cuts; and the General Strike was called, on 3 May 1926. It was surprisingly widespread, though the trade union movement was almost totally unprepared for it. The government hastily organized emergency supplies and rallied support, greatly helped by its monopoly of the mass media (the strikers made a great mistake in closing down the newspapers), and on 12 May the General Strike ended, in wholesale defeat. There had been no Labour plans for the struggle, so it was scarcely surprising that the strike failed, but even if it had 'succeeded', what would 'success' have meant? The Labour Party was quite unwilling to overthrow the constitution and usurp power, yet the strike could only have been effective had the government resigned, which it could only do following defeat in the House of Commons. And to have reversed the wage cuts would only have led to even faster falls in the sale of coal. Britain had revalued its currency by returning to the gold standard in 1925. Not a single Labour voice was raised against it – only Keynes' was – so that a successful strike while the country remained on the gold standard was a contradiction in terms: money wages would have risen, so would costs, sales would have fallen and so would employment.

Ramsay MacDonald and his government resumed office in 1929. This time they were the largest party in the House of Commons, though still not an absolute majority and still subject to the two-year suspensory power of the House of Lords. This time the Liberals were a less serious threat to them, electorally, though Lloyd George's campaign, inspired by some of the best minds in the country – notably Keynes' – was conducted on the basis of a programme that was to prove successful in Sweden and in the United States under Roosevelt. It is ironical that, had Lloyd George been elected instead of Ramsay MacDonald, and had that chronically dishonest but exceptionally able man carried out his programme, British liberalism might have preceded Swedish social democracy and the New Deal with a social democratic semi-Keynesian solution to the unemployment problem.

MacDonald's government had three interrelated problems to deal with. The first was the international economic crisis. Almost simultaneously with the election, the New York Stock Exchange boom collapsed, and a cumulative panic seized the world money markets. By 1931, after the *Credit Anstalt* collapse in Vienna, the crisis was of a severity that surpassed anything that had happened before. The pound, as the world's leading trading currency, was continuously threatened, and the Labour government was determined to maintain the gold standard. Their reasons for this were twofold: the respectable one was that they were told, and believed, that if Britain abandoned the gold standard, international trade would collapse, and the British export markets would disappear. The disreputable reason was that they could not think of anything else to do, though Keynes and Ernest Bevin, the leader of the Transport and General Workers Union, had a plan for a managed economy that was to prove eminently satisfactory.

Against this background of growing international monetary crisis, the Labour government was struggling to maintain world peace. After the Versailles Treaty of 1919, the United States had retreated into isolationism. This settlement, left to Britain and France to police, had never worked well and came increasingly under strain. In 1923 and 1924 MacDonald tried hard to make the League of Nations effective. He and Arthur Henderson tried again in 1929–31. In those years the world came nearer to a universal peace settlement than at any time to come. Almost complete disarmament was achieved, except for Japan, but as troubles broke out, it was clear that no general settlement was capable of being held against determined aggressors – the Japanese in the Far East in the case of Manchuria; the Italians, when Mussolini came to power in 1922 with a doctrine of militant nationalism; and the additional threat of a revival of German militarism, should Hitler and the National Socialists come into office. Ramsay MacDonald was justifiably vilified later for his helplessness in the face of the economic problem, but internationally his record was good. Had he been able to achieve an *entente*, acting through the League, it is just conceivable that the Second World War might have been averted.

The major crisis, however, which the government faced every day and neglected to tackle every day, was unemployment, which mounted steadily. As it grew, poverty and distress became more acute, especially in the Labour constituencies in Scotland, Wales and the north of England. Inevitably, payments out of public funds rose. They were insufficient to alleviate distress and their mode of disbursement – as a public charity – was humiliating and offensive to the unemployed, while the outflows were sufficient to alarm financial opinion about the state of the Treasury. Thus the government had two utterly irreconcilable pressures put upon it. The first was to alleviate its supporters' distress. The second was to keep public expenditure down in the hope of avoiding a loss of confidence in London as a financial centre. The tension was resolved by a complete capitulation to the need for confidence. Fundamentally this was due to the absence of any theory for coping with unemployment and to the absence of any boldness that was prepared to act without a theory. Margaret Bondfield, the Minister of Labour, was a weak and unimaginative politician. Philip Snowden, the trade unionist who was Chancellor of the Exchequer, was an ignorant and stupid man, determined to be as reactionary as possible. The left had no leaders. There was no pragmatic middle-of-the-road man to lead the Labour Party out of the horror. Sir Oswald Mosley, an attractive rising politician, resigned from the government but made the understandable error of starting a new party. It was not at that time fascist but its foundation meant that Mosley and his supporters were no longer able to influence Labour policy. The political pressures on the government were all reactionary. The Conservative Party was deeply worried about the national finances. The Liberal Party made the government pass an Anomalies Act which reduced the number of unemployed able to claim benefit, pushing the unfortunate people straight into the arms of the Poor Law.

Meanwhile, throughout 1931, attempts were made to secure foreign loans, while the government did literally nothing about the economy and virtually nothing about social reform. It is difficult to see what they could have done, given the limitations of the ideas prevalent at the time. The only intellectual alternative to laissez-faire was Marxism and (it must be emphasized) what was happening in Russia at that time gave no indication that Marxist-Leninism offered any alternative save revolutionary terror. It must be recalled too, that, though bad, conditions were not as bad as all that in large parts of the country. The falling price level meant that people in safe jobs (teachers, civil servants) or in prospering industries, were increasing their real incomes steadily. Only in the crisis years 1931–2 did many of their incomes fall, both in money and real terms. And people with capital, however little, had a great deal to lose if capital values collapsed. Prudence dictated, therefore, the avoidance of panic or of unorthodox measures that inclined people towards panic. Britain was still a free trade country. Any drastic attempt to raise employment would have entailed not only going off the gold standard but a significant shift to protection and, probably, to controls on capital movement. By 1936 Britain had done the first two, and Germany had done all three; but five years is not an exceptionally long time when ideas and attitudes are involved.

Labour's policies and views from 1929 to 1931 profoundly affected opinion about social democracy. In the first place, a number of people, like Mosley, came to the conclusion that a quasi-military organization of society, such as Mussolini had achieved in Italy, was necessary to bring Britain back to greatness. In Germany, where the depression was far worse and militarism more popular, many social democratic voters went over to Hitler. In Britain a few intellectuals went over to communism but most people did not. It is interesting to speculate why. Life in Britain was not too bad. Life in Russia, especially with the famine in the Ukraine, was terrible; and the ghastly irony of Stalin's 'comrades, life is better, life is brighter' speech, while millions starved, thousands were in prison, and thousands were shot, was not lost on the British working people. But, above all, when the Conservatives came back into office, in September 1931 (under the guise of a National government), economic recovery began, first by abandoning the gold standard and adopting protection, and secondly by a housing boom, largely resulting from low interest rates, which in turn were due to Neville Chamberlain's sensible policy at the Treasury. From 1931 until the middle of the Second World War, Labour not only had no real alternative programme to offer to pragmatic conservatism, but it was exceedingly doubtful whether it could govern at all, since its record from 1929 to

1931 had been so miserable. When Labour's fortunes were restored it was largely because of foreign and social policy, and the economic policy advocated was contrasted not with Chamberlain's success at the Treasury but with Lloyd George's disasters in 1921 and Snowden's in 1931. Thus were the Conservatives blamed for a Liberal and a Labour failure.

The mode of Labour's collapse in 1931 was dramatic and the very substance of myth. As the summer wore on, unemployment mounted and foreign confidence fell. Foreign loans helped to support the pound. Then a committee under Sir George May reported that substantial cuts were necessary in social expenditure, including unemployment relief, if the pound were to be saved. The government was in agony; ministers tried to avoid the implications of the cuts and it was rumoured that the cabinet was split. This promptly caused foreign confidence in the pound to wane still further, for it was feared that a Labour government might ignore the May Committee's recommendations. It is now known that this rumour was untrue. The cabinet was in fact united on the principle of cutting expenditure; the argument was about where the cuts were to fall. As the crisis grew more desperate MacDonald and Snowden formed the opinion that the only hope was to form a coalition to save the pound; after the pound was saved, it appears that he hoped to resume normal party arrangements and, presumably, to reappear as a Labour leader. Yet he took no serious steps to tell his colleagues, or the Labour Party, that this was his intention. He went to the king, came back and dismissed his colleagues, and formed a new government. The Labour Party was hopelessly split: a rump supported MacDonald but the great majority voted to expel him and the rump from the Labour Party. The new government went off the gold standard. It won a vast electoral victory; the Labour Party was virtually wiped out, having only forty-six Members of Parliament, including only one ex-cabinet minister, George Lansbury, an insignificant figure of some moral stature, who became the leader. But Labour, leaderless and defeated, had a valuable alibi. MacDonald had always been a traitor, it was said, and he had long since planned to do a deal. Betrayed, not defeated, Labour could console itself. The fact that it had no policies at all was conveniently forgotten.

Labour 1931-8

The defeat of 1931, reducing the Labour Party to forty-six Members of Parliament, and giving the Conservatives an overwhelming victory, could have led to the complete disappearance of the Labour Party. A scenario may be imagined in which the steady improvement in economic conditions that followed the bottom of the slump in 1932 was followed by a widespread adoption of Keynes' ideas, advanced in *The General Theory of Interest, Employment and Money*, in the winter of 1935-6, and representing an intellectual breakthrough of the greatest importance on the question of how to manage a capitalist economy in order to achieve full employment. Had the ideas been adopted, say by 1940, as they were increasingly (in Sweden and in America particularly), then the radical commitment to a social democratic party might have disappeared. A party system would have survived but it would (perhaps) have been far more like the American or German party system in the 1960s, or the British party system before 1914. It may well be the case, indeed, that British politics in the 1960s provided a justification for this view; that in a post-Keynesian economy, a social democratic party had no distinct ideological basis. That it was not so in the 1930s was due almost entirely to the international situation and to the slowness of the recovery from the depression. A great deal must be attributed, too, to the power of party loyalty. Studies seem to have shown that the pattern of voting loyalty, once established, is hard to break. Labour had established itself, before 1931, as the party for which over half of the manual working class habitually voted. In 1935 this pattern re-established itself, as indeed it probably would have done in 1931 had a few months – or even weeks – elapsed between the 'betrayal' by MacDonald and the election, so that the Labour Party could have adopted candidates and prepared to fight the election.

The period up to 1935 was largely preoccupied by the problems of the unemployed and the impoverished. Despite the drift towards communism of a number of intellectuals, from Kim Philby, the master-spy, to John Strachey, and the Webbs, the bulk of the intelligent working class rejected the Soviet Union as a system of terror sustained by lies. The preoccupation of the Labour Party was with social welfare and, in this connection, its victory in the London elections in 1933 was important. Herbert Morrison became the leader of the London County Council, the biggest local authority in the country, and promptly began to press through small but important reforms. Thus, increasingly, Labour turned to the practicalities of government. Herbert Morrison, who had been Minister of Transport from 1929 to 1931, was also the originator of another pioneering piece of work. A bill of his to establish a public board to own London Transport – the London Passenger Transport Board – was enacted by the National government, and it established the procedure by which industries and services could be taken into public ownership in the Labour government of 1945–51. A board was established which ran the industry, under an Act of Parliament, generally subject to the minister's directions but independent in its day-to-day operations, which were carried out on normal commercial principles. Thus Herbert Morrison, by putting London ahead in social welfare, hospitals and education, and by establishing a model of a statutory board, set the pattern for social development.

When to this was added the development of the techniques for maintaining full employment, Labour by 1938 had a domestic strategy for economic and social development which was wholly in advance of the strategy with which it had faced the experience of the 1931 depression. There was also the experience of Sweden and of Roosevelt's New Deal – discussed later – to show that radical governments could defeat the bankers and could use the power of the government to undertake significant programmes of economic development and social reconstruction. The atmosphere had changed significantly; a new generation had arrived which no longer believed in laissez-faire, which no longer saw Bolsheviks under the bed when socialism was discussed, but (paradoxically) thought of Roosevelt and the Swedes.

But the biggest change of all was the darkening international situation in which there were a number of separate issues that brought the Labour Party support. They were virtually incompatible but each had such moral overtones that the diversity was swamped by a bellowing of righteousness, which had the immense advantage of putting the Conservative government in the wrong whatever it did, whether it rearmed or disarmed, whether it appeased Hitler or was bellicose to him, whether it intervened in Spain or whether it did not. The first of these causes was the League of Nations and disarmament. Mac-Donald had an excellent record internationally, in his support for the League and in his campaign for international disarmament. Henderson, the Foreign Secretary in the 1929 government, remained as chairman of the international conference on peace in Geneva, which finally adjourned, with Henderson dying and nothing achieved. But the belief remained that if the League were strengthened peace could be maintained, and the League of Nations Union and the Peace Pledge Union jointly showed how enormous was the support for an active policy to build up the League of Nations. The celebrated 'King and Country' debate at Oxford, when the Oxford Union voted by a majority that it would not fight for king and country was not primarily a pacifist motion; it was in fact a vote that they would only fight for an international cause. But support for the League was also connected with pacifism. Lansbury, the leader of the Labour Party, was a pacifist, as had been Ramsay MacDonald, and the pacifist feeling was widespread as a revulsion after the horrors of the First World War and from a sense that it had been utterly unnecessary – merely due to dim politicians and corrupt generals – and had settled no substantive issue. On the other hand, those who wished to use the League to deter aggression had necessarily to argue for rearmament.

After 1934 this became a live issue. The social democrats were the first victims of the German Nazis, also of the terror in Vienna waged by Nazi sympathizers against the Social Democratic authorities. As refugees fled to Britain, Labour Party leaders like Hugh Dalton realized that German militarism would once more have to be fought, and pressed for rearmament. Then after the 1935 election Ernest Bevin took the issue to the Labour Party Conference and overthrew Lansbury. Thenceforward Labour was in principle committed to armaments, though in practice every step towards rearmament was opposed. The arguments for opposing it were not entirely specious: it was feared that the National government would use the arms not against the Nazis but against the communists. It was argued, therefore, that before rearmament could proceed, foreign policy would have to be changed.

The Spanish Civil War brought this issue to a head. The British government adopted a policy of non-intervention. As the Spanish army was in revolt, and it was aided by Italy and Germany, the Republican government was almost bound to lose, especially as Russian support was feeble and the Republicans were themselves split up into four major groups, with the Stalinists more anxious to attack their allies than the enemy. Inexorably the Falangists – the Spanish fascists – swept across Spain, and the heroic resistance of the Spanish people served only to prolong the agony. The war grew more barbarous, and Guernica, where for the first time aerial bombardment was used as a weapon of terror against a civilian population, showed what a future war would be like. Social democrats rallied to support the Republic and some brave spirits went off to fight in the Major Attlee Battalion of the International Brigade. Labour was aware of a fascist axis of Germany and Italy, determined on aggression and turning on the social democrats with terror. As the anti-semitic persecution intensified in Germany, the Jewish refugees added to Labour's feelings, since the Jewish community was by tradition a Labour group.

The Comintern changed its policy in 1936 and supported the notion of popular fronts against fascism. Its earlier policy had been one of welcoming the destruction of bourgeois reformers. Consequently, no love was lost between the two parties. On the change of policy, the British communists sought to set up a popular front which would press ahead with a military alliance between Russia, France and Britain. The Labour Party indignantly rejected it, supposing (correctly) that this was but one more tactic of infiltration. With the Spanish Civil War lost, with rearmament proceeding apace, and with the humiliation of Munich when the British prime minister signed away Czechoslovakia's frontiers to Hitler, Labour became even more aware of its place as a British radical party, whose duty it would be to rally the country against totalitarianism. When, in 1939, the Nazi–Soviet Pact was signed, the Labour leaders felt justified in their forebodings about the communists. Despite the fact that some of the best Labour people had been expelled from the Labour Party because of the popular front issue, the party was united in its view of Hitler and Mussolini.

Thus, from 1931 to 1939, Labour had become a national party once more. It had a domestic policy and in a muddled way, it had a patriotic foreign policy, which was to be its best guarantee of future success. Hitler and the Communists hated the Social Democrats. They hated Hitler and Stalin, in turn, which was understandable and right.

8 The rise of authoritarian politics and some alternatives

The rise of authoritarian politics

Lenin seized power in St Petersburg in 1917. In 1922 Mussolini marched on Rome. In 1928 Salazar took office in Lisbon. In January 1933 Hitler won the German election.

Lenin's successors remained the only communist government in the world, but the working-class organizations in many countries turned increasingly to communism as their political philosophy, and their pattern of behaviour came to be rigidly controlled by the Communist International (the Comintern) in Moscow. Thus, for capitalist governments in many countries, the real opposition seemed to be the Bolsheviks, acting as agents of Moscow. In France, Germany, Italy and Spain, for example, the communists came to control important working-class organizations which henceforth were treated as outside the normal political process. To the capitalists, moderate socialists were often identified with the communists; to the communists, on the other hand, the socialist parties seemed the worst kind of bourgeois lackeys. In the crisis of 1932, in Germany, the communists fought the socialists, taking the view that the Nazis – in their view the party of monopoly capitalism – would be succeeded by communism. Thus left-wing politics were rent by schism.

Fascism and Nazism had dissimilar roots but increasingly they had common policies and a common ideology. They were nationalist, and arose from a sense of national humiliation that became widespread as governments appeared increasingly impotent in the face of international financial movements. They identified as the enemy international finance, which they labelled Jewish; the Nazis regarded German Jews as rootless aliens and agents of international finance. Some of the Jews, however, it was held, were agents of Bolshevism. Both cases were aided by the fact that many international bankers and some international communists were Jews – so also were some bakers, furriers and boxers.

Nazism asserted the supremacy of the state, as embodying the true will of the people: its members were prepared to use the state to run the economy, achieve full employment, regulate wages, and remove poverty. The liberal institutions were swept aside. But nationalism and state power meant, also, strong armed forces and territorial aggression. A virile nation would have a big army, and would use that army to conquer territories in the colonies and among inferior peoples, which meant, first, the Balkans, and secondly Africa. The campaigns against Ethiopia, Poland, and Russia followed inevitably.

Both Nazism and fascism dissolved the trade unions and formed them again as expressions of national unity (a process also adopted in Russia by the communists). Totalitarian régimes, as their name implies, wanted unity rather than diversity, and sought to unite all people of one race (whatever that might mean) into one national unit. Hitler rejected religion, though he tolerated it. The fascists, Salazar in Portugal, Mussolini in Italy, and Franco in Spain, were blessed by the Pope. In some respects fascist practice embodied Roman Catholic doctrine. The corporate state, in which all people in one trade co-operated rather than competed, in which free thought and expression were forbidden lest they led to disunity and godlessness, represented the culmination of the counter-revolution and a return to pseudo-medieval modes of thought. It was an utter repudiation of 'godless capitalism' no less than of 'godless communism'. Pope Pius XII, who blessed German troops fighting against the Allied armies to liberate Europe from Nazism, was right to regard fascism as an embodiment of his philosophy (which was subsequently repudiated by Pope John XXIII and the Second Vatican Council).

Yet, ironically, fascism and Nazism, which represented the repudiation of the philosophical basis on which capitalism was built, received virtually unanimous support from the business classes. Krupp, for example, was to be sent to prison by the

Allies for war crimes, so keen was his support of Hitler. The businessmen prospered because of rising demand caused by increased public expenditure, because genuine trade union activity was forbidden, and because their capital assets and gains were not taken from them.

It seemed as though the communists had a case, and that Nazism and fascism (which they lumped together generically under the label of fascism) were the political embodiment of monopoly capitalism. The régimes enjoyed the support of big and small business. They made trade unions illegal. They threw the opposition into jail and killed the more active. They talked, openly, in imperialist terms.

But, in fact, what they did was so much the antithesis of capitalism as to render the terms 'monopoly-capitalist-fascist' a total paradox. The businessmen under capitalism had sought profit wherever and however they could. The Nazis (especially) took control of the economy. It was, moreover, inefficient control, save in the one aim of building up military strength swiftly. The Nazi régime ran an economy tied hand and foot by government regulations, and the prosperity of the German people, up to almost the point of collapse in 1945, was due to the systematic looting of the occupied territories. Private international trade was virtually abolished, in the sense that trade was conducted entirely by government permission and increasingly through government agencies. The intellectual freedom, freedom to travel, rights of free speech and of assembly, which were all abolished, had been essential concomitants of capitalism and had followed it wherever it had gone. Capitalism had been defiantly internationalist and had reluctantly recognized national boundaries. The spirit of xenophobia and the cult of aryan blood were directly antipathetic to it. Capitalists had had a rationalist, pragmatic, scientific spirit. Nazism was inspired by Nietzsche and fascism was blessed by the Pope.

Indeed, almost the only evidence for the charge that fascism was increasingly capitalism in jackboots was the fact that it persecuted socialists, communists and trade unionists. But as it also persecuted liberals, Jews and democrats, that proved nothing.

In the Spanish Civil War, which was fought from 1936 to 1939, both sides sought foreign assistance. Out of the complexities of that conflict two points emerged. The first was that the communists would turn their weapons as quickly on democrats, anarchists and Trotskyites as on fascists, and that their main aim was power, not the cause of the working class (except in the purely tautological sense that they identified their own interests as by definition those of the working class). The second was that fascism, in any of its forms, was a cult of violence and irrationality that was totally alien to the forms of government and the independence of thought which had characterized capitalist régimes. Further, it was to be seen later that capitalism was not only capable of reforming itself, but that it could defeat Nazism. But the question remained – whether the successor societies to the devastation that occurred in the Second World War could be called capitalist at all, or whether some other name might not better describe them.

Italy

After unification in 1870 Italy remained a country that was still a collection of widely differing traditions, societies and economies. In the highly developed cities there were socialist movements, which were small; but to be nationalist was to be radical, and to be radical was to be anti-clerical. Thus, in the country of the Pope, political attitudes were determined by reaction to his stance. In such a context, the socialist movement was but one part of a nationalist, radical, anti-clerical movement.

In 1915 Italy entered the war on the allied side as a result of the secret London treaties, the purpose of which was to give the fringe of Italian territories under Austrian control to the United Kingdom of Italy. The war was at first disastrous, though the Italian army fought with great heroism, and victory was only achieved ultimately at very great cost of men and material. The dismemberment of Austria-Hungary did not fully satisfy Italian demands and expectations. By 1919, Italy was war weary, and felt that it had been tricked and led into a futile war. The war demands of the London Treaties were not met; yet the Italian socialists were 'renouncers' – that is, they wanted only Italian-speaking territories to be allocated to Italy. Thus, by 1919, Italian nationalism was in a highly confused and neurotic state, and the socialists had got themselves into a hopelessly false position. To these difficulties was added the classical dilemma. The Catholics had not taken part in Italian politics because the secular Italian state was not recognized by the hierarchy; in 1918 the position was reversed and a Catholic Popular Party was organized. Its strength lay in the countryside, and it made quick advances. The positive entry of the Catholic Church into politics was an important step, if only because it had the effect of driving the socialists into paroxysms of anti-clericalism.

The socialists were not only violently anti-clerical, they also adopted a revolutionary programme and posture, though they were totally unprepared for a revolution. Yet, closely allied to Moscow, they gained a large vote in the 1919 elections. The nationalists, however, inspired by people like d'Annunzio, were far more prepared for violence than the socialists. As the postwar economic problems intensified, industrial and social difficulties mounted. Mussolini, an ex-socialist, emerged as leader of the fascists, who were a mixture of nationalists, radicals and thugs. As the Socialist Party fell into increasing ideological difficulties, the fascist Blackshirts took over town after town, breaking up meetings, terrorizing trade unions. Over all this trouble presided a series of ephemeral and hopelessly ineffective governments.

Fascism was violently patriotic and therefore violently opposed to the socialists, who were not only internationalists but were also manifestly dominated by Moscow. Fascism was violently anti-parliamentary, and parliamentary government was not working. Fascism was for strong state action to right social ills – and there were plenty of ills, including rural poverty and exploitation, unemployment, soaring prices and mass discontent. Mussolini thus became a hero of the masses, a rallying point for the army, a defender of the bourgeoisie (frightened of the large socialist vote in the industrial cities in 1919), and, oddly, a hero to the priests. The Popular Party, under the pressure of intolerable social unrest and seeking to outbid the socialists, had become too radical for the Pope. In 1922 he ordered all priests to leave politics, which literally took the heart out of the Popular Party.

Thus, in 1922, when Mussolini's Blackshirts 'marched' on Rome – it was actually an unopposed motorcade – they were welcomed by Pius XI as restoring order, welcomed by the bourgeoisie as preventing revolution, and welcomed by many of the poor as nationalist reformers.

Italian socialism was gradually made illegal and terrorized. In 1924 the socialist leader, Matteotti, was murdered. The trial of his murderers, who were fascists, was a farce: the guilty men were amnestied and opposition to the régime was suppressed. Tribunals were set up to try political offences; fascist labour unions replaced trade unions; and socialist leaders either emigrated or were imprisoned.

Mussolini's success was not only important in itself, because it put an end to Italian socialism for twenty years, but because it indicated an alternative path for Europe. Fascism was not originally an international movement, and it never became one in the sense that it was a centrally directed affair, like communism. It did, however, become an extremely important international fashion. It was authoritarian, and by stressing the importance of effective government it offered an alternative to the depressing political chaos into which many countries fell. It had a patriotic rhetoric which was, for many people, infinitely more attractive than the rhetoric of internationalism. As the Third World revealed, from the 1940s on, nationalism was by far the most widespread political force of the twentieth century. Fascism laid emphasis upon national unity rather than upon class war and this, again, was attractive to those who disliked civil strife. It had a rhetoric – and possibly a genuine concern – for radical action to improve the lot of workers and peasants. It was, it claimed, socialism without the class war. It offered jobs and opportunities to the working class, especially in the armed forces and para-military formations, yet it did not attack the wealthy. Fascism started out as a variant of socialism, based chiefly on the working class; it became petit bourgeois; and it ended up as a front for powerful capitalists. Mussolini's emulators, especially Hitler, introduced anti-semitism and other detestable elements into their systems; but in the 1920s Mussolini's draining of the Pontine Marshes, his creation of autostrada, his efficiency, were not as reprehensible in the eyes of the outside world as they later seemed in a different and infinitely more vicious context.

France

Long before the First World War, the French social democrats were well-established and influential. *The Section Française de l'Internationale Ouvrière* (SFIO) was an attempt to unite the different French factions in the socialist movement. Disputes were frequent. But Jean Jaurès (1859–1914) was a leader who commanded great respect. Though he would have welcomed participation in bourgeois governments, he opposed those socialists who joined the French cabinet. The reason for this was important. The French party regarded itself as internationalist and anti-militarist; its very title indicated its position as a local section of the Second International. Kautsky had succeeded in getting the Second International to pass a resolution declaring the aim of socialist parties to be power, achieved by electoral procedures; but that participation in dribs and drabs in predominantly anti-socialist governments weakened rather than strengthened the socialist cause. Since socialism represented a clear break with liberalism and radicalism, rather than a continuance with them, this doctrine was logical and sound. But it ignored a central fact – that parliamentary politics required flexibility if they were to be successfully conducted, and that such flexibility might well require coalitions, electoral arrangements and other compromises, especially when the democratic régime was itself in danger. After the fall of Napoleon III and the repression of the Commune, the Third Republic had virtually continuous instability. Despite the prosperity of France and its supreme achievements in civilization, there were constant threats to the régime from monarchists, from Boulanger, and from ex-Bonapartists. The Dreyfus case, when a Jewish army officer was falsely accused and convicted of spying for the Prussians, and it took years to reverse his conviction, epitomized the weakness of the Republic and its institutions, faced with the power of the army; and for progressives (including socialists) the vindication of the Republic against the anti-Dreyfusards was of cardinal importance. Jaurès wished to save the Republic, for if the SFIO were to achieve a majority, there had to be a republic for it to gain a majority in. The Kautsky resolution, therefore, deprived him both of flexibility and the means of helping the Republic.

Then came the First World War. It blew up suddenly, Jaurès was immediately assassinated by a right-wing fanatic, and the socialists, viewing the German social democrats (who mostly supported the war) as traitors to internationalism, fell in behind the French government. It was a case of national defence and national defence was permitted to socialists. Two of the leaders joined the government (Marcel Sembat and Jules Guesde) and later Albert Thomas joined it as Minister of Munitions.

As the war went on, however, and the terrible slaughter of the French army occurred, opposition to it began to mount. At first there was doubt about socialist participation in the government; also there was a feeling that the war should be ended – a feeling strongly encouraged by the Russian Revolution. The French, as allies of the Russians, were deeply involved in Russian affairs; and the apparent triumph of Russian socialism gave new hope to the French socialists, for whom there was a prospect of a socialist conference to end the war and bring about a socialist (and internationalist) peace. But at this point the socialists split: the majority wanted to see Kerensky continue the war; the minority, especially after the Bolshevik Revolution, supported the Leninist demand for peace and revolution. Strikes broke out, and once more the French socialist movement was split. The socialists refused to join Painlevé's government in September 1917, and by October 1918 they were opposing war credits and were determined to support international socialist action to stop the war. But by then the war was ending.

Jean Longuet, Marx's grandson, was leader of the moderates. Like the German socialists, he supported the achievement of socialism by democratic and constitutional means, though at a quicker pace than Jaurès and other French socialists would have done. The reason for speed, of course, was the Russian Revolution and the imminence of socialism throughout the world. Above all, in contrast to the French socialists at the beginning of the war, the moderates blamed the war on capitalism and regarded the achievement of a just, socialist peace as their major political aim. The significance of Longuet's emergence as their leader with this posture was that the pro-Bolshevik revolutionary left was out-manoeuvred and out-gunned; and the extreme left, in any case, consisted largely of syndicalists and quasi-anarchists. Thus when the war ended France was a completely non-revolutionary country.

The end of the war was marked by a trade union demand for a just peace, and for social and economic reforms, such as the eight-hour day. In 1919 there were mass demonstrations and Parliament passed the Eight Hours' Law, but in fact the trade unions were beaten. The French trade unions (organized in the *Confédération Générale de Travail* – CGT) were independent of politics, and therefore their defeat was not as politically significant as the defeats of the British trade unions. On the other hand, the Socialist Party was not rooted in the day-to-day struggles of the industrial workers: it was far more a debating society. Debates now raged about whether the SFIO should join the Third International – the Comintern. It was decided not to do so, but the debates helped to fracture the party and became even more fratricidal when it was badly defeated by Clemenceau in November 1919.

After a series of manoeuvres, the French sent a delegation to the Moscow Conference of the Third International. The delegation recommended that the SFIO should affiliate, and at the Tours Congress, in December 1920, an overwhelming majority voted to do so. The right wing thereupon left the party, which was transformed into the Communist Party. Thus the Communists became the major French working-class party, with all the party organization, newspaper, and funds. The Congress had made French socialism communist just as the Emperor Constantine had made the Empire Christian.

The right wing (including the moderates) set up a new socialist party, handicapped by having no organization but helped by the fact that most socialist Members of Parliament refused to become communists. The struggle from then onwards was between the Communist Party and the SFIO, with the Communists always on the attack. The government was strong; it defeated the trade unions in their great strike of 1920, and subsequently the French working-class movement degenerated into desperate groups of rivals. France was not a predominantly industrial country for the bulk of the population was engaged in agriculture. The working class was now weak and divided, leaving the socialists, who were the party of the intellectuals and school-teachers, with no effective electoral base.

The decline in French socialism caused the Communists to demand, in 1922, a united front of working-class parties, but the socialists (who were becoming more and more a petty bourgeois party) formed local electoral alliances with the radicals. In France, to be progressive was to be anti-clerical and to support the principles of the revolution; to be socialist was increasingly to be communist. The SFIO was thus progressive but not socialist. In the 1924 election the Communists were badly beaten, but electoral alliance with the radicals gave the socialists over a hundred seats in the Chamber. They gave support to Edouard Hérriot's radical government which shifted French policy towards internationalism, evacuated the Ruhr, supported the Dawes Plan, and joined Ramsay Mac-Donald in the attempt to build up international institutions. Thus the socialists, in supporting Hérriot, supported internationalism, and their popularity continued to increase, especially as the Communists sporadically expelled people who were not slavish followers of Moscow and who then rejoined the SFIO. Some of these were Trotskyites, others became more orthodox social democrats. But whatever their views they strengthened the left in the SFIO, and pressed (some of them, at least) for an electoral pact with the Communists. The main parliamentary strength of the SFIO was prepared not only to support Hérriot but also to participate in a coalition with the radicals. However, they were unable to get party support to enter Poincaré's more solidly right-wing government, which stabilized the franc.

In the later 1920s France had not only a stable franc but, like America, genuine prosperity. In the circumstances it was difficult for any party arguing for major changes in society to gain a convincing vote. Thus in the 1928 election the Communists lost seats, while the socialists, growing ever more respectable, just about held their own. Throughout the 1931 slump, which affected France less than any other major country, the parliamentary position was held, and in 1932 the Communists again lost seats, while the socialists made small gains. There were frequent approaches to socialist deputies to join the Radical governments; and, though some of the deputies were more than willing, the Party Congress always refused permission.

Meanwhile the trade union movement, considerably

attenuated, abandoned its revolutionary and syndicalist posture and concentrated on reforms. It was a small body, without significant power, and its members' allegiances were split between the Communists and the SFIO.

All in all, the French socialist party, despite continual ideological disputes, contributed little to French life from 1914 to 1932. Its main contribution was to keep the main element of the petty bourgeois, small civil servant vote in the republican arena and to support the Republic. The Republic was little threatened, however. France was peaceful, exhausted by the war, but victorious and reasonably progressive. It could look at defeated Germany's upheavals with contempt; and, with rapidly changing governments, it could look at Mussolini's Italy with some interest but no great concern. Exhaustion and contentment, however, were not to keep the peace for long.

French prosperity continued well into 1932. The franc was stabilized by Poincaré in 1928 at a low level, and an export boom followed. But eventually the world depression became so severe that it spread to France, causing incomes to fall and a slight rise in unemployment. This was a situation that was to prove critical. Anti-clericalism in France had been important since Voltaire, but it is often forgotten how important clericalism, aristocracy and the right are too. France had an economic and social structure which had remained unaltered in substance, despite the changes in the legal structure that the Republic had brought about, and which left power firmly in the hands of the upper bourgeoisie. Thus, whenever the bourgeois Parliament seemed more farcical or corrupt than usual, powerful people turned their thoughts towards absolutism. France, in its days of glory, had been absolutist. The Third Republic, despite the cultural achievements of the civilization over which it presided, had few claims to glory; for the war of 1914–18 had been won largely by the Allies and, in the last analysis, by the Americans. Had the French been alone it would have been another Sedan. In the circumstances, the Third Republic was, it seemed, a tawdry substitute for French glory. Ever since 1871 the upper bourgeoisie had attacked the Republic.

In 1922 Mussolini had brought a similar régime to an end in Italy. His style of fascism was attractive to advocates of 'sound government'. Italy seemed to be governed efficiently. The godless communists and socialists were suppressed. The Jews were discouraged from being too prominent in public life. The army and navy were strengthened and honoured. The French right, with its intellectual heroes, drawn to a sort of pessimistic eschatological view of the world, tended to support the *Action Française* of Charles Maurras and the *Croix de Feu* of De la Rocque, which were but pale reflections of militant reaction. But as Russian communism grew in power and horror, as Nazism revived German militarism, and as fascist Italy 'put its house in order', more and more French people felt the need for a virile régime based on law, order, the Church and the traditional verities. On the left, the intelligentsia was communist and anti-clerical; on the right it was clerical and fascist; in the middle was the Republic, defended, it seemed, only by its corrupt politicians. The Stavisky scandal, which rumbled on from 1927 to 1934, implied that fraudulent financiers could be defended by politicians, including prime ministers, just as the army had been defended by politicians in the Dreyfus case, but for what to the right seemed infinitely less worthy motives.

The right grew more and more militant. Daladier came into office and, to gain SFIO support, dismissed the extremely right-wing *Préfet* of Paris, Jean Chiappe. In February 1934 the right-wing militants attempted to capture the Chamber of Deputies, during the debate of Daladier's justification of his actions. They almost succeeded. Daladier resigned. The immediate effect was a retort by the left in the form of strikes, organized jointly by communist and socialist trade unions. The left, having seen the fall of the Weimar Republic, and seeing the rise of fascist Italy, was as ready to believe in an international right-wing conspiracy to overthrow republican institutions as the right was prepared to believe in an international left-wing conspiracy. The result of this confrontation was a great rallying of working people to the trade unions and the formation of the *Front Populaire* – a coalition of socialists and communists, to fight fascism.

Throughout 1934 the Stavisky scandal continued to cause political disruption – soon after Daladier's resignation his successor Doumergue also resigned – while the economic situation deteriorated. When Britain went off the gold standard in 1931

France remained on it, and by doing so lost her competitive position in world markets. Exports fell, and workers and farmers suffered serious falls in income. The peasants thereupon became a strong addition to the right-wing forces. In this situation, the new prime minister – an ex-socialist, Pierre Laval – increased the tension by intensifying the deflation: food prices fell and the peasants became more militant, initiating tax strikes. Laval, in order to placate the radicals, acted with increasing violence by suppressing the militant organizations like the *Croix de Feu*. Strangely enough, this firmness was successful, and the left strengthened its anti-fascist agitation.

Laval was in a difficult position. He was determined to maintain order and to preserve the franc. He was also acutely conscious of German rearmament and of Italian demands for Nice and Savoy. He tried to keep the Nazis and fascists apart by agreeing to allow Mussolini to attack Abyssinia without French intervention, and in December 1935 he got the British Foreign Secretary, Sir Samuel Hoare, to agree to stop British sanctions, which had been invoked against Italy. The agreement was published and there was a strong British reaction against it. Hoare resigned and Laval's position was made far more difficult. In March 1936 the Germans reoccupied the Rhineland, making another war more likely, and in July 1936 General Franco rose in revolt against the Spanish Republic. France, with a discredited republican régime, a deflation, a militant right, and a communist-dominated left, was now surrounded by countries where military-minded dictators were on the march.

In mid-1936 the general election returned the SFIO, under Léon Blum, as the largest party, and the Communist Party, as a result of the *Front Populaire*, also had seventy-two seats – a gain of sixty. Blum formed a government which the Communists supported but did not join and which had radical ministers. It was the first major Popular Front government in the West, its support ranging from Marxists, both Trotskyite and Stalinist, to right-wing liberals. Immediately after the election a great wave of strikes broke out, for better industrial conditions. Blum forced the employers to accept their demands and enacted a forty-hour week and holidays with pay. His government opened, therefore, with the biggest single achievement of a socialist government in any major country. But, inevitably, price rises followed immediately and a devaluation of the franc had to be arranged. By June 1937 the reforms had to be followed by a 'pause'; a financial panic threatened and Blum resigned, to serve under a radical, Chautemps.

Meanwhile the Spanish Civil War raged. Blum followed the British in a policy of non-intervention. This not only left Spain to the mercies of the Italians, Germans and Russians, but alienated the left, especially the Communists. The right were already furious with Blum, for being a socialist and a Jew, for his wage awards, and for not supporting Franco.

Chautemps had to devalue the franc a second time and, after the socialists had left office, he resigned, to be succeeded by Blum. The international situation deteriorated steadily. Hitler occupied Austria and threatened Czechoslovakia. Franco was winning in Spain. After a month, Blum resigned again and Daladier resumed office. It was his government that signed the Munich agreement, in September 1938. This was a momentous act. Not only did it show that Hitler could be refused nothing and that the British, French and Russians would not ally themselves against him, but it indicated that France could not act alone (as it had done in the Ruhr fifteen years earlier). Czechoslovakia was a close ally of France. By betraying the Czechoslovak cause the Daladier government destroyed their own international credibility.

Thus, by the end of 1938, the French were allied to Britain through the *Entente Cordiale*, they were nominally allied to the Soviet Union by the Franco-Soviet Pact of 1935, and they had enemies on all sides – Germany, Italy and Franco's Spain. Internally the Republic was despised by both the right and the left. The socialists, after the great wage awards of 1936, had caused a series of major economic crises; and they had jointly presided over a collapse of French foreign policy.

War broke out in September 1939, almost by default, between Britain and France on the one hand and Germany on the other, nominally to defend Poland. The Russians and the Germans occupied Poland. From then on there was a lull until, in May 1940, the attack through Belgium led to the turning of the Maginot Line and the collapse of France. The government fell, an armistice was signed, and all but south-east and central

France was occupied. The socialist party leaders were tried and imprisoned.

Thus the Third Republic collapsed, it seemed, from within. Its collapse was said to be due to bourgeois politics. The party that had been connected with it most was the radical party, but the SFIO had to accept a major part of the responsibility. The complete eclipse of French socialism together with the Third Republic seemed a fitting end to a sorry story. Yet within four years the socialists were once more in office in the Fourth Republic following the Liberation. The Resistance was the forcing bed of what seemed to be (though it was not) a new socialist party.

It can be seen that in the Third Republic the socialists had no policy that was relevant, either internally or externally, to French problems. The reason for their lack of policy was twofold. First, the game of bourgeois politics in which they were involved was almost bound to be ineffectual, since the game bore little relevance to the real seats of decision-making which, in France, were always the permanent institutions of the Republic. These survived empires, republics, communes and Vichys, and were unaffected by socialist and radical politics. But, secondly, French socialism, like British and German socialism, had no coherent and powerful doctrine. Its policy was determined by a relationship to Communist policy: to find a socialist policy, the SFIO looked at the Communists then did the same, or not, as seemed fit.

The New Deal

While in Europe social democracy suffered defeat after defeat, there was a different story to tell in America. In the nineteenth century, when socialism was being invented in Europe, in the United States the socialist movement was always weak. Trade union leaders came from European traditions, and tried to form a socialist movement. Populist movements sprang up. There were Utopian settlements. But there was no general socialist movement. The immigrant working class was organized politically in its local wards; many of the ward bosses were integral parts of the Democratic Party, though the Republican Party, with its deep roots in the northern struggle for the Union, also attracted many working-class supporters. America was democratic, and it seemed an open society, with great opportunities. To the European left, America was for long a promised land; and the European left, the American populists, and American legislators were equally disturbed by the growth of the great monopoly capitalists. Thus, in the European socialist mind America had a dual role: it was the land of opportunity and democracy; it was also the land of monopoly capitalism. Marxists attempted to account for this paradox by maintaining that the closure of the frontier had turned extensive exploitation into intensive exploitation and that the poor immigrants and the poor Negroes represented the exploited proletariat. America would increasingly become characteristic of monopoly capitalism.

In the middle of the slump, in 1932, Roosevelt won the Democratic nomination. He symbolized, as a cripple paralysed by poliomyelitis who had overcome his handicap, the overcoming of tribulation. This is not as fanciful as it might seem, since his campaign was rhetorical rather than practical. He campaigned, for example, for a balanced budget and a sound currency, which would have been disastrous; yet his appeal was that of somebody who would do something.

Franklin Delano Roosevelt, the wealthy poliomyelitis victim who was four times elected president of the United States, has many claims to be one of the greatest figures in American history, surpassed only perhaps by Lincoln and Washington. This is not mainly because of his contribution to the Allied victory in the Second World War, important though that was, but because he presided over the recovery of the American economy and the consequent revival of faith in American political institutions. It was the transformation of economic, social and political attitudes and institutions, which came to be known as the New Deal, that transformed capitalism. Taken together with the effects of the Second World War, a new social order was created which was so unlike capitalism – while having some common features – that it deserves a new name.

The New Deal was a confidence trick. 'The only thing we have to fear is fear itself' was Roosevelt's opening shot in the battle to revive confidence, and he succeeded in reviving it by a series of unorthodox measures. He took America off the gold standard and altered the basis of the currency and credit system, so that it was a managed currency – exactly the opposite to the system that Ricardo had recommended in England one hundred years before. Congress also passed laws to protect the reserves of the banks and to establish a proper central banking system. Thus the credit structure was able to resume activity, insulated from foreign crises. At the same time Britain and France had managed currencies, and Hitler (with his financial expert Schacht) had isolated Germany. International trade therefore depended upon a triangular arrangement between the banking systems of America, Britain and France, each economy successfully insulated by high tariff walls and import quotas.

The effective characteristic of the New Deal, and especially its first year, was hectic activity. It was as though governmental activity proved infectious. This reversal of the situation of before the First World War, when the less government activity there was the more business felt confident, was astonishing. What the New Deal actually did was to implement a number of policies, many of which were mutually contradictory. Roosevelt substantially increased expenditure on social security and welfare. The Public Works Agency increased its expenditure and was replaced by the Civil Works Administration and the Works Progress Administration which eventually, by the end of Roosevelt's second administration, employed one-fifth of the American labour force. The government also set about afforestation, soil conservation and other agricultural projects.

The National Recovery Administration effectively abolished the anti-monopoly laws and established codes of behaviour for different trades and industries. This policy was based upon a fallacy: industrial reconstruction could not succeed in reforming business when demand was so low. If demand picked up, organizational structures would change. This fallacy affected policy measures in Britain as well. But the Act, though it was soon declared unconstitutional, first embodied the principle of collective bargaining between trades unions and employers in American legislation. It also provided a body of administrators who were able to mastermind the rearmament programme which brought America into and through the Second World War. This defence programme became the basis of the post-Second World War Atlantic economy.

A similar fallacy was implicit in Roosevelt's Agricultural

Adjustment Act, which sought to control agricultural production and so to raise prices. Once more, although state regulation may have been necessary, since technological advances led to continuously increasing crops, and demand for food could not rise at the same rate, the juxtaposition of restricting output and hungry people represented a paradox that Roosevelt need not have accepted. Increasing demand would have revived agriculture and provided jobs in industry for surplus agricultural labour, as the experience of the Second World War showed.

Roosevelt's Social Security Act of 1935 marked a fifty-years belated conversion of America to Prussian social arrangements. It became a basis for modern society, because social security benefits provided a floor below which demand could not fall.

The clue to the New Deal, then, was in reviving public confidence rather than in its detailed measures. Its two successful measures, substantial public investment in public works, and a budget deficit, were not meant to be permanent and the latter – the deficit – was, indeed, unintended. Between them they boosted demand. This led to a tremendous revival of the economy. By 1937 output was above 1929 levels, investment was rising rapidly, unemployment was falling and prices were rising.

It was in 1937 that the test of New Deal pragmatism came. The recovery suddenly faltered. A great many of the New Deal Acts had been declared unconstitutional; the first *élan* of the administration had begun to wane and orthodox finance began to make itself felt again. Government receipts began to exceed government expenditures. Almost immediately unemployment rose again, prices fell, and investment (especially investment in stocks of raw materials) began to fall very quickly. By March 1938 it looked as though the depression might return in full force.

The international position was different, however. Germany was rearming at an increasing rate and had almost solved its unemployment problem. Britain had had six years of recovery and was also rearming. The international situation was tense, with civil war in Spain, Germany preparing to invade Czechoslovakia, and the Italians threatening their neighbours. Japan was advancing rapidly across China. In these circumstances, with an international currency situation that was tightly controlled, financial panics were now part of history rather than of present reality. The forces of inertia and inaction were no longer on the side of orthodox economics: they were on the side of countries that had decided to put foreign policy and armaments first.

Roosevelt decided to act, as he had acted in 1933, without closely considering the ultimate implications of his activities. He adopted deficit budgeting as a policy. He asked Congress to authorize a further big spending programme. The National Recovery Administration, and many other attempts at detailed intervention in the economy, were forgotten; Roosevelt decided to spend his way out of depression. This was the new orthodoxy. It was embodied in John Maynard Keynes' work, *The General Theory of Employment, Interest and Money*, published in 1936. Keynesian economics and armaments rivalry, together with scientific progress, underlay the new civilization. When Roosevelt began to rearm, early in 1940, he had an ideology at hand.

When he was inaugurated in 1933 the American economy was almost at a halt. In Europe, too, things were at their worst. Hitler was returned to power in just such circumstances. What Roosevelt did in his first hundred days (the comparison with the return from Elba to Waterloo might have seemed unfortunate), and in his New Deal, was to undertake a series of wildly contradictory actions, many of which worked, and for which a *post hoc* theoretical explanation had to be given. Roosevelt was not a Keynesian – regarding Keynes with hostility as an impractical theorist – but he accidentally undertook Keynesian policies, by massively increasing public expenditure, both on social welfare and on public investment, and by unbalancing the budget. This, together with his other measures to restore the confidence of the American people in themselves, 'worked' in the sense that unemployment fell substantially and that profits and prices recovered. How much of this was due to the normal recovery of the trade cycle, how much to Roosevelt, how much to international action (which was gradually reviving world trade on the basis of managed currencies and high tariffs) it is difficult to say.

What is important, however, is that Roosevelt represented the third possibility of recovery from the collapse of capitalism –

Hitler and Stalin being the others. He had the immense merit of being the leader of a great constitutional democracy and of using the power of the democratic state to restore the economy, to introduce welfare services and to recreate confidence. In essence what he did was not dissimilar to what governments were doing elsewhere – Baldwin and Chamberlain in Britain, for example – but it was the manner in which it was done that mattered.

In the American context Roosevelt was left-wing. Seen across the Atlantic it was easy to portray the Democratic Party as a social democratic party (which, of course, it was very far from being). Roosevelt was an orthodox liberal, somewhat to the right of Lloyd George, but he was represented as being almost socialist. His attacks on business orthodoxy, seen out of context, seemed socialist. The landmark of his administration that was seized upon was the Tennessee Valley Authority – the TVA – which used public investment to restore a derelict area. It became a place of left-wing pilgrimage. In fact the dams, the electricity generators, the housing, the soil reclamation, though important in themselves were a relatively minor part of Roosevelt's New Deal. But in the 1930s, when business orthodoxy was so tired and so dim, rhetoric and symbol was everything.

Similarly with Roosevelt's international policy. Until well on into 1940, America remained profoundly isolationist. Roosevelt, as a liberal patrician, was deeply shocked by Hitler and the other fascists, and he saw increasingly that in a world war America would inevitably be involved on the anti-Axis side. But he had to move circumspectly and extraordinarily cautiously. His rhetoric was important: he was given to peace moves, to appeals to Hitler, to proposals for conferences. What would have stopped Hitler would have been treaties and troops, but they had to wait until Hitler was foolish enough to declare war on America after the Japanese attack on Pearl Harbor in December 1941. Roosevelt earned, however, the entirely unjustified reputation of an active and ferocious anti-fascist, whereas poor Chamberlain (who, after all, did declare war on Hitler twenty-seven months before Hitler declared war on Roosevelt) was denigrated. The reason for this was that Roosevelt was the democratic hero and was assumed to have taken actions and positions that Europeans would have wished him to take. In this respect, the Republican attacks on Roosevelt for being both a socialist and an internationalist helped to invent a Roosevelt who never existed.

The significance of Roosevelt and the New Deal for the social democratic left was twofold. In America, apart from the communist conspirators there were hardly any socialists. To be on the left was to be a New Dealer. Elsewhere, to be a socialist meant increasingly to be a New Dealer, that is to adopt the policies, often imaginary, that were supposed to be part of the New Deal. Deficit budgeting, comprehensive redevelopment of depressed areas, social welfare measures, control of the banks and the Stock Market – all these seemed to be part of a socialist rather than a liberal programme. Partly this was due to the style of the New Deal which was essentially populist. Its verbal assaults on bankers were in the populist tradition; its zeal for the ordinary man was extraordinarily persuasive. Thus by 1936 or so a social democratic government that came to office in western Europe had a policy, and a model – Roosevelt's New Deal.

Sweden and Denmark

It has already been pointed out that Sweden and Denmark provided a model for social democrats elsewhere. Scandinavia was an island of security in the 1930s. With a long tradition of rural prosperity and constitutional rule, it consolidated a prosperous democratic system in the early decades of the twentieth century. Sweden, as a major industrial country, provided a model which reconciled social democracy with industrial progress. It suffered less from the slump than other countries, partly because its timber, wood pulp, and iron exports kept up both in volume and price, and partly because its economists devised, very early, counter-depressive measures. The great Swedish economists came (by another route) to the same conclusion as Keynes, that public expenditure could create employment. Sweden inherited a system of social security, on the Prussian model, which kept public expenditure up and like other Napoleonic countries it had a more than century-old tradition of major public works expenditure. When, in 1920, the Social Democrats became the largest party and formed a government, they had around them all the components of a post-Keynesian welfare state – pensions, a health scheme, an excellent education system, extensive public works – and it remained only for them to endorse the principle of unbalanced budgets. So successful were the Social Democrats in this policy that they were re-elected with an increased vote in 1921 and thereafter remained continuously in office.

Similarly, in Denmark a Social Democratic government was in office (in a coalition) from 1920, following essentially the same policy, though as Denmark had a very small industrial sector the agricultural policies of the government were central to its success. Denmark's agriculture rested upon a strong co-operative basis. By the use of co-operatives, and with state aid, Danish agriculture was kept technically ahead of the rest of Europe; and it was able to supply the growing British market for eggs, bacon and dairy products at decreasing prices.

Denmark, therefore, represented a rural society based on co-operative principles, utterly at variance with the collapse of industrial societies based on laissez-faire. The pure air of Scandinavia, the Oslo breakfasts of milk, fruit and eggs that produced tall, tanned, lithe, strong-toothed children, using well-designed wooden furniture and living in garden suburbs, all contrasted with the rickety, toothless populations that inhabited the hideous industrial slums of capitalist Europe. Scandinavia (like New Zealand) offered healthy living, with low infantile mortality rates and tremendous social and some aesthetic achievements.

The pull of the Scandinavian ideal cannot be over-estimated. Scandinavian health, education, social welfare, housing, and architecture – no mean indices of a standard of living – were streets ahead of the rest of Europe. That this was achieved by socialist governments, following non-orthodox fiscal and monetary policies, was no less important for other social democratic movements than were the achievements of the New Deal.

The Third World
Another alternative to authoritarianism was provided by Indian mysticism embodied in the highly political person of Gandhi. Gandhi was the first effective opponent of imperialism. And as imperialism had been defined as 'the highest stage of capitalism' by Lenin, it is important to look at it in the present context.

The Third World of developing nations, which was to play so large a part in the politics of the mid-twentieth century, was very much offstage in the 1920s and 1930s. The European colonial rivalries of the later Victorian years had gone, save for Hitler's rhetorical demands for the return of the German colonies sequestered at Versailles, and Mussolini's conquest of Abyssinia. Nationalism was chiefly centred in the successor states to the Austro-Hungarian Empire. In Africa and Asia it was barely stirring. The Chinese war lords were struggling for the control of China, Indian nationalists made periodic disturbances that got into the newspapers, but of general and widespread symptoms of colonial revolt there was no sign. According to Lenin, the colonial empires represented the source of profit to imperialist monopolists who had exhausted their profitable opportunities at home, and this was the accepted socialist reason for the existence of the empires. It was to remain the accepted interpretation, especially by the nationalists; indeed it was believed by the Labour British Foreign Secretary, Ernest Bevin, who was determined to keep bases in the oil-bearing Arab states in order to defend the standard of living of British workers. There is in fact little evidence that beyond the normal profits of trade there was any significant degree of exploitation of colonial empires by colonial powers. Political régimes and defence forces, as in India, were paid for by taxes on the indigenous populations; the French, especially, and to a lesser degree the British, particularly after the tariff reforms of 1931, gave advantages to their own businesses; the Belgian state and Belgian companies appear to have transferred funds substantially from the Congo to Belgium; but there was no evidence of general exploitation, in the sense in which treasure was looted from Latin America by the Spanish in the sixteenth and seventeenth centuries. Wages were low in Africa and Asia, but so was productivity. Minerals were extracted on a vast scale from South Africa and other territories but this was not in itself evidence of exploitation. The terms of trade of primary products fell as against manufactured products, but that was because of the depression. The export earnings of Africa and Asia were depressed. The falling prices of food and raw materials greatly helped those in the metropolitan countries who were in employment. On the other hand, the profits of businesses which dealt in primary products and those of the planters, the miners, and the agriculturists were diminished and in many cases eliminated by the falling prices.

What imperialism did was to establish firm and, to a degree, modern government, and to engender, by a reflex process, a series of nationalist movements whose purpose became one of taking over the government rather than one of sending the imperialists packing and reverting to pre-imperialist conditions. This was especially important in India, where large parts of the country were governed by British-protected princes, and in British Africa, where tribal chieftains and emirs also ruled directly, under British suzerainty. Modernization meant opposition to these rulers.

Indian nationalism had four aspects. One, which was unimportant, was agitation for greater independence by the princes, especially when they had been stopped from doing something outrageous to their own subjects. The second was opposition to British rule by modernizing politicians, often British-educated, who wished to take over the British functions. Third, there were modernizing politicians who were also socialists. These people, like Nehru, wished to use the British-created state to eliminate social evils (like untouchability) and to promote economic development. It was they who were represented as a major threat both to the British and to the Indian princes. Last, there were the religious leaders, like Gandhi, who wished to use the nationalist movement to lead India to a Tolstoyan, Utopian society which wholly rejected modern industrialism and which would be based on the simple life of asceticism, agriculture and handcraft industries. Though the Gandhians and the socialists made common cause, their aims were in fact in great conflict.

It was Gandhi who, by the doctrine of non-violent resistance, fasts to death, and the organizing of systematic unrest, became the leader of Indian nationalism. Despite the opposition of influential conservatives, both Labour and Conservative governments gave India considerable degrees of autonomy by 1935; but Gandhi and his supporters continued to work for complete independence.

By this agitation, Gandhi made two contributions to socialism: first, he brought the problems of colonialism and imperialism to the forefront of British opinion (there was no comparable shift in France), and secondly he offered a peasant brand of socialism to the world, which (by a process of assimilation) seemed to have more in common with social democracy than with communism. By 1936 the independence of India was in sight. The links between Indian and British socialists were close. It was possible that the developing world would choose socialism and not communism.

Thus nationalism, Gandhi's doctrines, and socialism came together in a blend, just as forty years before, vegetarianism, mysticism, Irish nationalism and socialism had been linked. The British left, especially, was anti-colonialist, because of its opposition to tyranny and its dislike of the governing class that found so much to do in the Empire. The old concept of radical imperialism had died, though it was very strong in France. The French Revolution had always been for export, especially since Napoleon's conquest of Europe; the French left remained convinced that France had a civilizing mission in North Africa, Central Africa, the Levant and Indo-China, and that a rise in the standard of living could be achieved by French state action. These radical differences of approach were to be revealed after 1945 when the British abandoned their Empire and the French fought to retain theirs.

9 War and peace

Spain and the Civil War

The development of social democracy in reaction to the slump has now been examined. The great test of industrial society turned out, however, to be not the slump but war. Rumblings of war – in Manchuria in 1931, in Spain in 1936, in Ethiopia in 1936 – all presaged the Second World War of 1939 to 1945. This was a war initially between democracies on the one side and Hitler on the other. Then Russia was invaded in 1941. Out of all this, new political and economic forms emerged of course. In many ways, however, it was not the slump, nor the Second World War, that was the big element in the development of the social democratic posture in the late 1930s and the 1940s, but the Spanish Civil War. That this was so was not because of Spain itself but because of the forces that intervened there. Spain became a symbol and a myth. The story of the civil war became a saga of the socialist movement – a saga that had something, but not much, to do with what actually happened in Spain.

In the 1930s Spain was a relatively backward and stagnant nation, socially and politically. Barcelona was the only really developed industrial city, and it was the home of a local nationalist (or federalist) movement, which had anarchist doctrines based on Proudhon, Sorel and Bakunin. In the 1920s the anarchists were attempting to crush industrial development. The constitutional monarchy was increasingly ineffective. Primo de Rivera, the military dictator, took over as a mayor of the palace and in the late 1920s, as world trade grew, Spain seemed increasingly prosperous and peaceful. The Spanish socialists had fought the usual struggle about communism and had not joined the Comintern. They supported Primo de Rivera and helped him to develop trade unions. Thus, in some respects, Spanish socialists were almost prototype fascists – national socialists, supporting a strong government, using the government to strengthen the trade unions, and supporting a national dictator. However, within a few years they were to join the other forces of the left in the civil war against Franco and the Falange.

In 1930 the king dismissed Primo de Rivero. In 1931 the monarchy itself fell and a Republic was established which removed some of the Church's privileges, expropriating (with compensation) some big estates and forbidding teaching by religious orders. In Spain neither the Church nor the army supported the constitutional monarchy and they detested the Republic. As the economy deteriorated with the slump, Spain increasingly fell apart. There were two brands of monarchists – Carlists, intensely reactionary, Alfonsists, slightly less so – and there were also fascists, drawing on the example of Mussolini (successfully governing a Latin country), the army (colonels and generals), the Catholic centre, the Communists, the anarchists, the regional nationalists, the traditional political parties, and the Social Democrats. In 1933 Primo de Rivera's son José entered politics, founding the Falange Español, which was fascist – believing in 'national unity', in violence, and in repression of atheistic communism (which included almost everybody who was not a militaristic, totalitarian, credulous Roman Catholic).

In 1933 a right-wing government came into power and began to undo the reforms; revolts broke out and the situation deteriorated rapidly. The Falange was small and powerless, until in 1936 the Popular Front of the left won the election against the Catholic-monarchist National Front. The generals and the Carlists plotted to overthrow the Republic. In this they were joined by the Falange. José Primo de Rivera was imprisoned and when the rising occurred in July 1936 he was shot. The Falange thus became the political expression of the revolting generals, though Franco became head of state without discussion with the Falange.

The overthrow of the Spanish Republic was, therefore,

mainly military. Yet to the outside world it seemed a part of international fascism, partly because Mussolini and then Hitler supported Franco, and because the communists, rallying to the support of the Republic, denounced the generals as fascists.

Even the phrase 'rallying to the support of the Republic' is untrue. The Republic in Madrid consisted of a socialist and liberal anti-clerical government. In Barcelona it was an anarcho-syndicalist Catalan nationalist movement. In Bilbao it was the Basques. By September 1936 the rebels held much of Spain, nearly to Madrid; by early 1937 they had occupied Malaga and much of the Basque country. Caballero, who had been Primo de Rivera's Minister of Labour, became prime minister in September 1936 and tried to organize a united popular front, to fight the army. Since the army had gone over to the rebels, resistance was sporadic and local; the central government had little power to order things to be done. It had to cajole. Above all, it needed arms; Caballero sought them from abroad. Germany and Italy supported Franco and the generals. The Soviet Union began to send some aid to the government. To stop the fight between fascism and communism being enacted through Spain, Blum, the French Socialist prime minister, appealed for a policy of non-intervention by all governments, especially not to supply arms. Britain, France, Germany, Italy, the Soviet Union and Portugal were among the twenty-seven nations that signed the Non-Intervention Pact. In fact, since Franco had the army, this was a heavily anti-government act. It was made more so by the fact that Italy sent armies to fight for Franco, and the Germans sent a considerable quantity of arms, especially planes and munitions. They also blockaded the Spanish ports so that the government could get few if any arms.

Socialists and democrats throughout Europe thought they saw a militaristic, mostly fascist régime of immense beastliness fighting and defeating genuine workers' armies, unquestionably led by brave socialists, anarchists and democrats. The propaganda against fascism was enormous; some young men went and fought in the International Brigade. What was less clearly seen was that the Communists were increasingly taking over the republican fight and that (as in Yugoslavia six years later) at least as much of their effort went into destroying socialists, anarchists and Catalan nationalists as in fighting the fascists. These people were denounced as Trotskyists, since it was the height of the Stalin terror in Russia. Thus in Barcelona, at the time of the greatest Basque struggle, there was a bitter fight between the anarchists and the Communists. The Communists seized the opportunity to demand central control of the war – which meant their taking control – and Largo Caballero fell from office, to be replaced by Negrín.

Gradually, in one heroic battle after another, the non-fascists were defeated, until by February 1939 Franco was victorious. The republican leaders fled. Their supporters were imprisoned and murdered by the hundred thousand, and refugees were herded into camps on the French frontier.

What the world saw was that a socialist government had been attacked by the fascists who had been supported by the army, the Church, the landowners and the business classes. Fascists from Germany and Italy had sent massive support. Right-wing governments elsewhere had boycotted the Republic and had established the conditions by which it was bound to fail to equip its army. The people of Spain had nevertheless fought heroically, assisted by foreign comrades in the International Brigade. What the world did not see was that the republican front had been a congeries of factions and that the Communists had behaved ruthlessly towards their rivals. They saw the Soviet Union as a major supporter of the Popular Front government and not as a vindictive partisan of Stalinism against other left-wing parties.

In 1939 came the Nazi–Soviet pact. For two years Hitler and Stalin were allies, but after Hitler's invasion of Russia in June 1941 this period was forgotten. The rise of resistance movements to Hitler's occupied Europe recreated the Spanish War: as had been the case in Spain, the resistance fought an unorthodox guerrilla war and did so as part of a Popular Front, including all anti-fascist elements and especially the communists.

The Spanish Civil War thus showed socialists that unity with the communists was possible. It showed informed socialists, like Orwell and the Labour Party, that such unity could be used by the communists to take over a popular front. It showed uninformed socialists that the only defence against fascist capitalism was a popular front.

The Second World War

When the Germans and Russians invaded Poland in 1939, and the Russians invaded Finland a little later, the long-threatened war broke out. The communists denounced the war as a capitalist conspiracy, and in the occupied areas of Poland and Finland the social democrats were among the first to be arrested. Thus, though Hitler's régime was evil and his aggression beyond reasonable doubt, for a considerable part of the left the war did not at first have an ideological content. This absence of ideology was partly explained by the absence of war – a virtual lull until April 1940, so that it seemed to many people that it was just the First World War resumed, a matter for generals and Foreign Offices. In ten weeks, between early April and later June, 1940, however, the whole context changed. The Germans occupied Denmark, Norway, Holland, Belgium and France. Italy came into the war. All the countries occupied were liberal democracies, several of them with social democratic governments. The war changed its character overnight. It seemed as though the fascist countries, with the tacit support of the communists and the Soviet Union, would conquer all Europe. Social democrats like Blum were among those early arrested.

In Britain, the Labour Party rallied to the defence of the country, and was instrumental in arranging for the resignation of the Conservative prime minister, Chamberlain (branded as 'the man of Munich', whom all parties had applauded vigorously only twenty months before), and the succession to his office of Winston Churchill. Thereafter, for a year, the British fought the Germans and Italians virtually alone. The communist newspaper *The Daily Worker* was banned because of its pro-German sympathies but, such people apart, the country was virtually united in its opposition to the Axis powers. The war went badly, despite the British victory in the Battle of Britain. In early 1941 the Balkans were lost and there were defeats in North Africa. The sea war (the Battle of the Atlantic) was almost lost, too.

This period of the war was of great importance for social democracy. In Europe resistance was organized by social democrats and liberals, with communist opposition. The later version that was put about, that the communists organized the resistance, was wholly untrue. In Britain, the Labour Party took some of the most prominent departments and was largely responsible for domestic policy – Ernest Bevin at the Ministry of Labour, Herbert Morrison at the Home Office, and Clement Attlee as deputy prime minister. As we have seen, in the process they and their colleagues, and the temporary civil servants who came in with the new government, invented what was to be known as the welfare state, and British industry was also wholly taken over by government regulation.

The process was an important one because the Labour government elected in 1945 adopted the whole wartime pattern of government intervention as its own, and what happened in the war was largely identified as social democracy. Virtually all the resources of the country were devoted to a common purpose. If the purpose were peaceful, it was argued, then all social and economic problems could easily be solved. The fact that all the national resources could be used depended on a remarkable spirit of national unity: the wartime coalition government was a genuine coalition and not a 'National' government, as the government of 1931–40 had been, which was predominantly Conservative. The national unity rested upon a principle of conscription of property and manpower: few, if any, individual rights were regarded as absolute. Yet at the same time a remarkable degree of freedom of expression was guaranteed. Allied to this was a sharp reduction in poverty, and a rise in living standards of the manual working class, associated with full employment, improved welfare benefits, price control, and food rationing. Public expenditure rose to unprecedented heights, without catastrophe, and many ordinary people felt better off. There was, too, an Owenite simplicity of life and thought that was sedulously encouraged by the radio and by the films and press. It seemed like an ideal socialist state – plain living, high thinking, fairly prosperous, united, well groomed and reasonably free. The British entered into a period of well justified self-congratulation which was to become the Labour Party's substitute for an ideology.

The disasters of the war, which were compensated for by the sense of being the only nation that was actually fighting Hitler, were intensified by the German invasion of its ally, Russia, in June 1941. The German armies conquered the whole of the Ukraine, the Baltic republics, and White Russia, parts of the Caucasus, and invaded Russia itself. Had Hitler not been so utterly xenophobic it is possible that the republics that were occupied would have welcomed him as a liberator. Large parts of the population undoubtedly did so, until his occupying forces showed themselves to be as brutal as the Stalinists. The immediate effect of the invasion of the Soviet Union, however, was to switch communist propaganda to a tremendous attack on Hitler and whole-hearted support for the war. In December 1941 the Japanese attacked Pearl Harbor and the war became virtually world-wide. Until the end of 1942, after the victories of El Alamein in Egypt, of Stalingrad and of the Midway Sea, it looked as though Germany, Italy and Japan were winning. Thereafter, slowly through 1943, and with ever growing speed through 1944, the victory of the Allied Powers was assured. Strange allies – the increasingly social democratic British government, headed by the anachronistic but brilliant Churchill, the New Deal American government, headed by the ageing Roosevelt, and communist Russia, headed by a tyrant, Stalin, whose excesses were at least as bad as Hitler's, and possibly, in terms of the numbers he killed and his long-term consequences, worse.

In Europe the underground was increasingly penetrated by the communists and in countries like Yugoslavia and Greece a great deal of the fighting was between communists and non-communists, rather than against the Germans. This produced fundamental problems later, because the social democrats were identified by communist propaganda as pro-fascist, even on occasion pro-Hitler. In France and Italy, on the other hand, 'popular front' liberation movements developed. Again, the communists for the most part seized control, and the social democrats were to be placed in the awkward position of having to assert themselves against the communists, which (objectively speaking) would mean that they would be forced to choose the anti-communist side. This side would have in it elements that remained pro-Nazi, which after June 1941 was something that drove the communists to frenzy.

From 1943 onwards, the leadership of the European social

democratic movement was seized by the British Labour Party. The Swedes were neutral and so their influence was negligible. The British Labour Party was winning the war and intended to win the peace. Retrospectively, this represented an immensely formative period.

In foreign policy, Labour was in favour of granting independence to India and of positive colonial development policies in Africa that might, in two or three generations, lead to African independence. European socialists were thus committed, morally, to colonial development towards independence. This was to put the French socialists into difficulties over Algeria, for the British had few territories in their possession where there were large numbers of white settlers, of some generations' standing, in the midst of an indigenous population. Labour thus fervently supported the idea of the United Nations, which, in contrast to the League of Nations, was to have power to maintain peace. Its power depended on the unity of America and Russia. This unity, which occasionally took the form of ganging-up against Churchill, was strengthened by Roosevelt's optimism about Stalin. But a curious role, which was pure fantasy, was evolved for Britain by the social democrats. Labour, it was held, was ideologically half American and half Russian. Socialism implied collectivism economically, as in Russia, and liberalism politically, as in America. Britain would thus be the honest broker. It could also interpret the world to the two great continental empires of America and Russia, because the British were a 'sea people', with contacts, through their Commonwealth (as the Empire had become), with all races and all places. This lunatic notion, totally disregarding the reality of Russia's tyranny, of Britain's weakness and total involvement in the future of the United States, became the dominant motif of social democratic theorists, the basis of the Common Market (rapidly captured by French technocrats and German industrialists), and the ostensible reason for the attacks on Bevin's postwar foreign policy of forging links with the United States.

Domestically, Labour favoured the continuation of wartime economic controls, except over labour, and the extension of public authority by nationalizing coal, electricity, gas, transport and steel (the so-called 'basic' industries). Especially it was in favour of bulk purchase of imports, bulk purchase agreements on trade with other countries, and the continuation of food and raw materials rationing. The major landmark was the adoption by the government and the Treasury of Keynes' economic policies. A government statement on full employment endorsed the principle of maintaining the level of demand by fiscal action, including unbalanced budgets. Thus Labour's policy was one of high taxation, using the budget as an economic regulator, low interest rates (the war was financed at three per cent), and physical controls over many aspects of economic life.

Socially, the coalition government accepted the Beveridge scheme of social insurance, designed to end the Poor Law, and the conception of a National Health Service, and it initiated in the Education Act of 1944 a major programme of educational reform. Thus Labour's domestic social policy was almost all derived from the war. It was later to be shown that the wartime dislocations had only been acceptable because of the response of public authorities in actively coping with the resulting personal crises. For example, the hospital services were nationalized in the war, to cope with air-raid casualties, and it would have been impossible to unscramble them at the end of the war. The social security system had to deal generously, quickly and efficiently with the wives and children of men at war, with evacuees, and with innumerable other cases. A return to pre-war attitudes was impossible.

When the war ended, the impression was widespread that it had been won by 'social democracy' in action.

Wartime and the world economy
The progress of the war illustrated the thesis that peace was indivisible, a thesis enunciated by Litvinov, the Russian Commissar for Foreign Affairs, in the abortive negotiations to prevent war. Its outbreak clearly refuted the hypothesis that war was an extension of monopoly-capitalist imperialism. The war was between communists and nazis, capitalists and fascists, democracies and totalitarian states, with alliances formed accidentally between those attacked and those doing the attacking. The only common features in all these combats were the expansionist aims of the three countries, Germany, Italy and Japan, which had militarist-fascist dictatorships, the inability of other

states to join together in defence, and the rivalry between the communists and the democrats, seen most strikingly in Spain, and then in the German–Soviet pact of 1939. There was more in common between Hitler and Stalin than between the capitalists in Germany and the capitalists in Britain. To describe the war as a struggle between monopoly-capitalists is a fantasy.

Yet the war completed the end of traditional capitalism. It led, first of all, to the end of the traditional international monetary system. The British, especially, sold some of their overseas assets (during the year that they fought alone, from June 1940 to June 1941) and accumulated large overseas debts. The Americans, on the other hand, became creditors on a massive scale. Thus the conditions for recommencing international trade after the war were, first of all, an international system of payments started *de novo*, at the Bretton Woods Conference, with the establishment of the International Monetary Fund, and secondly the use of the American surplus to extend credits to other trading partners on a systematic basis, which occurred through the Marshall Plan. Thus international trade ceased in any sense to be regulated by an automatic mechanism.

Internally, even in countries of extreme laissez-faire philosophy, the anti-slump measures were developed, in the process of rearmament and of total conflict, into an almost all-embracing system of governmental control. In Britain, where this process extended furthest, there was direction of labour and consumption affecting almost the whole labour force, control of prices, rationing of consumer goods, allocation of raw materials, and government determination of the final output pattern. The war was financed on Keynesian principles, partly by saving but mainly through very high taxation, so that the inflation was very small. Interestingly enough this enormous increase in government intervention led to little diminution in the standard of living. Full production and full employment were achieved, and for many working-class families adequate incomes were received for the first time. The capacity for output at full employment seemed, by pre-war standards, prodigious. At the same time what came to be known as 'the welfare state' was in fact invented. Whole sections of the population became entitled to welfare benefits and medical care to which they had previously not been entitled.

The situation in America was even more astonishing. By 1943, ten years after Roosevelt's inauguration in conditions of economic collapse, American output levels were higher than ever before, levels of real income were higher than ever before, and the output of war *matériel* and the size of the armed forces were without parallel. Thus government control plus the capital equipment and skilled labour force of a post-capitalist economy could achieve extraordinary output levels. The same was even true of Russia, the country that suffered most from the war. Despite the 'scorched-earth' policy, which destroyed virtually all capital equipment in the areas captured by the Germans, despite millions of deaths, output levels in the Soviet Union remained surprisingly high, and though there were grave shortages of all kinds, some sort of economic existence continued. It looked as though Keynes was right and that the problem of production was solved provided government intervened sufficiently and ensured that demand was high enough.

Managed international trade and managed economies therefore followed logically from the war. So, too, did the welfare state. Once it was seen that the output capacity of the economy was such that none need be paupers, and that government support could supply the necessary income in cash and in kind, the European countries moved over to comprehensive social security programmes and systems to provide free or heavily subsidized health care. Britain lagged behind Europe and the United States in social security (largely because of its extremely conservative trade union movement), but it led with its free comprehensive National Health Service.

The political consequences of the war were tremendous. First, the new international alignments, following the destruction of German and Japanese power, were centred on America and Russia. The postwar era was to be a Cold War, occasionally hotting up, between these two systems of alliances. The old empires which had survived the First World War – the British, French and Dutch – collapsed, the most notable event being the independence of India in 1947. To an important extent the capitalist assets and political interests of the imperialists in the colonial territories were taken over by the United States, lending some verisimilitude to the Russian charge that the 'liberation' of the colonial territories was merely an episode in an inter-imperialist struggle. On the other hand, the Russians succeeded to the imperialist heritage in the Balkans and eastern Europe and took far more open political control there than the Americans did anywhere, except in South Korea and South Vietnam. A power struggle between military alliances was a more plausible description of what was happening than an inter-imperialist conflict.

Within these new alignments, socialism and communism had a new status. Communism as a world power, based on Russia and China, might be tyrannical and inefficient, but it obviously worked well enough to threaten the military conquest of the world. Socialism was a vague and often contradictory creed (like most creeds), but it was the accepted creed of many postwar governments, from Britain to India, from France to Mexico. Moreover, especially in western Europe, much of their social and industrial legislation became a permanent part of the legislative code of their countries. Partly this represented a full recognition of working-class parties within the political system, but it was also a rejection of the older capitalist ethos. Pragmatism with respect to the role of government in society was associated with an inner conviction that government action was almost inevitable in conditions of crisis. This was a reversal of capitalist ideology, so complete as to justify the abandonment of the word.

Finally, once again the war enormously accelerated technological and scientific development – radar, missiles, nuclear weapons, penicillin are all examples – and in the Cold War the scientific-military establishment became institutionalized. It developed a logic and a path of development of its own, dragging governments and the economy after it. Wernher von Braun, who had tried to destroy London for Hitler, sent Americans to the moon. The American economy was organized round Wernher von Braun. So was the Russian. Capitalism was over, and the age of science had arrived.

The Labour victory and European socialism
On 26 July 1945 the results of the election held three weeks earlier became known in Britain. For the first time Labour had won an overwhelming electoral victory – 365 seats – though

less than half the total votes cast. It was probably the biggest boost that social democracy had ever had. The great war leader, Churchill, was dismissed. A clean break with the past was indicated. Wartime socialism was to be used to win the peace.

Throughout Europe a similar pattern showed itself. Social democrats were in office in Scandinavia. They entered governments in France, Italy, Belgium, Holland, Czechoslovakia, and in other eastern European states. Labour, as the government of the leading victorious country of Europe, was the leader of what looked like an international tide.

Its initial policies were clear. In important respects they were never changed. The 'rethinking' of the 1950s was a revision of an orthodoxy that was established in 1945; and that orthodoxy was an endorsement of wartime policies. (Socialism, not diplomacy, now became war by other means.) The Labour Party's first job was demobilization. This demobilization took an astonishingly long time – over a year longer than in the United States – allegedly because of a shortage of shipping, but in reality because 'fairness' dominated everything. A scheme was worked out by which a combination of age and length of service released people from the armed forces. Fairness was more important than speed. This preoccupation with fairness ran through many Labour policies. Rationing of food, clothes, raw materials, petrol, and some other commodities was maintained, often at lower than wartime levels and at considerable sacrifices of consumer satisfaction, because it was 'fair'. In Europe, on the other hand, rationing broke down, both because there was a large agricultural population who ate and sold as they liked, and because, in the war, to evade regulations was the mark of a patriot.

An additional reason for slow demobilization was the fear of a slump. After a brief boom, the First World War had been followed by an acute depression as wartime demand fell off; a similar reaction was expected in 1946. In fact the opposite occurred. The pent-up demand for goods was enormous. It was added to by the collapse of the continental European economy: aid had to be given to Germany and to some of the Allied countries. A world dollar shortage developed. British and European exports had collapsed. The United States and Canada became the major suppliers of food, raw materials and manufactured goods. A major loan from the United States and Canada was negotiated for Britain. A condition of the loan was free convertibility of the pound and dollar in mid-1947. This was a critical decision. Not only did it tie the British economy irrevocably to that of the United States but it made clear that the nature of the tie was to be on the basis of the Bretton Woods agreements on the expansion of world trade. The socialist arguments for bulk trading agreements between governments and for a tightly controlled autarchic economy were doomed. Since eastern Europe was forced by the Soviet Union to adopt this path, the Iron Curtain was created by different international trading procedures. This determination of the trade pattern was endorsed by the Marshall Plan which, though available to eastern European countries, was rejected by them on Russian orders.

Economically, then, the trading arrangements adopted in 1945 and 1946 committed Britain to the restoration of a market economy. But meanwhile the wartime controls were perpetuated and a peacetime administrative apparatus was constructed entirely on a wartime model. This provided a strong contrast with Europe, where the peacetime administration (except in Scandinavia) had been run down and the wartime administration was unacceptable. Social democrats in Europe were collaborating with communists in some cases and liberals in others to create new institutions. These institutions could not rest upon the high degree of detailed control that was adopted in Britain because the mechanics of government were not adapted to their efficient functioning. The problems in Europe, were also of a different order. In Germany and Austria, the country was divided into four occupation zones and the economy had collapsed. In Italy, too, the economy had virtually collapsed. In France, the country was functioning, but only just, and hardship was widespread. In eastern Europe there was widespread destruction and poverty.

Therefore, what Britain did seemed to continental countries to be both unattainable – an ideal – and remote from the European reality. In Europe the real question was whether the existing political system would be replaced by a communist régime. In areas occupied by the Red Army, the communists were dominant. In Italy and France they provided an alternative to the temporary régimes that prevailed and an alternative that might be voted in at any time. In Britain the Communist Party was minute, though its influence in some trade unions was important and some of the Labour Members of Parliament were also under-cover members of the Communist Party.

The Labour government initiated a programme of nationalization. First were the Bank of England and the airlines. Then followed coal, railways and some road transport, gas and electricity. All these activities were already heavily controlled by the government, so that the immediate impact of the change was small, especially as the vesting dates (January 1947 for coal, January 1948 for the railways) were some time in the future. A similar pattern of nationalization occurred in many European countries, where the consequences, as in Britain, were few. In France some of the banks and some manufacturing industries were included. In Italy, the state remained in the field of industrial development, using Mussolini's state finance corporation for the purpose.

Labour continued the Herbert Morrison policy of arranging the nationalized industries under state corporations, which resembled in most respects the larger privately owned corporations. There was no worker participation, as there would have been under syndicalism, and there was no consumer control, as in the co-operative movement. It followed that the vast bureaucratic organizations running big industries had few friends – the private industrialists disliked them, and the socialist organizations distrusted them. As most of the industries (except electricity) that were nationalized were making heavy losses, it was inevitable that nationalization would very rapidly become a potent source of unpopularity for the Labour Party. Socialists were angry at the large compensation payments made to the private shareholders; taxpayers resented the losses; the workers found that the managers they worked under were the same as in private ownership. It was indeed unfortunate that immediately after the nationalization of coal there should have been a very severe winter. The country ran out of coal, electricity supplies were cut, everyone was cold and millions were thrown temporarily out of work. Labour never really recovered from this disaster.

On the social side, Labour carried on wartime reforms which set a pattern for Europe. It was, indeed, a pattern that in many respects was improved upon by the Europeans. First, in 1946, the National Insurance and National Industrial Injury Acts were passed which, for flat-rate contributions, gave flat-rate benefits to the retired, the sick and the unemployed. (Family allowances had already been instituted by the coalition government.) Then the National Health Service Act was passed, providing a comprehensive, free medical service for the whole community, including hospitals, general practitioners, drugs, dentistry and preventive services. These Acts came into force on 5 July 1948, but already, by early 1946, they represented the hallmark of social democracy. The 'welfare state', which provided universal free benefits in health and welfare, was opposed to the old conception of benefits only for the poor; the universality implied both equality and 'fairness' – or fraternity. To the rationing system, with everybody getting the same small quantity of meat, sugar, fats and clothes, was added equal old age pensions, equal health care, and a stab at equal housing, for the Labour government initiated a big local authority housing programme designed to provide the majority of houses in the country.

Thus by 1946 the Labour government's domestic programme was clearly outlined. Its foreign policy was already radically shifting. Labour had been elected as a mediator between capitalism (the United States) and communism. Ernest Bevin, the Foreign Secretary, maintained the Anglo-American alliance, and it soon appeared evident that there was no wish on the part of the communists to maintain the Anglo-Russian alliance. The details of this period are still obscure but the main outline of the story appears to be that Stalin determined to hold on to his gains in eastern Europe, to eliminate the social democrats there, and to try to capture the countries of western Europe not occupied by the Red Army through internal subversion. Thus in 1946 the Communists withdrew from the French government. In Germany, four-power control rapidly dwindled into an eastern zone occupied by the Red Army to which Britain and the United States had limited access, and three western zones that were administered within an allied framework. The Labour government determined 'to keep America in Europe' at any cost, since (in their view) the Versailles Treaty and the League of Nations had been wrecked by American non-participation. Thus, both financially and in foreign policy, the Attlee government planned to keep closely in step with American foreign policy and, far from Labour being an intermediary between capitalism and communism, to make America and Europe the adversaries of communism.

Euphoria and crisis

The election of the Labour government in Britain in 1945 was the high point of social democratic euphoria. Though many of their aims – prosperity, the substantial elimination of poverty and wider educational opportunity – were to be achieved, they were to be achieved, not by the introduction of socialism, but by social reform, in a world deeply divided by the issue of communism.

Ernest Bevin's attitude to communism was affected by two major experiences. The first was his defeat of communist infiltration in his trade union, the Transport and General Workers' Union. He had experienced every type of conspiracy to capture the union, including practices later to be revealed in court in the Electrical Trades Union case. Bevin's second experience was in foreign policy. The Greek communists had captured the Resistance in Greece and had used their success to try to overthrow the régime which had returned with the British liberation of Greece in December 1944. A civil war broke out, with British troops helping the non-communist government. When Bevin continued this policy after July 1945, with clear evidence of a communist determination to make Greece a communist republic by any means, he was subjected to every kind of vilification, especially by the Communists and their allies in the Labour Party. By late 1946, with the Red Army not demobilized and with the American troops almost all returned to the United States, the British troops alone seemed to defend Greece and Turkey against communist invasion. The invasion would no doubt have taken the form it subsequently did in Hungary in 1956 and in Czechoslovakia in 1968, of helping the local communists to restore order. But the threat seemed real enough. The British government therefore reaffirmed continually the need to defend Europe against communism.

1946 was therefore a curious year. On the one hand was the euphoria of victory. Rarely in modern times had a régime been so utterly defeated as Nazi Germany had been. The defeat had been followed by substantial electoral victories for the socialists almost wherever elections were held. The restoration of Europe, it seemed, would be a rebirth – a rebirth of a socialist Europe. The full horrors of Stalinism, which propaganda had suppressed during the war, were as yet almost unknown. The general public, and especially the politically conscious, hoped for a rapprochement between the socialist governments of the West and the communist governments of the East. Formally the governments in eastern Europe were coalitions, built round a strong Communist Party, but still coalitions. Familiar social democrats were in office, especially in Czechoslovakia – Beneš and Masaryk – and Rumania and Bulgaria were still monarchies with young kings. It seemed as though all countries would become Denmarks or Swedens, if luck held and goodwill was not thwarted by vested interests. That was why Bevin seemed to many to be the evil genius of socialism, for it was he who constantly spoke out about the conditions in eastern Europe and about the plans of the Soviet Union to subvert and possibly to invade the West.

Bevin seemed the odd man out. Yet in Greece the Civil War raged. In Palestine, too, the Jews sought to expand the area of Jewish settlement. The Arabs protested. Bevin supported the Arabs, allegedly because he feared for British oil interests in Arab countries. It seemed that, despite the Labour government, the Foreign Office was exerting all its powers to exercise a non-socialist foreign policy, and that President Truman, who succeeded Roosevelt in April 1945, was swinging America into supporting British imperialism. Though it was the declared policy of Labour to give India independence, there was great difficulty in finding an agreed successor government since the Muslims and the Hindus could not agree on a unified state. Thus, internationally, it could plausibly be argued that Bevin and the Labour government were deliberately preventing world peace and socialism from achieving a just triumph.

The early euphoria of economic recovery, helped everywhere by demobilization and the overcoming of some of the more gross of the problems left by the war, was giving way to a slowing up and then a regression into chaos. Britain ran first into an acute problem of fuel supplies, which revealed the more general economic difficulty of continuous pressure of too much demand on limited resources. Underlying this difficulty was the balance of payments problem. Before the war Britain's imports had always exceeded its exports but the difference was usually made up by earnings on overseas assets. Many of these assets had been sold to finance imports during the war and very substantial debts had been built up. To meet the gap between imports and exports it was now necessary for Britain to limit imports and to step up exports. This determined the whole economic strategy of the Labour government. The pound became convertible in 1947, and within a few days the run on the reserves was so great that convertibility had to be stopped. It was, in the circumstances, impossible for Britain to adopt a 'socialist' economic policy, since imports were almost at a minimum and hope of trade with the devastated Soviet Union was illusory. A 'socialist' economic policy of high production would have required higher imports of raw materials. Many raw materials were not available and the rest could not be afforded. The European problem was a different one: the industrial structure of France, Italy and Germany was so disoriented that chronic imbalance developed. These imbalances could to some extent be overcome by imports, though with the world shortage of food and raw materials it was impossible to overcome the more desperate problems. By mid-1947 the situation looked almost hopeless. There was a growing feeling that the communists might win the Italian elections and that the big French Communist Party would be able to take over France. On the other hand, the European economic problem was different from Britain's, because once the pump had been primed, their overseas earnings position looked far more favourable.

Britain's balance of payments difficulties precipitated a solution to the problem. After the fuel crisis, in early 1947, the Labour government told President Truman's administration that it could no longer afford to maintain substantial forces in Greece to protect Greece and Turkey. President Truman then enunciated 'the Truman doctrine', which the communists identified as the beginning of the Cold War. This doctrine implied that the Yalta settlement, made in 1945 between

Russia, America and Britain, which divided Europe into spheres of influence, could not be overthrown and that the Americans would rearm and station troops in Europe in order to prevent Soviet aggression. This dramatic reversal of American disarmament represented a triumph for Ernest Bevin. His principal fear, that the Americans would withdraw from Europe as they had done in 1919, was allayed. The Americans were now involved in Europe. This meant ultimately that social democrats abandoned the notion of building a bridge between America and communism.

Some of them had abandoned the notion already. Throughout Europe, however, some social democrats allied themselves with the communists. This happened in Italy and France. A number of fellow-travellers were expelled from the Labour Party. Thus in France and Germany the left was predominantly communist, while in Britain, Holland and Scandinavia it was social democrat. The non-fellow-travelling social democrats (except in Sweden) were pro-American; and this meant that the pro-American splinter groups in France and Italy were allied with the growing centre parties against the left.

There had been a significant resurgence of moderate Catholic parties in Europe. After the war, with the disappearance of extreme right-wing, pro-fascist organizations, the moderates had formed parties on the basis of a religious, democratic, radical programme. The Christian Democratic Party was one such in Italy; the *Mouvement Républicain Populaire* was a similar formation in France. One simple point may be made here about these bourgeois parties: they were anti-communist. As the Cold War intensified, one of their major attractions was their anti-communism. But as the historian H. R. Trevor-Roper has remarked, before the Second World War the bourgeoisie supported fascism because it was anti-communist. These Catholic and liberal parties were not fascist. Their ideological basis was remarkably similar to that of the Labour Party. It was anti-communist but it supported the idea of an organic community based on generous social services. In Italy and France the Christian Democratic Party and MRP were supporters of a considerable degree of government intervention in the economy. Above all, they were democrats and supported republican democratic institutions. When the social democrats allied themselves with the Christian Democrats, therefore, they were not (at that period) allying themselves to laissez-faire parties.

In Germany the situation was to be different. There, the Communist Party was to be both illegal and unpopular, because of its behaviour in the Soviet occupation zone, where Ulbricht, the Communist dictator, was one of the worst Stalinist tyrants. The Christian Democrats became convinced supporters of laissez-faire (though initiating a very significant structure of social security). Therefore, in what was to become Western Germany, the social democrats were opposed to the Christian Democrats.

Thus, in western Europe as a whole, there were parties in office which had similar views, but in France and Italy they were Christian Democrats, with moderate social democrat support, while in Britain and Scandinavia they were social democrats. It was this situation that caused the communist parties to regard the social democrats as lackeys of the Christian Democrats whom they saw, in turn, as American capitalist-front parties. The drift to supporting 'capitalism' was, however, a later phenomenon of christian democracy: in 1947 and 1948 its orientation was towards a Labour Party type of government, especially in the field of the social services. It was Adenauer and Erhard who, by liberating Germany from its complex system of economic controls, subsequently created the 'free enterprise' boom of the 1950s – the so-called German economic miracle – which made christian democracy pro-capitalist.

In 1947 the German economic miracle was far away. The communists were consolidating their power in eastern Europe and it seemed as though they might gain France and Italy. An invasion of Greece seemed possible, despite the Truman doctrine. As the year wore on, economic difficulties intensified. It was in this context that the American Secretary of State, General Marshall, spoke of a recovery programme for Europe, supported by the United States but representing a co-operative multilateral effort by the European countries, including the Soviet bloc. His idea was enthusiastically endorsed by Bevin. Negotiations began. Eventually, despite a wish by Czechoslovakia and Poland to join in, the European Recovery Programme – known as the Marshall Plan – was initiated for all western European nations. The mechanism was that the United States paid dollars into a pool in Europe. European nations also made contributions to this pool and withdrawals were made to support programmes for recovery. Thus, for a nation like Britain, the actual aid was zero; the dollars from the pool covered the dollar deficit in the British balance of payments, while the pounds put into the pool by Britain covered the other nations' pound deficits. The principal recipients of aid were Western Germany, France and Italy.

By the end of 1947, Western Europe had set out on two paths, both in close alliance with the United States. Rearmament was the first, and this was to culminate in a co-ordination of arms policies through the North Atlantic Treaty (NATO). The second was economic recovery through the European Recovery Programme (the Marshall Plan) which entailed a systematic dismantling of trade restrictions between European countries and between Europe and America. These two programmes set the pattern for the 1950s.

European social democracy, therefore, had to fit into a picture of increasingly close relations with the United States, both militarily and economically. It faced, too, a dramatic intensification of Stalinism in Eastern Europe. Squeezed between these two giants, far from being a bridge, social democracy became a chasm of empty ideology and failing policies. Its social and industrial policies existed on the bounty of America and its very survival depended on the American nuclear umbrella.

The Cold War

The introduction of the Marshall Plan in 1948, and American rearmament, saved the western economy. But 1948 was dramatic in other respects. The Cold War became a terrible reality. In Czechoslovakia the Communists created a terrorist state, and with Masaryk's suicide or (more probably) murder, it was clear that no social democrat could survive in a communist régime unless he recanted. In Hungary socialists were executed after a sham trial, and elsewhere in eastern Europe the socialists were imprisoned, or disappeared. The Greek Civil War was virtually ended, with victory for the monarchists. Significantly helping this victory was the fact that Yugoslavia – a supply base for Greek Communist guerrilla fighters – defected from Stalin's empire. Thus, for the first time since Trotsky was expelled from the Communist Party, the Stalinists split.

The Yugoslav developments followed an increasing number of defections from communism. Arthur Koestler and others published innumerable books and articles explaining why they had left the Communist Party. Some became Roman Catholics or Quakers. The defections were dramatized by developments in the United States where it was revealed that a network of communists had worked for many years in the Federal government and conspired to overthrow the United States. It became an era of the unmasking of spies – the Rosenbergs and other atom spies, and Alger Hiss – leading increasingly to a strongly anti-communist spirit which reached its extreme form in Senator McCarthy's campaign against liberal democrats who had sympathized with causes that were now known to have been infiltrated by communists. Distasteful though the campaign was, it has to be said that there was evidence that communists had infiltrated many liberal organizations, though there was little evidence that they had been successful in affecting public policy as a result.

For socialists, the most significant causes of defection were given by those who claimed that Stalin had perverted communism. They drew attention to the Russian oppression of other nationalities: this was primarily the cause of Tito's Yugoslavia's break with Stalin. They spoke of the terrible tyranny in Russia – the shooting and exiling of millions of people, of the purges and the Stalin terror, of the incredibly arbitrary nature of Soviet rule. Above all, Stalin threatened the world with a renewed war. He was a man for whom little could be said.

His acolytes, who were many, said a lot: they denied that Stalin had aggressive intentions, despite the clear evidence of Czechoslovakia. That they explained away by saying that the Czechs wanted it and that Stalin was forestalling an American move to 'liberate' eastern Europe. They denied that there were persecutions in Russia. They denied that there was anti-semitism.

The socialists who were deceived were many, and they were chiefly to be found in countries with large communist parties. The social democrats proper reaffirmed their belief in democratic, constitutional, representative government. They aligned themselves with America. Two things then occurred that were important. The first was the siege of Berlin – a four-power zone in the midst of Soviet-occupied Germany – by the Soviet occupation forces. It was decided by the American, British and French governments to run an airlift into Berlin. This was done. It dramatized both the threat of communism and the military response that was necessary to deal with it. The immediate cause of the siege was the establishment of the German Federal Republic in 1948, to cover the three western occupation zones. In the general election the Christian Democratic Party gained a major victory, with the Social Democrats as the opposition. This victory represented the beginning of a major electoral recession of social democracy throughout the West. It was followed by a dramatic improvement in the German economic performance and by a steady diminution in the reputation and standing of social democratic parties.

The year 1948 marked, then, a major development in the Cold War – the organization of the West around America, both for defence and for economics. President Truman, to everybody's astonishment, was re-elected in 1948, but America had decisively shifted its position towards militant anti-communism. It had shifted because of China (where the communists were in the process of driving Chiang Kai-shek, America's ally, off the mainland), because of Berlin, because of what was happening in eastern Europe, because of spies within – because it all added up to a threat that the Soviet Union was about to embark on an aggressive war to conquer all Europe, as China was being conquered. Voices were raised to suggest a pre-emptive atomic war against the Soviet Union. Bertrand Russell was one of those who held that it was highly necessary to defeat communism, at almost any cost, before communism had the power and the ability to send atomic bombs to the West.

In this situation, the choices were agonizing for socialists. Should they support the tyrannies of Russia or the capitalists of America? Book after book tumbled into the bookshops arguing that the Soviet Union need not necessarily have gone sour. It was due to Stalin. Stalin, in turn, was due to the isolation of the Soviet Union, beginning with allied intervention in favour of the Whites in 1919, followed by the *cordon sanitaire*, followed by the postwar Anglo-American alliance. This highly selective reading of history, which ignored the Comintern, the Nazi–Soviet pact, and the occupation of Europe east of the Elbe by the Red Army, made a great impression, especially in Yugoslavia and India.

India was emerging as the light of the East. In 1947 the British had withdrawn from the Indian Empire and two successor states had been established – India and Pakistan – whose inhabitants had fallen upon each other with terrifying ferocity. More than a million people were killed in less than a month. After this slaughter, India set itself up as a sanctimonious, secular, socialist state, led by Pandit Nehru. Its brand of socialism owed a great deal to that incompatible trio of Tolstoy and the Webbs. Gandhi was an old-fashioned, Tolstoyan, vegetarian pacifist. He was convinced – and others were too – that India had become independent of the British because passive resistance had driven them out. This happened, unfortunately, not to be true. They had withdrawn because they were bankrupt and could not afford an army to occupy India, because of American pressure, and because the Labour Party sincerely believed in self-determination. Yet Gandhi, who was almost immediately assassinated, started a myth, which was to be very potent, that passive resistance would be more successful than armed resistance to invasion. If this were so, then the Cold War could be fought with spiritual and costless weapons.

Thus India, home of passive resistance, became a socialist Mecca. Its role, taken over from the British Labour Party of 1945, was to be a bridge between communism and capitalism. A great many left-wing economists were hired to draw up innumerable and conflicting plans for industrial development, agricultural improvement, educational advance, taxation reform, expropriation of the rich and endowment of the poor, birth control and health reform. The bureaucracy swelled to an enormous size. As Gunnar Myrdal, one of the most enthusiastic advisers, was to point out in 1968, nothing happened. Mother India continued unchanged, traditional to the last, and defeated in war by the Chinese and the Pakistanis. But in 1949 socialist euphoria was at its height; the only regret was that the Webbs were dead. They would have loved it.

George Orwell was one of those who, faced with the reality of Stalinism in the Spanish Civil War in 1937, had chosen democracy. His view hardened as the Second World War developed and pro-Soviet propaganda became dominant on the left. Modern technology and the absence of any moral restraints had given a socialist state total power over its inhabitants. Not only could they be thrown in jail, tortured and executed, as they had been in Germany, Italy and Russia, but their very existence could be denied. History could be rewritten, as Soviet history was rewritten to exclude Trotsky and other unpersons. People could only live, work, marry and have children by permission of the state and the party. Unlike medieval Catholicism or other earlier tyrannies, the twentieth century was yielding to a tyranny of a drab industrial kind with no redeeming features. Its art was despicable; its social tone typified by the ration card, the queue, the overall as a uniform, the factory with its endless canned music, mass recreation. In such a society, the very ideals of socialism – of diversity and equality, of freedom and fraternity – were meaningless. His two books – *Animal Farm* and *1984* – enunciating his view of the Soviet horror, were the authentic voice of English socialism. Yet the alternative, an enthusiastic prosecution of the Cold War, seemed to imply a wholesale adoption of Americanism. America which, periodically, had been the Golden Land of the left – especially under Roosevelt – had now become a McCarthyite ogre.

Yet it had to be admitted that it seemed as though capitalism was overtaking social democracy. While Britain was rationed and poor, Belgium had recovered without rationing. Travellers' tales of steaks, silk stockings and American cars brought sneers to the lips of the English, accustomed to look upon Belgium as a Breughelesque mixture of vulgar hedonism and working-class neglect. But the German economic miracle was beginning to work. Despite the Marshall Plan, the British economy faltered; in 1949 a major devaluation was necessary. Rationing continued for years after the end of the war. In early 1950 the Labour government was re-elected, but with a tiny margin of a majority. It looked as if the end of social democracy was at hand. Europe, far from copying the Labour government, as seemed probable in 1945, was reviving under American guidance and with free enterprise.

A major philosophical shift was occurring. Though the Labour Party had identified itself with rationing, detailed control of the economy, and fair shares, its theorists had argued that the duty of a social democratic government was to ensure full employment and an equitable distribution of the national income. Thereafter the price mechanism would ensure that consumers' satisfaction was maximized. This thesis, advanced in the 1930s by Abba Lerner, was now proposed in Britain by James Meade and Arthur Lewis. A more confused writer, Barbara Wootton, had advocated 'planning'. But planning had been identified with detailed bureaucratic control; an alternative was a long-term strategic view of the economy. But this long-term view was tarnished by the echo of the Soviet Five-Year Plan. There seemed no middle way. *The Economist* newspaper, edited by Geoffrey Crowther, advocated an alternative: maintain full employment and let the economy rip. But full employment should be defined as rather more men competing for rather fewer jobs. In contrast, then, to the socialist price theorists, Crowther would have maintained as 'full employment' what would have entailed a degree of unemployment which was unacceptable to the Labour government and the trade unions. To adopt this policy, however, seemed to lead to two difficulties – an internal level of demand that caused the threat of continually rising prices and wages, and a pressure of demand that continually drew in imports at a higher level than export earnings could finance. Both tendencies, the price rise and the import propensity, were contained only by severe physical controls over the economy. These controls included a prices and wages freeze, rationing, raw material allocation, and a paraphernalia of controls that were increasingly avoided and were increasingly arbitrary and inefficient. 'Set the people free' became a powerful slogan which was offset by the fear that if Labour left office, mass unemployment would return and the welfare state (especially the National Health Service) would be dismantled.

The Labour Chancellors of the Exchequer – Sir Stafford Cripps and Hugh Gaitskell – adopted a version of Keynesian control of the economy that had two defects: it did not work and it was electorally unpopular. If the total demand on resources was estimated to exceed the resources available, then the budget surplus was used to deflate the economy. Since the total demands on the economy continually exceeded the available resources, taxes were always being put up. There was a steady rise in output but the rise was masked by continually increasing taxes. As Europe became more prosperous it seemed ironical that one of the victors should still have rationing while in the rest of western Europe petrol, food, and other goods should be freely available. The situation was worsened, in 1950, by the outbreak of the Korean War.

The American and British governments undertook vast rearmament programmes, the first effect of which was a rapid rise of prices of primary goods, which adversely affected Britain's import bill. The second effect was a big increase in public expenditure for defence. This led to a further Gaitskell budget to raise taxes and a cutback in welfare services. It seemed as though the Cold War had not only led to a postponement of Elysium; it was now leading to a dismantling of the welfare state.

At this point the leading representative of the left wing of the Labour Party, Aneurin Bevan, who had been Minister of Health, resigned, together with two acolytes – Wilson (later to become prime minister) and Freeman (to be given various diplomatic appointments by his co-resigner). Cripps and Bevin died. The Labour government dithered on until, in October 1951, it was narrowly defeated at the polls by Winston Churchill and the Conservatives.

Thus, western European socialism lost its leading socialist government. Its achievements were solid – full employment, a welfare state, a move out of Empire and a Western Alliance. But other European countries, notably Germany, achieved all these without a reputation for sanctimonious austerity and mindless bureaucratic controls. And it rapidly became apparent that Labour, by keeping Britain out of a European federation and involving it in enormous military programmes, had left a legacy which was to handicap the country for at least twenty years.

Managerial capitalism

The end of the war and the immediate period of dislocation was followed by a burst of production the like of which had never been seen. By 1950 world output levels attained unprecedented heights. International trade revived. Full employment was maintained. Productivity rose to record levels. The devastation of the war was fully repaired by 1952, although armaments expenditure was only slightly reduced from its wartime levels. Above all, political stability was established throughout the world (compared with the interwar instability) in régimes of all political types.

In this context, what did 'capitalism' mean, if anything? The communist dictatorships lumped together all the American allies, and the benevolent neutrals, as capitalist régimes. What was their characteristic?

Many of them had parliamentary systems, which varied in effectiveness, but there were some dictatorships (notably Spain, Portugal and the Latin American military dictatorships). In the major countries, Germany, Italy, France, Britain, Canada, America, as well as the smaller western European states, the parliamentary régimes were associated with personal liberty, freedom of speech and freedom of movement. This was in striking contrast to communist and fascist régimes. The liberal tolerance that marked the countries of western Europe and North America, and their associated states in Australasia and Japan, was a creation of capitalism, and almost uniquely associated with it. To the extent, therefore, that political liberalism was synonymous with capitalism, the West was capitalist.

It was capitalist in another sense. Despite the extension of state ownership of industry, especially to public utilities like railways, electricity and coal, the bulk of industry and commerce was in private hands. It was from this private sector that the greater part of the rise in productivity came. The achievements were prodigious. Agricultural output, for example, rose so rapidly as a result of technical improvements in food production that the western countries achieved food surpluses by the mid-1950s, even in conditions of full employment when demand was high. Europe passed through a housing boom greater than that of the United States in the 1920s. Above all, the output of consumer durables – cars, television and radio sets, laundry equipment, kitchen equipment – increased by leaps and bounds. There was a transformation of the standard of living. Many of the products and services were new, and rested upon steady technical progress in many fields. The older industries – coal, steel, railways – were gradually either run down or their output growth slackened as new industries took their place. Chemicals, plastics, light engineering based on aluminium and new alloys, electronics, and biologically based products represented the new advances.

Industry (and the very rapidly expanding service sector) took new organizational forms, and these were what came to be known as managerial capitalism. Industry tended to organize in federations and trade organizations, to negotiate with government and the trade unions. Competition, in significant respects, was replaced by co-operation. This was represented most dramatically, perhaps, in France in the French planning system. The industrialists, civil servants and trade unions in an industry proposed targets for their output, and negotiations took place with other industries to see that the supplies of materials, capital goods and skills, and markets for the final goods were available. While it was probably the case that what caused the effective modernization of France was the continually rising demand for final goods, springing from the steady inflation of the currency under the Fourth Republic, the co-operation of the state and industry did not slow up technical advance and probably helped it.

Though much technical progress was due to small firms that grew rapidly as they exploited new markets available for new products (Xerox is an example), the typical postwar firm was an international giant corporation, with thousands of employees and shareholders and a professional management. It was the characteristics of these firms that caused the term 'managerial capitalism' to be invented.

The firm was an entity in itself in which it was possible to serve, as in a church or an army, for one's working life, to give absolute loyalty, and to expect in return care and concern for one and one's family for a whole lifetime – death and retirement benefits, care in sickness, housing, medical care, education, and a sense of personal worth based on an identification with the firm's ideals.

The firm ploughed back its own surplus and rarely turned to outside sources for capital. The shareholders, a transient body, consisting often of insurance companies, pension funds and other institutional investors, were treated as *rentiers*, expecting a conventional return, and in no serious sense the 'owners' of the firm. The firm had obligations, it was said, to see that its shareholders were fairly treated, but its true obligations were to its employees, its customers, and to society in general. A 'good' firm would therefore offer its employees steady employment in good conditions, for good wages, and it would expect in return considerable loyalty. It would go to great lengths to encourage democratic consultation and participation especially in industrial relations.

It would sell a product, or a series of products, that it genuinely believed to be an essential element of the good life.

In the market that came into existence, depending on advertising, and with competition between different products rather than between prices, the atmosphere of insincerity indissolubly linked with over-assertion was palpable. But, to the outsider, the 'company man's' belief in his product seemed obviously sincere and (to be fair) it was often justified.

The firm owed a duty to the community. Its executives would serve the government voluntarily (as Macnamara left Ford to become Secretary of Defense, or Catherwood left British Aluminium to serve the National Economic Development Office); they would encourage science and the arts; they would encourage youth movements and provide welfare facilities for the communities where their factories were.

Underlying this was a philosophy of responsible management. The management of the firm often had little or no financial stake in it. They served it for a salary. Their self-respect depended on recognition of their disinterested service for the company and its ideals. Management became a profession with its own codes of behaviour, its own education and training process. The emphasis was on responsibility to workers, the community and to customers (with shareholders as an afterthought).

The similarities to the great professions of medicine, law and the Church, were obvious, and so, too, were the similarities to the civil service and the army, with their selfless anonymity, their concept of service to the community rather than self-aggrandizement, and of a balanced and objective approach to all questions.

It was this type of man, in this spirit, who dealt with the

postwar problems. Their astonishing success in raising productivity, in solving social problems and in beginning to tackle international political questions, was the dominant feature of the 1950s and the early 1960s. Managerial capitalism was not capitalism. It also had its flaws. It ignored the real problems of the poor countries, nationalism, and the loss of morale among the really poor in the affluent countries.

Was it still capitalism?

Scientific advance dragged the world along after 1945. No sooner was a discovery made than attempts were made to see whether it had any conceivable technological applications. The finance for the development was always forthcoming, usually from government. Once the development had occurred, it was exploited. A new market was invented (as for television) and rapidly saturated.

Thus the original ethic of capitalism had been reversed. Far from the market initiating the conditions for technical progress, the opposite occurred. Technical development led to a market.

Capital no longer sought solely profit, but rather, a variety of objectives, of which the security and responsibility of the firm were the chief. A big corporation, like US Steel, or Ford, or Imperial Chemical Industries, closely resembled a publicly owned corporation, like the National Coal Board or the *Société Nationale des Chemins de Fer*. Its capital came from internal sources, and its profits were used for further investment and research. *Rentiers* accepted a conventional return.

The market was managed by advertisers and mediated through large chains of retailers. Price competition ceased to exist as a major means of transmitting market decisions.

Above all, government took a central role in three key areas. First, in promoting scientific research and technological development, often as a byproduct of military endeavour. This was the engine of the economy.

Next, economic development depended on the skills and education of the labour force. This was almost wholly a governmental responsibility. The astonishing recovery of Germany after the Second World War, and the development of Japan, for example, owed everything to the skills of the labour force.

Thirdly, as social problems revealed themselves, only governmental agencies could attempt to cope with them. The western civilization, based on huge conurbations, spread throughout the world. The whole east coast of North America, from Washington to Boston, the west coast from San Francisco to San Diego, Chicago, London, the Rotterdam complex, the Ruhr, Paris, Milan, Tokyo – all these great conurbations generated social problems on a terrific and terrifying scale. Crime, traffic control, ghettoes with hideous slums and acute poverty among immigrant groups, lawlessness, riots, drugs – all these represented threats to the postwar order. Private initiative could offer palliatives but it was widely agreed that a major programme of social reconstruction was both inevitable and desirable, and that only public bodies could achieve it.

Thus the role of government, in promoting science and technology, providing education and coping with social breakdown, was central to the economy. In addition, the corporate ethic and its liberal political counterpart seemed to be worthy but irrelevant.

There was, first of all, the problem of the developing countries. Two thousand million people lived outside affluence, and they were neglected by the concept of managerial capitalism. It would require international effort to raise their living standards, and their political struggles threatened constantly to disturb the delicate balance of terror between the American and Russian alliances. This was a geo-political problem to which managerial capitalism seemed irrelevant. Its solution – not a once-for-all solution, but a working through its problems to some sort of constructive and positive action – depended on international action at a governmental, political level, on much the same lines as the scientific-military complex tackled the problems of the arms race. Indeed, all proposals for coping with the Third World of underdevelopment depended on some analogy with the military-scientific approach to strategy.

Next, as the managers comforted themselves with an ideology of benevolence, students and the disenchanted denounced it as paternalistic and as a manifestation of the rationalist, technological outlook which had come to dominate the world, and which, in their view, was destroying it literally (because of the probability of nuclear and biological warfare) and metaphorically, because of the deterioration in the quality of the culture and its increasingly mechanistic nature which had destroyed the springs of originality, freshness and vitality.

The most telling point was that in many respects Russian society and western society were similar. The corporate identity, the dominance of science and technology, the culture – all had strong common features. There were grounds for calling the new society the scientific-military society.

The major difference was a significant one. Though under attack, liberal politics survived, battered but still upright. It was uniquely associated with capitalism. If capitalism meant liberalism, then there was a case for saying capitalism was still going on. But if the communist states could go liberal (as Czechoslovakia and Yugoslavia seemed at one time likely to do) the case would fall. Liberalism would be a political concept independent of the forces of industrial ownership and control, and capitalism would pass into history.

10 Rethinking

The attempt to redefine socialism

The Labour government's narrow defeat in the 1951 general election had marked the end of the wartime brand of social democracy. The era of world shortages of food and raw materials was almost over. The Cold War was a well-established fact. In a significant sense, the wartime socialist high tide had receded. Adenauer and the Christian Democrats were in office in Western Germany and the *Weltwirtschaftswunder* was underway; economic miracles led to a reassessment of capitalism in its new and successful form.

There were several aspects of society in the 1950s that called into question not only wartime socialism but the very concept of democratic socialism itself. There was, first of all, the problem of the Soviet Union. Despite the persistent tendency of people on the left to blame the 'capitalist' powers – especially America – for everything, the undeniable horror of Stalin's Russia became daily more apparent. There was tyranny in eastern Europe, followed by the violent crushing of the Hungarian revolt in 1956 by the Soviet armed forces. Krushchev's speech at the Twentieth Congress of the Soviet Communist Party revealed that even communists knew of Stalin's tyranny. And there were good reasons for believing that in essentials Russian communism had not changed. On the other hand, from about 1958 to 1967 there were signs of a 'thaw', both internally and externally. And, in addition, the first Russian spacecraft, Sputnik, suggested that authoritarianism of a Soviet kind was compatible with high technological and possibly scientific achievement. The split with Yugoslavia in 1948 and with China later, suggested that communism was becoming far less monolithic; the suggestion even developed that, as Soviet society 'matured', it would become far more like the technocratic, military, capitalist society of North America. Since socialism defined itself by reference to communism, a change – whether actual or perceived – in the nature of communism meant a change in the nature of socialism. It would be held, for example, that, though socialism should take steps to prevent the emergence of a Stalin, it should also try to see that a Sputnik should be produced. Could democratic socialism create the conditions for massive nuclear weapons, for interplanetary flight, for the hideously expensive investment needed to rival Russia's technico-military achievements?

The second aspect of society in the 1950s that was important was the transformation of the United States. The election of General Eisenhower as president in 1952 and his appointment of John Foster Dulles as his Secretary of State led to a phase of militant, verbal anti-communism, which seemed to confirm the switch of America's posture from the left of world politics to the far right – a militant defender of capitalism that was prepared to use and to maintain right-wing authoritarian régimes in office in order to stop communism. Thus socialism, far from adopting the American posture on world affairs as it had tended to do in Roosevelt's time, was tempted to define itself as a more moderate alternative to communism.

This was most obviously seen in the Third World of the developing countries. India and Pakistan became independent in 1947; Ceylon and Burma followed; then the Middle East. In the mid-1950s this independence movement spread to Africa. Through the United Nations and regional organizations the Third World declared itself to be 'non-aligned', neither pro-Russian nor pro-American. Its acceptance of quantities of American aid, and of lesser amounts from the Soviet Union, represented no ideological commitment; it was the payment, rather, of conscience money by the rich to the poor. Since Dulles was in the habit of claiming that everyone who was not for him was against him, this had the effect of making the Third World seem pro-Soviet, especially when, as in Africa, the metropolitan country (in that case France) waged war against the insurgents. It was in the American interest to support its NATO allies; it became, therefore, simple propaganda for the Soviet

Union to support the nationalists. In addition to this identification of the nationalist cause with the anti-Western cause, another factor had to be taken into account. Countries as diverse in social structure, religion and economic development as India, Egypt and Indonesia declared themselves to be socialist countries. This socialism of the Third World involved nationalism, strong central government, a high degree of economic planning, and (in principle) the expropriation of the large landowners and industrialists. In all these countries the problems of the landless peasantry loomed large, and socialism came increasingly to be defined as a conscious attempt, by use of the state, to improve the conditions of the rural poor. This also involved an attack on international companies, often of American or British origin, which appeared to dominate particular areas of the country or sectors of the economy, or to monopolize foreign trade.

'Right-wing' socialists like Gaitskell inclined more towards America and became violently anti-communist while 'left-wing' socialists like Nenni inclined violently against America and more towards the Russians. Socialists therefore were forced to react to the Cold War, aligning increasingly with the concerns of the socialist Third World, and especially with the prime minister of India, Pandit Nehru. Socialism came to mean the development of international institutions which would reallocate world resources to ensure the rapid growth of the economies of the poor countries. It meant, increasingly, the struggle for colonial freedom and for racial equality. Racial discrimination in the United States, apartheid in South Africa, the struggle in Algeria and Vietnam – all these became symbols which were socialist symbols, as the Spanish Republican cause had once been.

But perhaps the most profound effect on socialism was that caused by full employment and rapid economic growth in western Europe and North America. The rates of growth of the German, Italian and French economies were without precedent. Japan, with growth rates occasionally reaching nine per cent a year, was outstanding. Even Great Britain and the United States achieved growth rates that were remarkably high compared with earlier periods. National incomes per head doubled over periods of ten to fifteen years. World trade grew even faster. This was achieved in economies that were neither capitalist, in the laissez-faire sense, nor socialist in the Moscow sense. They had big welfare budgets. France especially had a national planning system. They sought to achieve full employment, generally speaking, by fiscal and monetary means (though both Germany and the United States eschewed unbalanced budgets). International machinery was created to make world trade flow as freely and smoothly as possible. Big companies and nationalized corporations worked side by side, and in terms of management and labour relations were indistinguishable. The firms, the state and the trade unions seemed to collaborate and not to fight.

Two important books defined the new society – Andrew Shonfield's *Modern Capitalism* and J. K. Galbraith's *The Affluent Society*. Both made the point that the socialist diagnosis of capitalism was no longer relevant. Whatever it was, modern capitalism was not a society that waged imperialist war within itself. It did not impoverish the working class. It did not run into constant problems of unemployment and misery. On the contrary, it led to rapid economic growth and mounting prosperity; the very existence of the social services depended on prosperity.

The socialist case could not rely, therefore, on the grounds that common ownership of the means of production, distribution and exchange was necessary for prosperity. The communist countries, on the contrary, where nationalization prevailed, were drab and impoverished: a modern industrial power like Czechoslovakia had clearly slipped back since it was taken over by the communists. Gaitskell, therefore, who succeeded Attlee as leader of the Labour Party in 1955, sought unsuccessfully to make it drop its vestigial socialist commitment to this kind of economic policy. The German Social Democratic Party dropped its commitment. The Socialist International – the meeting of social democratic parties – sought to redefine socialism.

It did so in terms of the struggle for social and radical equality, the desire for peace and the desire to build up the public outlays on health, education, welfare, and the environment, to use the affluence of modern industrialism to create a more adequate and satisfying life.

It is this thesis – which was the Gaitskell thesis – that was to be adopted as the main socialist theme. Its inadequacy, the 1960s would reveal. That its philosophy was one for civilized men could hardly be doubted. Its practice was, however, another matter.

Equality and poverty

Socialism meant equality, so Crosland and others held, after the process of revisionism had gone far enough to cast doubt upon public ownership of the means of production, distribution and exchange as the basis of socialism. What were the causes of inequality and, more pragmatically, what were to be the means of moving the world towards greater equality? Those were the socialist questions.

Inequality had many dimensions. It could be inequality between races, between sexes or between generations. It could be inequality of status, as between slave, serf and freeman. It could be inequality of incomes, or inequality of capital, or inequality of social status. Thus it had to be defined and measured before it could be explained. For this measurement and assessment Crosland turned to the social sciences.

As has been seen, the social sciences had an important role in socialist theory and practice. The earliest socialists, from Proudhon, Marx and Comte onwards, claimed that their socialism was 'scientific' – that is, that their analysis of the course of events was objectively true and corresponded to scientific criteria of observation and analysis. But a new group of sciences – calling themselves social sciences – had now grown up with economics and psychology as the prime examples. To Marxists these were not sciences at all, but apologias for bourgeois society.

Socialists differed from Marxists in accepting the methodology of the social sciences, whether in economics, psychology, sociology, social anthropology or statistics. The methodology was rooted in statistical and mathematical techniques, with emphasis upon accurate observation and upon the importance of the validation of prediction. In the course of the development of these 'scientific' social sciences, the place of social and political philosophy, of moral and aesthetic judgement, tended increasingly to be cast as mere value judgements. The implication was that the social sciences were neutral tools for discerning the truth, that judgements about society were matters of individual choice, which could not be objectively discussed and which were, indeed, often mere rhetoric.

If socialism were scientific, therefore, it implied an acceptance not only of the methodology but of the findings of the social sciences. If Marx predicted increasing mass unemployment in capitalist economies, and Keynes explained what caused mass unemployment, then Keynes' work was more socialist – because more scientific – than Marx's. Marx became merely another exploded scientist, whose tomb was erected on the long highway of scientific truth. Socialism thus became identified with social engineering – the manipulation of society, on the analogy of engineering, to attain given results. But what results? How were the targets to be set?

One appealing answer lay in the argument that certain values – truth, justice, kindness, compassion – were implicit in certain modes of life, and that the patient unravelling of complex social problems would enable difficulties to be worked through in detail, which would enable people to contain social evil. It would be hard to deny that in many respects life had become more tolerable because of patient investigation: that pedagogy, medicine, penology, for example, were immeasurably more effective and more humane because of the application of scientific methods. The use of general statements – such as that 'human nature will never alter' – was purposeless, because such assertions could only be understood in particular contexts, when they would be seen to be absurd. The patient, step-by-step approach to social questions was a way to enlarge the area of human choice, since it made what happened to people more open to rational discussion. In such a context, steps toward more equality, or towards greater social justice were not part of some grandiose scheme for human improvement, but rational choices, dictated by humane criteria, in highly specific contexts. Often, desirable aims would be in conflict and it would be necessary to trade off gains in one direction against losses in another.

The question for socialists, then, was not so much the ends as the means. The ends – equality, justice, freedom – resolved themselves (in the detail of any situation) into the humane alternative. Did the totality of these choices add up to a consistent pattern of social action, involving the use of the power of the state, that might be called socialism?

The sociologist Richard Titmuss would have answered the question affirmatively. Because the problems showed a consistent pattern, it was almost axiomatic that solutions to the problems would show a consistent pattern of response.

What was the consistency of the problems? It seemed that study of the problems of poverty and deprivation suggested that growing national incomes – the economics of affluence – created distress at a rate possibly as fast as it was alleviated, distress which was different in form but similar in nature. It was as though industrial society had a centrifugal tendency; as development took place, those at a disadvantage were flung out and fell through society to the bottom. In industrial societies there were the elderly, the mentally and physically handicapped, oppressed minority groups like blacks, widows, children from large families and all those, who because they owned no capital and could not earn very much, if anything, became the 'poor' – the absolutely and relatively deprived. Further, as change accelerated, the number of victims of change increased; there was, thus, a constant tendency for the number of deprived people to increase. Thus inequality could be seen as a function of change. Change itself – industrialization and automation – acting within the social context of bourgeois institutions, thus became the systematic cause of inequality, suffering and injustice.

The response to these problems was a growing network of publicly-provided social services. In the first place there was a growing political pressure from the underprivileged for the redress of their ills. There was also a growing body of professional people who wished to exercise their skills free from the pressures of the marketplace – doctors, teachers, social workers – and whose professional judgements involved radical reallocations of resources. To deal with an accident victim, for example, many thousands of dollars worth of medical skills would be needed, and then he and his family might need social security payments for many years, rehousing and other social provisions. Whether the accident was incurred in war, or in employment, on the roads, or at home, might affect his legal status as a claimant of insurance benefits but his social needs were the same. Only the state, it was argued, could make this provision to the victim whose rights sprang from his needs and not from the legal status of the accident that caused those needs.

Thus it was that the violent changes of the Second World War were cushioned by the growth of public provision. This public provision was based on equal treatment of equal needs; the socialist principle of to each according to his needs was therefore adopted; and this entailed progressive taxation – from each according to his ability. The growth of the social services was egalitarian; and to sustain them, the public ownership of the profits of industry and trade was essential. Whether the profits came directly by nationalization, or indirectly by taxation, was almost immaterial. That, roughly, was the egalitarian case.

The affluent society

The affluent society was geared to rapid growth. It was a society with a high propensity to invest, and it was this high level of investment which explained the full employment levels achieved. Even in the occasional periods of slackening of growth, unemployment rarely rose above four per cent in the United States, which was the industrialized country with the highest unemployment levels and which measured its unemployment in such a way that it was always apparently several percentage points above that of the rest of the world. The national income per head rose rapidly and this led to much higher consumption expenditure, especially in the income-elastic areas of consumer durables. For the industrial world outside the United States the 1950s were the years of the car, the television, the washing machine and the refrigerator. There was a dramatic improvement in housing and in the standard of clothing, food and holidays of ordinary people. In the United States, the most prosperous country in the world, many millions of people were sufficiently rich to live in a way hitherto confined to the upper-middle class. Nor was it true that the social services were neglected. Education expenditure rose to 5 to 7 per cent of the gross national products of most industrial countries. Expenditure on medical services was largely publicly subsidized and reached 4 to 6 per cent of the gross national product (it was lowest in Britain with a comprehensive National Health Service and highest in the United States with a substantial private sector). Social security benefits, especially in France and Germany, rose rapidly, on a basis closely related to earnings. Only in Britain, often regarded as the most left-wing of the industrial countries, were social security payments substantially on a flat-rate benefit basis.

The economic underpinning of this affluence was high investment. High investment was determined by high profit rates, which in turn depended on rapidly and steadily rising demand. This depended, in turn, on rapid rises in wages and salaries, which were guaranteed by the full-employment conditions that prevailed, in which employers could usually grant wage rises without pricing their products out of the market. Demand was also kept up by rapidly growing international trade, a growth that was accelerated by the successive measures adopted internationally to reduce or abolish tariffs, quotas and other obstacles to trade, as in the General Agreement on Tariffs and Trade and the tariff-free areas like the European Economic Community. Growing public expenditure, especially on social welfare, and steady expenditure on defence, also kept up demand. In such conditions there was a rising demand, especially for housing, consumer durable goods and services (particularly transport); this led to rising investment, and this high rate of investment led to accelerated technological progress.

The firms that provided this high investment and fast technological progress were unlike the businesses which had built up capitalism. In the first place they were often very big and international, employing many thousands of people and hundreds of millions of dollars of capital in many countries. They did not compete as the neo-classical models said, where many small firms offered the same product, but by offering different products, whose sales they ensured by vigorous advertising and selling effort. Nor were they, like traditional entrepreneurs, concerned mainly with maximizing profits. Rather, there was a division of ownership and control. Hundreds of thousands of shareholders were scattered throughout the property-owning classes: many of them held shares indirectly through pension funds, insurance companies and mutual funds, few of them had long-term loyalties to the firms in which they had stock; when the price of shares fell they sold; when the price rose they bought. The management of the companies was in the hands of a professional class of managers, for the greater part salaried, whose loyalty was to the corporation as such. This loyalty was to make the company grow in size and reputation; to market a product of high repute; to serve the public weal by disinterested service; and to be good employers. The net surplus of the country was thus distributed between consumers, workers and stockholders on an equitable basis. The large corporation behaved in fact as a public trustee; and its corporate philosophy was almost indistinguishable from that of the publicly owned body or nationalized industry.

It followed then that modern capitalism was welfare capitalism. The corporations sought steady markets, co-operated with the state and were good employers. They produced sound products and they invested in long-term development and research. In such circumstances to talk of the class war seemed preposterous.

In the 1950s American thinkers pronounced the end of ideologies. Increasingly, as prosperity achieved by high investment, scientific research and technological innovation affected country after country, it would lead to a growing assimilation of ideas and attitudes. The Soviet Union, Europe, America, would all live in a materialist society, using the same artefacts and strangely similar in ideas and outlook. The class war would be over and so would the Cold War. The role of the state would be to provide social services and an economic infrastructure. This might be a public planned economy as in the Soviet Union; or a semi-planned society as in France; but it would in fact be indistinguishable from America.

Two sorts of objection existed to this view. One was the protest of the Third World, that it was excluded from this prosperity, and (along with blacks in the United States) it was prepared to fight for its rights. The other was the challenge to the weight of materialism. Galbraith and others asked what sort of society was being created? It was the creation of useless object after useless object. Consumers' needs were invented by advertising; perfectly usable objects were thrown away because advertising made them obsolete; all spiritual life was atrophied. Meanwhile, the good life depended on public outlays on education and culture, and on preserving the natural and historic environment; and the poor stood outside the gates of the city of affluence. The balance of public and private spending needed to be radically changed.

This became the slogan of social democracy. Socialism returned to its primitive roots. It was against affluence.

Socialism and the Third World

In the context of the growing Vietnam War, and the profound changes which had taken place since 1945 throughout the formerly colonized areas of the world, socialism tended to be increasingly defined in terms of the needs of the developing nations. These nations found western-style political institutions fitted ill with their circumstances. Many of them became military dictatorships; some, like Algeria, became 'people's democracies' on the Cuban or Yugoslav model. These régimes required solidarity and intense nationalism, and opposition was met by imprisonment, exile or death. Many of the régimes adopted hostile attitudes to each other; there was the perennial Arab–Israeli conflict, wars in Africa, the Vietnam War, the Indo–Pakistan War, and military confrontations in south-east Asia. All these wars had to be 'contained' for fear of sparking off a Russo–American nuclear war.

Within each country, except Cuba, Algeria and a handful of others, the military régimes tended to stop short of radical redistribution of the land, nationalization of domestic industry, and other measures of socialist development, and tended as a result to be dismissed as American puppets by their opponents. There was little doubt that some régimes were installed by the Americans and maintained in office by them – the Dominican Republic and the Saigon Vietnam régimes being instances – but elsewhere it seemed that America had become involved, sometimes against the better judgement of the Department of State, as part of the competition for influence with the Soviet Union or China.

The identification of socialism with poverty, and with hitherto despised racial groups like the Africans, was inevitable. It looked (probably erroneously) as though the prosperity of the West was a reciprocal of the poverty of the East; it could be argued that compensation and blood-money had to be paid.

What was less easy to understand was the degree to which socialism was identified with nationalism. People who would have blushed at patriotic fervour at home found patriotic rubbish moving in Lagos, Hanoi or Havana. It was no less rubbish for being black or yellow rubbish, just as tyranny and murder were no less tyranny and murder for being black or yellow.

Socialism and pragmatism in Europe

The socialists experienced mixed political success in Europe between 1944 and 1960. In France, for example, the Social Democrats served in many governments from 1944 to 1958. In 1946 the Communists left the government and de Gaulle resigned. Thereafter the prime minister was frequently a socialist. There were four main parties – the Communists, the socialists, the Catholic Social Democratic Party, and the radicals. The Communist Party, increasingly intransigent and increasingly in a minority, stood apart from the governmental process, leaving affairs to the other groups in successive coalitions.

These coalition governments achieved a great deal both economically and socially. Some of the economy was nationalized, but the biggest change in the French economy was the introduction of a new concept of central planning. The French *Commissariat au Plan* was established at the heart of government, its task being mainly to plan physical investment in the public sector and by a process of consultation and encouragement to plan investment in the private sector as well. The result was a significant advance in the rate of economic growth and the redevelopment of France.

The weakness of the economy was the rate of domestic inflation, which was related to weakness in the external balance. The inflation was, in one respect, a strength, because under inflation the level of profit continually grows and this encourages investment. It led, however, to a sense of threat and weakness, to which the chronic instability of the régime contributed. The external balance was cushioned by American aid, through the European Recovery Program, and by frequent devaluations. France thus had rapid economic growth and a substantial social reform programme, especially in education, where from the point of view of numbers of students, France led Europe.

The weakness of the régime was political. It was unable to control wage demands and unable to stop inflation. Its foreign policy was necessarily tied to a desire to restore the French position in the world but this desire was inhibited by the weakness of the balance of payments. France entered the North Atlantic Alliance. It also took a leading part in the movement which culminated in the Treaty of Rome and the establishment of the European Economic Community.

French socialism was therefore interpreted as economic growth, social reform and European unity, an interpretation largely due to the influence of the moderate Catholic reformers, similar to those in office in Germany and Italy. The Common Market, which was the institutional form taken by the movement for European unity, was basically a liberal Catholic conception.

The opposition to this concept was threefold. The Communist Party, which had the traditional support of a number of working-class people, was a close follower of the Moscow line and, as the French government allied itself firmly with the North Atlantic group, this meant that the Communist Party was profoundly opposed to the régime. In this they were joined by the Gaullists, who were intensely nationalist and who completely rejected the concept of a North American and a European world in which individual nationalist loyalties would be subsumed into a wider internationalism. This nationalism was accentuated by the inability of the Fourth Republic governments to settle the French colonial problem. In the first place there was the war in Vietnam, leading to the humiliating defeat and withdrawal of 1954. This blow was bad enough but the Algerian situation was worse.

Algeria was not a colony. Like Ireland under the Union with Great Britain, it was constitutionally an integral part of France and many Algerians were French or of French descent. The simple solution of withdrawing from Algeria seemed to involve betraying compatriots, as well as abandoning the 'civilizing mission' of France – the leaders of Algeria were all products of high French culture.

Algeria divided France. The army and the Gaullists were determined not to leave, but to subdue the nationalists; the communists and the left were determined to leave Algeria; the governments vacillated. The socialists, on the whole, sided with the army. The philosophical debate was of great significance.

On the one side the Marxists and democratic socialists, deeply concerned about colonialism, regarded the Fourth Republic as a contemptible engine of bourgeois repression. The most distinguished French thinkers – Sartre, for example – who were ex-Marxists, or neo-Marxists, found Algeria the test of their commitment to humane values and to the support of revolutionary forces. On the other side, the army and the Gaullist socialists developed a concept of radical nationalism, which would use the paternal strength of the army to regenerate France and to purify its civilization. No French thinker of any distinction supported the moderate social policy and parliamentary institutions of the Fourth Republic.

The Republic collapsed in 1958 and de Gaulle assumed power, establishing a familiar type of plebiscitary presidency, such as Napoleon III had maintained. By a series of moves of political genius, worthy of Gladstone or Parnell, Roosevelt or Bismarck, he withdrew from Algeria. Gradually, too, he extricated himself from the growing internationalism of European policy. He also managed to reverse the adverse balance of payments and to attract considerable quantities of gold to France.

Thus, by the mid-1960s, de Gaulle had consolidated the economic and social achievements of the Fourth Republic, he had ended the colonial problem, and he had achieved an independent foreign policy. To a considerable degree political activity had stopped in France. Parliament was far less important than it had been since it lacked the effective power to make or break governments. The socialist movement, split by Algeria, had to a considerable degree become Gaullist. Opposition to the régime by socialists was sporadic and ineffective, and was to remain so through the student uprising of May 1968, and after the resignation of de Gaulle himself.

In Britain, socialism passed through successive crises in the 1950s. There is no doubt that despite Labour's striking achievements in social policy, it was identified in the public mind with austerity and rationing. Before 1955, however, the Conservatives restored a great deal of the free market and consumption levels rose, while there was no reduction in social benefits nor any rise in unemployment. The fears that the Conservatives would dismantle the welfare state and introduce mass unemployment were allayed and in 1955 they won the general election with a big majority. This electoral defeat accelerated the process of the Labour Party's rethinking of strategy, policies and philosophy.

Hugh Gaitskell succeeded Attlee as Labour leader after the 1955 election. His first major political act was a confrontation with the Conservatives over the Anglo–French–Israeli invasion of Suez. During the period leading up to the invasion, and during the invasion, the Labour Party for the most part attacked the government violently. For once, the Labour Party was almost united in its support of two tried policies – anti-colonialism and backing for the United Nations – without regard to the narrow interests of the country. Thus Gaitskell opened his period as leader with strong and wide support. The exception was an important one: the majority of working-class voters supported the invasion. Their sense of patriotism and nationalism was outraged by the internationalism of the Labour leadership. This was to be important in the 1959 election.

During the period from 1955 a major debate took place about the future of socialism. Up to 1959 this debate was concerned with the policy of the impending Labour government, which it was expected would be elected in 1959. After the defeat of the Labour Party in that election, the debate was more ferocious because what now seemed to be in question was whether or not the Labour Party would survive at all.

The debate was about three things. The first was whether or not the economic problem had fundamentally been solved. The great growth of affluence in North America and western Europe had eroded many of the socialist positions. The Keynesian solution to the question of unemployment seemed to have been successful and had been followed by economic growth in a process that was continuous and irreversible. There was little point in socialism as such if its aim was to overthrow the system in order to achieve what the system was already doing. Gaitskell, as an economist, was concerned to improve economic management and he found it less successful in Britain than elsewhere; but in essence his criticisms were criticisms of detail. Despite casual references to international monetary problems, neither he nor his colleagues foresaw the monetary crises of the later 1960s.

Because the economic problem was solved (and those who denied this did so for visceral rather than intellectual reasons) nationalization became irrelevant. There might be particular arguments for particular cases but, in general, nationalization would not accelerate economic growth. Nationalization and economic controls had been and remained extremely unpopular. Why saddle the Labour Party with an ideological commitment to a goal whose interest was purely sentimental? This became an issue of great significance – especially *à propos* of steel – but Gaitskell's position was, broadly speaking, adopted.

Assuming steady economic growth, socialism became a doctrine about three things. The first was the division of the spoils. A proportion of the population seemed to be missed out by economic growth. It was necessary to build up the social services to eliminate poverty. This would lead to a far more egalitarian society. The thesis was that technical and economic progress had outdistanced social change – that a dynamic economy was held back by an outmoded social structure. The social services were to be lavishly endowed with the fruits of economic growth and the whole policy rested on the assumption that the latter would continue and accelerate.

The second pillar of socialist doctrine was the quality of life. Society had to be made more equal and more just but it also had to be made more liberal and more beautiful. The reform of the penal system, the removal of penalties for homosexuality, the legalization of abortion, the removal of puritan restrictions of all kinds, were some aspects of liberalism. Another aspect was an attempt to strengthen democratic institutions, in politics, in industry and in society.

The third platform of revisionist socialism was an attempt to redress the balance of the world by helping the developing nations, both through aid and through institutions in international trade, which would raise the prices of primary products.

The attacks on this reform movement came from those who held that the capitalist economy was bound to run into crisis; that the affluent society was debasing the culture and leading to increased alienation of the workers from the dominant social values; and that the world crisis, shown in the Third World, would bring down the institutions both of the West and of Russia, which were designed to entrench a powerful bureaucratic class.

Gaitskell died and his former opponent Wilson was elected leader of the Labour Party. In 1964 Labour won a narrow electoral victory and in 1966 a much larger majority. In the event it followed Gaitskell's policy, enlarging the social services and introducing or supporting a great deal of liberal legislation.

But two major problems affected it. The first was that the economy got increasingly out of control, mainly because of the growing international monetary crisis, which centred on Britain and inhibited any policies that appeared to threaten the balance of payments. The repeated crises in the external balance, which led to devaluation and then to further difficulties, also led to a low rate of economic growth – which removed the basis of the Gaitskellite programme of financing the growing social services from the fruits of economic development. It also destroyed much of the credibility of the government, especially with the working people, who were subjected to constantly increasing prices, rising tax rates and wage control.

The crises also inhibited foreign policy. Wilson's government was a supporter of the United States' war in Vietnam; its independent foreign policy crashed on to the rocks of the monetary questions; it was unable to help the Third World.

By the late 1960s, the question was no longer what was the content of revised socialism. It appeared that revisionist socialism had died. It had been replaced by nationalist scientific-militarism, which was in control of many countries and which would determine the future, if any, of the world.

The New Frontier

The election of J. F. Kennedy in 1960, by a hairsbreadth, marked an apparently radical change in the style of American government. It was in fact symptomatic of changes that occurred in the late 1950s, and early 1960s throughout the industrialized world.

The significance of Kennedy for democratic socialism lay more in his rhetoric than in his actions. He adopted wholeheartedly the view that the affluent society had overcome the economic problems that had beset earlier societies. By accelerating public expenditure he raised the United States' growth rate; by accelerating the growth rate, the United States became more affluent than ever before. The administration devised programmes for an attack on poverty. Kennedy's concern was for the poor – for improving their housing, their environment, their health, their education and their incomes. Thus there were Poverty Programs, Urban Programs, Health-Care Programs, and Education Programs. Many of these were enacted only after Kennedy's assassination in Dallas, Texas, in 1963, and pushed through by his successor Lyndon B. Johnson, in his Great Society Program, but in essence the diagnosis of the situation was the one expounded by the men and women brought to Washington by Kennedy in what was known as the New Frontier.

This New Frontier was a rhetorical device for making the discoveries – or alleged discoveries – of the social sciences palatable. In the first place, it was now known that social problems appeared in clusters; that social disadvantages were cumulative; to tackle any one in isolation was to attack a symptom for increasingly, the roots of inequality were to be seen in the whole environment of the disadvantaged. It would not be enough to raise material standards only – though politically and economically that would be a heroic enough task – but the deeper sources of motivation for achievement had to be tapped. This implied a co-ordinated programme of reform – socio-psychological action of a kind that had never been attempted before and about which little was known even in theory – in order to achieve a radical transformation of society.

It was this attitude of the New Frontier that was enshrined in Crosland's dictum that equality of opportunity was not enough: the conditions had to be created which gave equality in the opportunity to acquire ability. It seemed as though ability was more an acquired rather than an inherited characteristic; and whatever the 'scientific' truth about 'ability' – which was certainly not an inherited characteristic like the colour of the eyes but a conglomerate of attitudes and talents – for public policy purposes it was a respectable assumption that the environment could be to some degree controlled whereas inheritance could not. The attack on the deprived environment, through a series of laws and the voting of substantial sums of money, was, therefore, the domestic policy of the New Frontier.

It involved, first, legislation about racial equality. The Supreme Court had ruled for some years that racial equality was guaranteed by the Constitution; the legislation proposed by the New Frontier (especially about voter registration) was designed to implement this guarantee. But racial equality was not merely a matter of formal equality of voting rights. It was necessary to have social equality if political equality were to be meaningful. Social inequality in the United States rested most strongly on the historic division between slave and free, and it would take profound efforts to overcome these inherited disadvantages.

In America, in essence, domestic policy of this sort had been predominantly a matter for the states, and the complexity of arranging for Federal intervention was one of the reasons for the slowness of the programme. It was also undertaken within a framework of constitutional law which both inhibited some action (the Federal government, for example, could not directly provide schools) and created situations with which the Federal government had to deal. The Supreme Court accelerated the process of civil rights for Negroes by a series of judgements; legislation followed to enforce these judgements.

Thus by the later 1960s American society was a complex of private and public initiatives. The majority – the great majority – of the population was richer than people in other countries, except Canada, Sweden and Switzerland. Educational outlays were greater than elsewhere and a higher proportion of young people was at school and college than elsewhere in the world. Social security was, in some respects, better than in Britain. It is true that health care was expensive and there was no comprehensive system of medical provision or insurance payments; yet this was due less to some innate capitalist weakness than to the extraordinary power of the American Medical Association in holding the community to ransom – a power that a complex Constitution enhanced (as it enhanced the power of all pressure groups). Racial inequality was obvious; yet the Negroes (except in some of the southern states) were not necessarily as relatively deprived as the urban poor of some other advanced countries or as the depressed rural minorities in the Soviet Union. Above all, representative political institutions worked in a constitutional framework. To strike a balance with the Soviet Union, it would be easy to say that all but the very poorest Americans were better off than the Russians, that education was better but the health service worse, but that above all the Americans had freedom of expression and democratic institutions.

Yet Lyndon Johnson's Great Society collapsed politically, to be followed by Nixon's election in 1968. The first reason was the war in Vietnam. Successive American presidents, but especially Kennedy and Johnson, became involved in a holding operation in Vietnam which in effect meant supporting a corrupt régime in the south against a communist régime in the north. Involvement in a civil war is always unwise; in this case it was catastrophic since it led to allegations that the 'true face' of American capitalism was revealed in Vietnam.

The next reason was black militancy. It has been repeatedly shown that when a depressed group begins to make economic, political or social gains it will become more militant. So it was with black Americans. This militancy, concentrated in the northern cities, attracted support from young radicals, already alienated from the Great Society by the Vietnam War, and drove many respectable people in the opposite direction, especially when it took the specific form of campus revolts, sit-ins and violence in the universities.

Thirdly, the Great Society's full employment policies added to America's unfavourable balance of payments situation, which jeopardized her position in the world monetary system and led to continuous price and wage rises which revived fears of a steady inflation. This in itself represented a threat to middle-class Americans, which redoubled their dislike of the democrats.

To be radical in America, therefore, meant to be identified with the anti-Vietnam cause, to sympathize with Cuba, to sympathize with the Negroes, and to regard these three problems as systematically connected – the responsibility of capitalism. More important, the collapse of cultural values – the impoverishment of American education, the cheapjack nature of American society – was regarded as being due to the same cause. The affluent society, far from being the Great Society, struck radicals as being rotten to the core. But, it has to be said, this diagnosis was an impressionistic one; and there was no coherent alternative, since Marxism (especially in the romantic revolutionary Cuban case) had proved to be equally bankrupt.

Democratic socialism

Democratic socialism was committed to constitutional action and not to revolution. Like Parnell's Irish Party, it had to achieve its aim through parliamentary institutions. This involved compromises. At what point the compromises involved betrayal was the perennial question. In part it depended on the nature of the constitution and of the attacks on it. Were Imperial Germany, fascist Italy or Gaullist France intolerable régimes that had to be violently overthrown? Or could they be reformed from within? If the attacks on the régime came from communists, or anarchists, or fascists, determined to establish a tyranny, should not a democratic socialist defend institutions that, however imperfect, guaranteed some sort of public order, some freedom from arbitrary arrest, some freedom from terror, and had some hope of reform? The answer depended partly on the degree of horror that was evoked by the attacks; John Dillon, the last leader of the Irish Parliamentary Party, said after the Irish Civil War that he would almost have preferred to continue the Union with Great Britain than live under the nationalist terror. A democratic socialist has often been in this position. He sees a choice between evils; he does not see a Utopia.

To be a democrat, therefore, is to regard the possibility of revolution as something to be avoided at almost all costs. To be a social democrat is, however, to hold that this constitutional parliamentary process can be used for social engineering to make society more rational. Rationality – and this is a huge claim – would, it is held, lead to a more desirable, a softer, more prosperous, more equal and more just society. Rationality involved the understanding of society. Social democracy, therefore, is the application through social engineering of the findings of the social sciences.

Democratic socialists, then, in contrast to the Marxists (who had a revealed doctrine) had the pragmatic, empirical application of transitory findings as the body of their approach. If, as often happened, the social sciences were wrong, or were wrongly interpreted, democratic socialism failed its own tests. In any event, too, the world has often, perhaps usually, preferred irrationality; in olden times it preferred religion and now it prefers nationalism.

The findings of economics on the causes of unemployment and economic growth drove democratic socialists to seek to use the power of the state to create employment and to hasten innovation by promoting investment. The process of economic policy-making involved the greater use of state power; but not necessarily its use in a direction of greater equality and social reform. The process of wage control, for example, which is an integral part of the programme for economic growth, necessarily involves a redistribution of the national product away from the wage-earning class. The building up of investment almost necessarily involves an increase in the level of profits. It does not necessarily follow, therefore, that economics will lead to socialism.

Nor does it follow that sociology will. The discovery of the extremely deep roots of inequality entails the possibility of extremely radical measures to uproot inequality – including the abolition of the family. Are democratic socialists prepared to accept a society of social isolates? Obviously not. Yet, to retain an organic society would involve the acceptance of inequality and of apparent irrationalities which were contrary to socialist principles.

Democratic socialism presumes an ordered society; if that ordered society is in a state of military readiness, militarism will always be the dominant of the two forces.

Another element which democratic socialism has found it increasingly difficult to cope with is trade unionism. Democratic socialism, like any socialism, is linked with a concept of the working class as the vanguard of the struggle for a better social order. Yet the trade unions, deeply sunk in bureaucratic lethargy, have rarely been seen as such except by their most addled bourgeois admirers. In the modern, post-capitalist world the trade unions are part of the bureaucratic power structure. To be radical is to be against them. A rational incomes policy requires their powers – like those of other oligopoly groups – to be controlled by the state in 'the public interest'. Yet the democratic socialist movement depends for its financial and organizational strength on the trade unions. Thus democratic socialism is bound to compromise its radicalism with reality; its concern with the future is affected by its history as a class party.

Some conclusions

Socialism has to be defined more by what it is not than by what it is. On the one side stands liberal capitalism, with its distrust of the state and its emphasis on competition and the liberation of the individual from many (not all) social principles of obligation. On the other side stands communism, with its totalitarian identification of the individual with the state and its identification of liberty with the realization by the individual of a collective social purpose. Socialists have sought to tread the middle way. In the Second World War English socialists like J. B. Priestley defined England's future as a country embracing the best of American capitalism and Russian communism (both allies of the British at that time); and throughout the 1930s and 1940s Sweden was held up as the example of a country which, while aiming at equality and prosperity by social intervention, managed to give its people the greatest degree of individual aberration from the mean. Legalized abortion on the welfare state seemed to be the symbol of an ideal socialist society, and was contrasted with the suppression of the Kulaks in the Soviet Union on the one hand and mass unemployment in America on the other.

Socialism, then, is best defined as a self-conscious middle way. Its original doctrine was opposition to capitalism, its later doctrine opposition to communism. But for many years communism and socialism were synonymous; after Marx they were regarded, by some, as separate successive historical stages, but the socialist movement was not yet split cleanly from communism. The split came when Bernstein and other thinkers differed from the majority of Marxists on the nature of revolution and the direction of the bourgeois state. For Bernstein, as for the Fabians, the state was a mechanism for social improvement and for the gradual achievement of socialism; for the Bolsheviks it was an instrument of the bourgeoisie, with no possibility of other use. After the Bolshevik seizure of power in Russia the division between socialists and communists attained an objective basis. Political and economic actions by the Soviet government showed clearly that the Bolsheviks were not liberals, were not gradualists, and that they were apostles of violent revolution throughout the world. Socialists were parliamentarians.

Thereafter, socialism represented as much a response to communism as an alternative to capitalism. Whenever communism moved, socialism felt bound to move too, rarely in a different direction. Socialism had become, by the late nineteenth century, part of the ordinary party system of liberal (and increasingly democratic) politics; socialist tactics and strategy were dictated more and more by the needs of the political situation in liberal countries; but socialist philosophy, when it came to take stock of where socialism was going, felt obliged to orient itself to the Soviet state. Because what was going on in the Soviet Union bore little if any direct relevance to the party politics of liberal states, socialist philosophy and socialist practice increasingly diverged.

It is difficult, therefore, to relate socialist practice directly to socialist philosophy, or to relate either to political and economic reality, since socialist practice has for the greater part been dictated by short-term parliamentary considerations, and socialist philosophy has been like the shadows on Plato's cave, reflected and refracted from capitalist societies to communism, and back to socialism, and then hastily related to what socialist parties were doing. To attempt to make socialist policies and principles consistent is self-evidently an impossible task, for both philosophical response and political urgency have led to innumerable accretions of policy and philosophy which are often incompatible one with another. But that is not unusual, for the same criticism could be made *mutatis mutandis* of liberal, communist, capitalist and Catholic apologias. Yet, one doubts whether the criticism of incoherence when laid at the door of communist doctrine would have much force, for – doctrine or not – communism in its various forms manifestly exists, and though its forms vary, they have many essential features in common. It is a matter for dispute whether socialism exists in the sense that communism does, and certainly, if it does exist, then the régimes that have called themselves or are called socialist have little indeed in common.

How, then, is socialism to be defined? It is, first of all, parliamentary in conception and in operation. In the dispute between capitalism and communism, the socialists accepted the parliamentary political structure which the communists denounced as irredeemably bourgeois. Socialists put Parliament at the centre of their political institutions. This was an inevitable consequence of their decision to achieve socialism by gaining a majority in existing parliamentary institutions. It meant that socialists were organized in parliamentary parties, and that 'after the achievement of socialism', the party system would continue. This was in direct contrast to the communist view that in a socialist society parties would cease to exist since the development of a classless society would remove the basis for political parties. The acceptance of parliamentary institutions as the central feature of a political system marked, therefore, a clear break with Marxist principles and practice. This is the essence of what is meant, in this book, by social democracy; and if the traditional shorthand 'socialism' is often used, the contrast with other 'socialist' systems (whether Marxist or national socialist) must never be forgotten.

Historically, then, Parliament was at the centre, and socialists were one party among others. As a party they put themselves on the left, in a continental semicircular chamber ranged between the communists on *their* left, and the radicals on their right. Socialists, therefore, defined themselves as on the left of the parliamentary system; whenever the centre moved to the left to socialists moved left as well, to preserve their original position. Thus, within the parliamentary system, the socialists were bound always to provide from their own members the most extreme of the parliamentary opposition (though, of course, there were extremists of the left and the right who were outside the parliamentary system); and at any particular time their orientation was bound to be part of the total orientation of the parliamentary system to the society in which it was functioning.

Their situation on the left meant that they were bound to choose the more populist course, and the more 'democratic' course, when choices were presented. The extension of the suffrage, first to all males, then to all adults, the extension of the right to elect officers and representatives in many institutions –

all this conception of radical democracy, 'one man one vote', equal constituencies, and the secret ballot – were taken over from the Chartists in England and, ultimately, from the American and French revolutionary doctrines. The socialists developed the conception of representative democracy along the most liberal lines in all the countries where they were active.

In contrast to the liberals, however, their concern for democracy was accompanied by a different view of the role of the state. Under liberal capitalism the state was, ultimately, a referee; the game was played by the capitalists. According to the communists the state was a corrupt referee: it rigged the match against the proletariat. According to the socialists, the increasing majority of voters would be working-class, and they would use the power of the state in their own interests. The nineteenth-century state, according to the Webbs and to later historians not of their persuasion, was a tremendous social invention, enabling the community to perform tasks that previously could not be performed at all. This was the case first of all in the social services, where education, health and social security could be provided free or cheaply with impressive consequences for the happiness and well-being of mankind, and secondly in the ownership and control of productive enterprises.

Thus, in practice, socialism came to mean the growing extension of state power through the public ownership of industry and the extension of social services. Bismarck's social security legislation was copied in Australia, and then in Britain, with socialist advocacy. The state railway enterprises of the continent formed the forerunners of extensive public holdings in business and commerce, ranging from agricultural credit corporations in Scandinavia to coalmines in Britain, and to airlines throughout the world.

The extension of state power was a further argument for public control. The analysis of capitalism's defects that underlay socialist policies laid stress upon the apparent fact that capitalism could produce goods but not sell them. The division between the owners of property, on the one hand, and the propertyless workers was seen as the cause of inequality of incomes, and an inequality that, in Marxist terms, would lead to the breakdown of capitalism because of the crisis of over-production in which what was produced could not be consumed because of the absence of purchasing power. Thus socialism was intended to be a mechanism to boost purchasing power. It was to do so by a redistribution of incomes away from the rich towards the poor. Under communism this would have been achieved by a general political convulsion in which the propertied would have been hanged from the nearest lamp-post, while their property was socialized. Under socialism the expropriation would be gradual: increasingly, society's surplus value would accrue directly to the state, and through progressive taxation the rich would be deprived of income which would be given to the poor. The rich, who saved, would be replaced by the poor, who would spend. This spending would also effect another change: production would now be of things made for use, rather than of vain fripperies made for the rich and sold for profit. 'Production for use and not for profit' was a slogan that carried with it many implications. One was derived from the utilitarian theory that extra goods gave greater satisfaction to those who were poor than to those who were rich. Another was that profit was a disreputable surplus derived from the exploitation of the poor, producing unnecessary goods for the wealthy.

The practical consequences of this view of profit were many. Inevitably egalitarian anti-profit measures were bound to commend themselves to socialists but the consequences for production and output were grave, for it turned out that capitalism had not solved the problem of production. This was seen most obviously in poor countries like India where a socialist government's most pressing problem was not distribution but output, but it was also seen in the third, fourth and fifth Labour governments in Britain (1945–51, 1964–70 and 1974–9) which were elected on egalitarian expenditure programmes but were forced to deal almost entirely with problems of production.

The difficulties of production were intrinsic to all societies, and a mistake had been made in believing that technical advance had gone so far that it would be possible easily and painlessly to incorporate it into physical capital and allow the production of abundance to proceed. The conditions for technical progress were complex, but they depended, certainly, upon the rapid and continuous accumulation of capital, which implied that a high proportion of total potential output would not be available for consumption but would have to be invested. If the rich were deprived of their surplus, which they had largely saved and made available for investment, then the state would have to save. This made 'production for use' according to social priorities (selling at or below cost) an unfeasible process for publicly owned industries. Increasingly, therefore, the debate about the ownership of property became a debate about how business was to be managed.

A publicly owned, democratically controlled economy is a concept that immediately raises the questions, who is to manage the enterprises and on what principles are they to be managed? For public ownership is not the same as public control; a series of socially owned enterprises operating on no common principle could be anarchic, and (in their various ways) despotic.

A variety of answers were given. The first, historically, was that workers should control their own enterprises and run them by consensus, or by majority rule. This co-operative conception, as applied to whole enterprises, was called syndicalism. It was a French conception, applied first in the 1848 Revolution, and later in small ways elsewhere, culminating in experiments in Yugoslavia in the 1950s and 1960s. It had many drawbacks, but two stood out. Managerial skill is rare; and an enterprise needs managerial skill and authority to be exercised if it is to survive. This is difficult if not impossible in the given conditions. Above all, even if this difficulty could be overcome, there was no general rule by which the output and pricing policies of each enterprise were to be determined. It was implicitly assumed that the economy would function 'normally' as it did under capitalism.

At the other extreme from workers' control was state control. A municipal tramway in Belgium, a state electricity company in Latin America, the state coal industry in Britain, could all be managed exactly as though they were privately owned corporations. Except that profits went to the state (or the losses were borne by the taxpayer) there was no difference that could be discerned, immediately. Thus, the management of state enterprises was a perennial topic of discussion. At one extreme, syndicalism came near to the fascist doctrine of corporatism, in which the state consisted of groups of people organized according to their working groups; at the other extreme, state control came near to the conception of the all-powerful state, which libertarian socialists had set out to oppose.

The problem of workers' control arose not only because socialism had a concern for public ownership. It arose too because socialists called themselves a working-class party. In fact, at most times, a majority of the working class, and especially working-class women, voted for right-wing parties, and in many countries – France, Italy, Germany – a majority of those voting for left-wing parties voted Communist. The socialists called themselves a working-class party for three reasons. It was their view that political parties represented different social groups – peasant parties represented the peasants, liberal parties represented the manufacturers and conservative parties represented the big landowners – and that they were the representatives of the working class. This sprang from their Marx-like interpretation of politics as a manifestation of the class struggle. In fact, the basis of party allegiance was far more complex than this simple-minded division would have suggested. The second reason for the socialist identification with the working class was the objective fact that in some countries they were the representatives of that part of the working class organized in trade unions (which was usually, though not always a minority of the manual workers). Thirdly, socialists were a working-class party by aspiration, in the sense that they desired to redistribute wealth, income and power to the working class. It was this aspect of socialist thought that led to the great preoccupation with equality, and the notion that liberal equality in political terms was virtually meaningless without an economic and social interpretation as well.

But equality with whom? Socialists were from the start internationalists, in the sense that they were opposed to war, which they thought to be an aspect of capitalist competition, and they were positively in favour of supra-national institutions. But they were also nationalists – any small racial, ethnic or linguistic group was sure of their support in its demands for independence. Socialists were also unprepared to extend the concept of equality to equality between nations in any but a legislative, political sense.

The rise of socialist theory, its compromise with practice, and its final collapse into a pragmatic justification for nationalist scientific-militarism, a world in which people succumb to nationalism, believe in science, and are led by generals, is the culmination of liberal theory and of a world-view that has dominated the West for centuries, though it is a nineteenth- and twentieth-century phenomenon. The central question for a century or more has been the place of socialism in a world which has been equipped with the means of material abundance by capitalism. In western Europe, socialism has compromised with capitalism to produce 'social democracy'; in the Soviet Union it is Marxist tyranny that is defined as socialism; and in the Third World it simply means military dictatorship. Where socialism retains its glamour, it is where there is still constitutional democracy. Could that democracy survive socialism?

Bibliography

Capitalism

The classical primary and secondary works on capitalism are legion. In this selection, the most interesting and accessible for the concerned reader are cited.

Classics

Adam Smith *The Wealth of Nations*

T. R. Malthus *An Essay on Population*

David Ricardo *Works* (ed. P. Sraffa)

Karl Marx *Capital*

John Stuart Mill *On Liberty*

Alfred Marshall *The Principles of Economics* London 1890

A. C. Pigou *The Economics of Welfare*

J. M. Keynes *The Economic Consequences of the Peace* London 1919
A Treatise on Money London 1930
The General Theory of Employment Interest and Money London 1936

J. A. Hobson *Imperialism*

Commentaries on capitalism

The most significant are:

Joseph Schumpeter *Capitalism, Socialism and Democracy* New York 1942

J. K. Galbraith *The Affluent Society* London 1958

Andrew Shonfield *Modern Capitalism* Oxford 1964

There are some general introductions to economic history:

J. B. Clough *The Economic Development of Western Civilization* New York 1959

Barry Supple *The Experience of Economic Growth; Case Studies in Economic History* New York 1963

Max Weber *General Economic History* New York 1961

The Ancient World and China

Jean-Philippe Levy *The Economic Life of the Ancient World* Chicago 1967

F. M. Heichelheim *An Ancient Economic History from the Paleolithic Age to the Migrations of the Germanic, Slavic and Arabic Nations* Leyden 1958 and 1964

C. P. Fitzgerald *A Concise History of East Asia* London 1966

Edwin O. Reischauer and John K. Fairbank *A History of East Asian Civilization* Boston 1960–64

J. Needham *Science and Civilization in China* Cambridge 1954–65

Early capitalism

Maurice Dobb *Studies in the Development of Capitalism* London 1946

Europe and the North Atlantic

Cambridge Economic History of Europe vols. I, II, III, VI Cambridge 1942–65

John Clapham *The Economic History of Modern Britain* 3 vols. Cambridge 1930–8

Henri Sée *Histoire Economique de la France* Paris 1948–51

Werner Sombart *Der Moderne Kapitalismus*, 3 vols. Munich 1921–8

Douglas C. North *Growth and Welfare in the American Past* Englewood Cliffs, N.J. 1966

Dudley Dillard *Economic Development of the North Atlantic Community* Englewood Cliffs, N.J. 1967

J. K. Galbraith *The Great Crash* Boston 1955

Simon Kuznets *National Income and Its Composition 1919–1938* New York 1954

League of Nations *World Economic Survey* Geneva 1932–44

Socialism

First is G. D. H. Cole's *A History of Socialist Thought*, 5 vols. London 1953–60, which is diffuse but essential reading.

There are a number of important historical works; some of the most interesting of relatively recent date are:

M. Beer *A History of British Socialism* London 1948

Alexander Gray *The Socialist Tradition* London 1946

P. Gay *The Dilemma of Democratic Socialism* New York 1952

D. Ligou *Histoire du Socialisme en France, 1871–1961* Paris 1962

Edouard Dolléan *Histoire du Mouvement Ouvrier* vols. 2 and 3 Paris 1939–53

Leszek Kolakowski *Main Currents of Marxism* 3 vols. Oxford 1978
H. Pelling *A Short History of the Labour Party* London 1961 gives a clear
account of the development of the Labour Party. Hugh Thomas *The
Spanish Civil War* London 1961 describes the failure of all moderate
movements, including social democracy, in Spain. E. J. Hobsbawm's
Industry and Empire London 1968 is especially helpful.

Of course, the works of Marx and Engels are essential reading.

Some important statements on modern democratic socialism are C. A. R.
Crosland *The Future of Socialism* London 1956; Evan Durbin *The Politics
of Democratic Socialism* London 1940; and Arthur Lewis *The Principles of
Economic Planning* London 1949.

John Strachey in his last books, *Contemporary Capitalism* London 1956 and
The End of Empire London 1959, made important contributions to the
theory of modern social democracy.

Gunnar Myrdal, especially in *Value in Social Theory* 1958, attacks the
notion of 'value-free' social services, and thus provides a basis for the
refusal to accept the market, or some other self-regulating mechanism, as a
basis of the social order.

Joan Robinson's *An Essay on Marxian Economics* London 1942, remains a
standard work on Marxist economics, studied from a social democratic
standpoint. Thomas Balogh's *The Economics of Poverty* London 1966 is also
relevant. For a criticism of neo-classical economics Nicholas Kaldor's
Essays on Value and Distribution London 1960 is especially helpful. Piero
Sraffa's *Production of Commodities by Means of Commodities* Cambridge
1960 has been called the most important economics book of the century; in
this context its importance lies in its profound reinterpretation of classical
economics. Robin Marris's *The Economic Theory of 'Managerial' Capitalism*
London 1964 will repay study.

Among sociological works that are relevant, R. H. Tawney's *Equality*
London 1931 is, of course, of central importance as is T. H. Marshall
Citizenship and Social Class London 1950. R. H. S. Crossmann (ed.) *The
God That Failed* London 1950 and Arthur Koestler in *The Yogi and the
Commissar* London 1945 are works that explain the background to a
non-Marxist alternative to Marx's view of society, based on disillusionment
with Stalinist Marxist régimes.

In recent German publications there is no better historical work than Carl
Schorske's *German Social Democracy 1905–1917* London 1955. For the
later period there is no good standard work in English.

J. L. Talmon's *The Origins of Totalitarian Democracy* (1952) is an important work for the pluralistic basis of social democracy. It relies in part on K. R. Popper's *The Open Society and Its Enemies* 2 vols. 4th edition London 1962. E. M. Forster *Two Cheers for Democracy* London 1951 expresses the moderate civilized tone in which politics ought to be conducted, as does A. J. P. Taylor in *English History 1914-45* Oxford 1965. George Lichtheim in his *Marxism* London 1961 takes a profoundly depressing view both of social democracy and of Marxism, which is a useful corrective to the view presented here.

Sir Isaiah Berlin in *Four Essays on Liberty* Oxford 1969 offers an interpretation of freedom in a democratic social order which most nearly accords with the view presented here.

Index

83
85
88